Africa Now

Africa Now is an exciting new series, published by Zed Books
in association with the internationally respected Nordic Africa
Institute. Featuring high-quality, cutting-edge research from
leading academics, the series addresses the big issues confronting
Africa today. Accessible but in-depth, and wide-ranging in its
scope, Africa Now engages with the critical political, economic,
sociological and development debates affecting the continent,
shedding new light on pressing concerns.

Nordic Africa Institute

The Nordic Africa Institute (Nordiska Afrikainstitutet) is a centre
for research, documentation and information on modern Africa.
Based in Uppsala, Sweden, the Institute is dedicated to providing
timely, critical and alternative research and analysis of Africa and
to cooperating with African researchers. As a hub and a meeting
place for a growing field of research and analysis, the Institute
strives to put knowledge of African issues within reach for scholars,
policy-makers, politicians, the media, students and the general
public. The Institute is financed jointly by the Nordic countries
(Denmark, Finland, Iceland, Norway and Sweden).

www.nai.uu.se

Forthcoming titles

Iman Hashim and Dorte Thorsen, *Child Migration in Africa*

Titles already published

Fantu Cheru and Cyril Obi (eds), *The Rise of China and India in
 Africa: Challenges, opportunities and critical interventions*

D1453306

About the editor

Ilda Lindell is a researcher at the Nordic Africa Institute and an associate professor of human geography at Stockholm University, Sweden. Her current research focuses on collective organizing in urban informal economies in Africa, including links to international movements and relations with other organized actors. She has authored book chapters and journal articles, including in *Urban Studies*, *Third World Quarterly*, *Habitat International* and *Geografiska Annaler*. She has edited a special issue in *African Studies Quarterly* (2010) on 'Between Exit and Voice: Informality and the Spaces of Popular Agency'. She is also the author of *Walking the Tight Rope: Informal Livelihoods and Social Networks in a West African City* (2002), which deals with processes of informalization and how urban dwellers are dealing with the changes.

Africa's informal workers

Collective agency, alliances and transnational organizing in urban Africa

edited by Ilda Lindell

Nordiska Afrikainstitutet
The Nordic Africa Institute

Zed Books
LONDON | NEW YORK

Africa's Informal Workers: Collective agency, alliances and transnational organizing in urban Africa was first published in association with the Nordic Africa Institute, PO Box 1703, SE-751 47 Uppsala, Sweden in 2010 by Zed Books Ltd, 7 Cynthia Street, London N1 9JF, UK and Room 400, 175 Fifth Avenue, New York, NY 10010, USA

www.zedbooks.co.uk
www.nai.uu.se

Editorial Copyright © Ilda Lindell 2010
Copyright in this collection © Zed Books 2010

The right of Ilda Lindell to be identified as the editor of this work has been asserted by her in accordance with the Copyright, Designs and Patents Act, 1988

Set in OurType Arnhem, Monotype Gill Sans Heavy and Elsner+Flake TechnoScript by Ewan Smith, London
Index: ed.emery@thefreeuniversity.net
Cover designed by Rogue Four Design
Cover images clockwise from top right: © Andy Johnstone/Panos Pictures, © Petterik Wiggers/Panos Pictures, © Mark Henley/Panos Pictures, © James Oatway/Panos Pictures, © Sven Torfinns/Panos Pictures, © George Osodi/ Panos Pictures.
Printed and bound in Great Britain by the MPG Books Group, Bodmin and King's Lynn

Distributed in the USA exclusively by Palgrave Macmillan, a division of St Martin's Press, LLC, 175 Fifth Avenue, New York, NY 10010, USA

A catalogue record for this book is available from the British Library
Library of Congress Cataloging in Publication Data available

ISBN 978 1 84813 451 5 hb
ISBN 978 1 84813 452 2 pb
ISBN 978 1 84813 453 9 eb

Contents

Acronyms

ANC	African National Congress
AFACEB	Association des Femmes d'Affaires et Chefs d'Entreprise du Bénin
APF	Anti-Privatization Forum
ASMAB	Association pour la Solidarité des Marchés du Bénin
AZIEA	Alliance for Zambia Informal Economy Associations
CBTA	Cross-Border Traders Association (Zambia)
CCIB	Chambre de Commerce et d'Industrie du Bénin
CIAWU	Commercial, Industrial and Allied Workers Union (Malawi)
COMESA	Common Market of Eastern and Southern Africa
COSATU	Congress of South African Trade Unions
CPP	Convention Peoples Party (Ghana)
DRC	Democratic Republic of Congo
FAOMAB	Fédération Nationale des Organisations et Associations des Marchés du Bénin (au Dantokpa)
GDLC	Ghana Dock Labour Company
GPVMB	Groupement Professionel des Vendeuses des Marchés du Bénin
HDI	Human Development Index
IEO	informal economy organization
ILO	International Labour Organization
KENASVIT	Kenya National Alliance of Street Vendors and Informal Traders
MCTU	Malawi Congress of Trade Unions
MDU	Maritime and Dockworkers Union (Ghana)
MSE	Micro and Small Enterprises
MUFIS	Malawi Union for the Informal Sector
NABW	National Association of Business Women (Malawi)
NAFDAC	National Agency for Food and Drug Administration and Control (Nigeria)
NGO	non-governmental organization
NLC	Nigeria Labour Congress
NUTGTWN	National Union of Textile, Garment and Tailoring Workers of Nigeria
RB	Renaissance du Bénin
SACP	South African Communist Party
SADC	South African Development Community
SAMWU	South African Municipal Workers' Union
SAP	structural adjustment programme
SOGEMA	Société de Gestion des Marchés de Cotonou

SYNAVAMAB	Syndicat National des Vendeurs et Vendeuses et Assimilés des Marchés du Bénin
UNACOBE	Union Nationale des Commerçantes du Bénin
UNACOIS	Union Nationale des Commerçants et Industriels du Sénégal
UNDP	United Nations Development Programme
UNIDO	United Nations Industrial Development Organization
USYNVEPID	Union Syndicale des Vendeuses et Vendeurs de Pièces Détachées et Divers du Marché de Dantokpa
UUSC	Unitarian Universalists Service Committee
WIEGO	Women in Informal Employment: Globalizing and Organizing

Introduction: the changing politics of informality – collective organizing, alliances and scales of engagement[1]

Ilda Lindell

Introduction

Processes of informalization and casualization of livelihoods loom large in the world today. While these phenomena are far from new and in many settings have deep historical roots, we seem to be witnessing new waves of informalization whereby an increasing number of people rely on forms of work beyond the purview of state regulation (Alsayyad 2004; Bryceson 2006; Cross and Morales 2007a). This is highly evident in cities in Africa and the South, where urban landscapes and economic structures have been deeply transformed by a wide range of informal activities.

Despite much writing on the persistence and growth of informal economies, our understanding of the politics of informality has been hampered by deeply entrenched views that tend to deprive people in the informal economy of agency. Much research on the 'informal sector' over several decades has devoted much effort to defining its features and understanding its potential for economic development, leaving political dimensions largely unexamined. Celebratory views that dominate mainstream policy and academic circles today emphasize the entrepreneurial capacities of 'the poor'. Ultimately, however, this 'aesthetic framing of the informal sector silences the voices and experiences of informal [...] workers' (Alsayyad 2004: 24 referring to Roy 2004b). Marxist approaches interpret the contemporary trends in terms of a 'downgrading of labour' and tend to allow little room for spaces of autonomy or resistance among informal workers. Praised or victimized, informal workers are seldom seen as political actors.[2]

The above limitations have led to approaches that attempt to give centre stage to the agency of people in the informal economy. The literature on urban livelihoods and household income strategies has helped uncover the diverse ways in which people get by in the face of shrinking formal employment (for example, Rakodi and Lloyd-Jones 2002). Other work has highlighted the diverse kinds of personal networks through which urbanites sustain their informal activities and incomes in the context of economic crisis (for example, Lourenço-Lindell 2002). Recent work has emphasized the capacities and opportunities that are generated through provisional connections and new and diffuse forms of collaboration among people of highly diverse cultural and social backgrounds in urban Africa (Simone 2004). Such fluid networks are seen as 'platforms for people to collaborate in "silent" but powerful ways' (ibid.: 13). More generally, there are growing calls for looking upon local informal economic practices not as merely marginal, acted upon, as manifestations of chaos and decay or as deviations from a Western normative ideal, but as providing the basis for social economies from which a different kind of urbanism can be envisioned (ibid.; Pieterse 2008). Such everyday informal practices are seen as one form of 'insurgent citizenship' (Pieterse 2008), one which has been well articulated by Asef Bayat (2004). Bayat depicts the politics of informal actors as taking the form of 'the quiet encroachment of the ordinary'. Such politics refers to the individual everyday practices through which the urban subaltern groups gradually appropriate space. Rather than engaging in collective demand-making, it is argued, informal actors act in a quiet and atomized fashion to address their immediate needs. The far-reaching effects of such individual practices are exceedingly evident in urban areas. However, individual everyday actions are not the only kind of political practices in which informal actors engage, or even their preferred mode of politics.[3]

Influential analyses across the political spectrum give little attention to the possibility of collective organization among people in the informal economy. In some cases, their organizations are dismissed as being of limited interest or of little relevance. In other cases, they are seen as outright incapable of collective mobilization. This capacity is reserved for the traditional working class, while informal workers are said to lack organizational capabilities (see Castells and Portes 1989; Bayat 2004: 90–93). This anthology provides a different picture. It examines the collective organizing initiatives that are multiplying in African informal economies, in the context of contemporary economic and political transformations. Collective action – while not necessarily progressive – opens possibilities for articulating interests and agendas, expressing grievances and claiming rights (Pieterse 2008: 95). It also creates opportunities for the collective articulation of alternative discourses on the informal economy and of new visions for the city. It makes possible collective engagement with a range of other actors, to negotiate, defy them or ally with them. Thus, collective organizing, in its various forms and orientations, is here seen as an important component of the contemporary politics of informality in Africa.

People making a living in the urban informal economy face great challenges today. The global and local forces that shape conditions and opportunities in the informal economy have been discussed at length before.[4] Neoliberal policies and the decline in formal employment opportunities have led to a dramatic increase in self-employment in most African cities, often resulting in intense competition in the informal economy (Bryceson 2006; Hansen and Vaa 2004).

At the same time, large firms in some contexts have found in the informal economy an important sphere of accumulation and increasingly make use of casual work, reportedly contributing to an increase in the precariousness of work (Castells and Portes 1989; Gallin 2001). In the context of economic liberalization, informal economies have also tended to become more deeply enmeshed in international commodity circuits and global economic processes. Clearly, the above trends have created new opportunities for some groups, but vulnerability has increased for many. Indeed, a diversity of groups today make use of the informal economy for a wide range of purposes, from survival to accumulation (Alsayyad 2004; Hansen and Vaa 2004; Lourenço-Lindell 2002).

As the numbers of people in the informal economy swell, governments and political elites seldom remain indifferent. Some governments opt for restrictive and violent measures towards segments of the informal workforce, a hostility that appears to be intensifying.[5] At the same time, many politicians have come to regard these growing crowds as 'vote banks' (Mitlin 2004). Concurrently, in the transition to multiparty politics, the urban informal economy has often become a sphere of intense political competition. The political terrain in which livelihood struggles are being fought is thus also changing.

This collection explores the collectively organized initiatives emerging around informal livelihood issues in the context of the above economic and political transformations. It uncovers the current diversification of such initiatives, which reflects the diversity of interests and actors in today's informal economies. Important changes in the dynamics and patterns of association in the informal economy come to light throughout the book.

Particular attention is given to the strategies of organized informal workers for political influence, their alliances and their multiple scales of collective engagement. Accordingly, the anthology is structured around three sets of central concerns. One major concern pertains to the politics in which collective organizations in the informal economy are today engaged and embedded. Given the urban anchorage of most of the examined organizations, one may think of it as an *urban* politics – and indeed, issues of urban governance come to the fore in many of the chapters. The politics of informality depicted in the book, however, is broader and involves relations with a range of local, national and international actors, as a number of the chapters show. The extent and ways in which such collective organizations attempt to influence dominating power, while surfacing in many of the contributions, are a central issue in the chapters in Part One of the collection. The state emerges as an important actor, although not the only one.

The growing diversity of organizing initiatives in the informal economy makes it pertinent to consider relations between different organized actors, and the tensions and alliances that may emerge. Such relations can be of many different kinds and involve a variety of actors. The collection inquires into one particular set of relations, those emerging from current attempts at organizing across the formal–informal 'divide'.[6] This is the key theme in the chapters in Part Two, which critically assess emerging relationships between trade unions and informal workers and the possibilities and challenges involved. The discussions also contribute to bridging another deep 'divide', that between labour studies and 'informal sector' studies. Finally, the collection explores the widening scales of collective organizing by some groups in the informal economy, in particular the internationalization of such organizing. The chapters in Part Three uncover how some groups increasingly participate in international movements, engage with international governing bodies and respond to some global processes. Such an inquiry counters a deeply entrenched view that confines the politics of informality to the local and national scene.

The developments discussed in Parts Two and Three embody arguably novel trends that are becoming visible both in Africa and beyond, and that are still scarcely researched. By addressing the above issues in specific economic, cultural and political contexts, the contributions in this volume provide a diverse picture of the politics and dynamics of collective organizing around informal livelihoods in Africa. The empirical focus is on sub-Saharan Africa, but many findings and discussions in this collection are of relevance for other regions of the South undergoing similar processes.

This introductory chapter provides a broad overview of the changing landscape of organizing initiatives in informal economies in Africa (and beyond). The next section provides some clarifications of and reflections on the term 'informal', while also raising certain critical issues that are discussed later in the chapter. The emergence of new organized actors using new discourses and strategies is then discussed. This is followed by an analysis of reconfiguring patterns and dynamics of association in the informal economy. This includes a discussion of the impacts of social and economic differentiation on the organizational environment and of the implications for our understanding of the collective identities of organized informal workers. The key themes in each of the three parts of the anthology are then introduced and discussed. First, relations with dominant power, in particular with the state, are discussed, with attention given to the complex political subjectivities of informal workers and to the multiple modalities of power and influence at work. Second, the perils and opportunities of organizing across the formal–informal 'divide' are examined. Third, the implications of the internationalization of collective organizing among informal workers are reflected upon. The general picture that will emerge is of a complex politics of informality, encompassing a highly diverse landscape of organized actors in the informal economy, the multiple power relations in which informal workers are inscribed and the multiple spatial scales at which they engage. The chapter concludes with a review of the individual contributions, highlighting insights of relevance for the key areas of concern outlined above.

Locating the 'informal'

First coined by Hart (1973), the concept of informality has had a long history that has been well covered elsewhere (among others, Potts 2008; Alsayyad 2004). In spite of considerable criticism and disagreement, the term continues to be widely used. Like many others, we use it in this book as a commonsense notion generally referring to economic activities that lie beyond or circumvent state regulation (Castells and Portes 1989).

Even such a minimalist definition as the one above requires clarification. First, using the notion of 'informality' does not necessarily involve a dualistic view of the economy as having two separate sectors, underpinned by unilinear assumptions of economic development, where the informal is understood as marginal, residual and a mere appendage to the formal economy.[7] Rather, the boundary between the formal and the informal economy is blurred. The two interconnect in varying degrees and in multiple ways and often contain elements of each other. Both feel the influence of the same global forces and, as noted many times before, ordinary citizens also straddle the two spheres as they pursue their income strategies. These are insights of relevance to understanding collective organizing and identities in the informal economy, as will be discussed later in this chapter. Second, the fact that informal activities lie outside the state regulatory system does not mean that they are 'unregulated'. Rather, relations in the informal economy are regulated through a multiplicity of rules, institutions and a variety of actors beyond the state (Meagher 2009; Lindell 2008a; Lourenço-Lindell 2002: 247–54; Roitman 2004) – including associations operating in the informal economy, as many chapters in this anthology show. Viewing the informal as unregulated contributes to a 'black box' understanding of the informal economy that renders invisible both the multiple power relations and the solidarity principles at work within it (Lourenço-Lindell 2002).

Third, while the above definition may be considered too general, it allows room for locally specific relations and forms of work, thus avoiding the disadvantages of strict and universal definitions. More precise definitions of informality need to be situated in specific contexts, as there is great geographical variation in the forms that economic informality takes and in the ways in which they relate to state regulation (Hansen and Vaa 2004: 10; Potts 2008: 163). In addition, the meanings that local actors attribute to informality are of relevance for understanding the symbolic struggles in which many associations engage and which are discussed in the next section. Fourth, independent of the modest analytical value of the term, 'informality' remains relevant as a category of practice – that is, the various ways in which different actors (state actors, international institutions, grassroots associations, etc.) may use the term to pursue certain agendas. Governments frequently use the term to mean 'outlaws' so as to legitimize repressive interventions (Potts 2008), while informal economy associations may use it in an assertive manner. These discursive uses of the term are key to the contemporary symbolic politics of informality, as further discussed below.

Some current definitions of informality have evolved to reflect the now widespread realization that the informal economy is, in most contexts, no longer restricted to the small-scale and survivalist activities of the poor, but is also a sphere of accumulation in which the non-poor operate. Such conceptions of the informal economy have been widened to capture these developments. Castells and Portes's (1989: 13–14) influential conceptualization highlights the 'unrecorded practices of large corporations', whereby production relations that are unregulated by the state become part of the flexibilization strategies of those corporations. The International Labour Organization (ILO) has also revised its definition of 'informal economy' to encompass informal work arrangements in both small-scale/unregistered enterprises and registered/large-scale firms – a definition that has largely been embraced by international activist networks (ILO 2002a, 2002b; WIEGO 2002: 11, 23). This revised definition relates to the ILO's new commitment to promoting 'decent work' across the formal–informal continuum. Informal employment has been redefined as *any* type of employment lacking secure contracts, social protection or worker benefits. This involves a diverse group of people, including the self-employed and own-account workers in unregistered enterprises; employers and their employees in such enterprises, including unpaid family workers; those employed informally by registered firms, including industrial casual and day workers and contract workers lacking worker benefits; and domestic workers (Carr and Chen 2004: 4; Chen et al. 2002: 5; WIEGO 2002: 11, 23).

These widened conceptualizations are appealing in that they call attention to the contemporary expansion of various forms of unprotected work as manifested in the parallel processes of informalization and casualization. However, they lump together a wide range of work situations, even if these share a common denominator, i.e. they evade state regulation. Some important distinctions, which have relevance for the central concerns in this collection, are worth highlighting. First, take for example the categories of casual workers and the self-employed, many of whom employ other people. These different categories are embedded in very different kinds of social relations, subject to very different types of constraints and vulnerabilities, may relate differently to state regulation and may also have different interests. These differences may shape, though not determine, the forms and contours of collective organizing. They warrant consideration of issues of conflict and unity as well as of collective identity and of the scope for collaboration and alliance among groups in the informal economy. As will be discussed later, however, common ground may be constructed where least expected. After all, labels such as 'casual workers', 'the self-employed', 'formal workers' and so on are socially constructed rather than fixed categories. Thus the way they relate to each other is a matter for empirical investigation.

Second, distinctions concerning the legality or illegality of informal activities are a matter of discussion and contention in the literature. The informal activities examined in this book pertain to goods and services usually considered as 'licit' – i.e. they pertain to the more common informal activities through which regular citizens in urban settings make a living and not to the more exceptional war-zone economies or criminal networks handling drugs, smuggled weapons and so on. The more usual informal activities of the sort treated in this book have also been classified by different analysts as being either legal or illegal, sometimes alluding to political implications.[8] In the latter case, differences in legality/illegality between, for example, casual workers and unlicensed traders have been said to explain why the latter groups are particularly exposed to the punitive actions of the state (Potts 2008). This may be so, but this relationship between illegal status and state disciplinary action or law enforcement interventions is certainly not automatic. The state can both appeal to the law and resort to the 'state of exception' (i.e. suspend the law) (Agamben 1998). The result is a situation of legal uncertainty for many people in the informal economy, as well as a blurring of the conceptual boundary between the legal and the illegal (the inside and the outside of the law). Rather than thinking of legality/illegality in terms of definite attributes and clear-cut boundaries, one can consider the social struggles involved in the shifting of those boundaries over time (Castells and Portes 1989: 33), the endeavours for recognition and the interpretive battles through which certain economic activities become legitimized or criminalized (Roitman 2004).

The categories of workers in the book include vendors, marketers, cross-border traders, casual port workers, casual waste collectors, informal manufacture workers and tailors. The settings in which they work are mainly urban.[9] People depending on these various kinds of informal work are, for reasons of convenience, interchangeably referred to in this chapter as 'informal actors', 'informals' or 'informal workers'. This unavoidably subsumes a great diversity of people, which is hopefully compensated for by an emphasis on diversity and differentiation in the informal economy.

The emergence of new organized actors

Civil associations have multiplied since the 1990s in Africa, particularly in urban areas (Aina 1997; Olukoshi 2005; Tostensen et al. 2001). Some of these associations have been induced by external funding agencies and on the initiative of powerful local groups. But there is also a growing number of grassroots organizations that are not necessarily subservient to those interests. Many are contesting current policies, claiming recognition, basic socio-economic rights and participation, as well as addressing various forms of exclusion (Aina 1997; Ballard 2005; Lindberg and Sverrisson 1997: 14). It is in this broader context of reconfiguring civil societies that we also see the emergence of a new generation of collective organizations around informal livelihood issues.

We witness today, across a variety of contexts in the South, the emergence of collective initiatives articulating a concern for vulnerable groups in the informal economy, engaging with key centres of power and contesting unfavourable policies and regulations in visible ways. The Self-Employed Women's Association (SEWA) in India could be considered one of the pioneers in this respect. Created in the early 1970s, it is today one of the world's largest informal economy organizations (Gallin 2004). It came to inspire the creation and agendas of organizations in other contexts, including in Africa, as well as the formation of grassroots networks across countries and regions. Many of these 'new' actors engage in advocacy and are making themselves visible through a variety of strategies, including the use of the media, publicity campaigns and protests. Many are also making use of litigation and the courts to assert the right to a livelihood, contest evictions and harassment (Cohen et al. 2000). In sub-Saharan Africa, while associations in the informal economy have often been described as 'inward-looking', i.e. mainly welfare- or business-oriented and circumscribed by kinship, ethnic and religious affinities (Mitullah 2003), the associational landscape is today more diverse, following trends in other regions in the South (see War on Want et al. 2006; Devenish and Skinner 2006; Setšabi 2006; chapter by Brown and Lyons, this volume).

An important development is that a number of informal economy organizations in different contexts are 'scaling up', potentially opening new possibilities for political intervention. They have created federated bodies at the national level in Kenya, Tanzania, Zambia, India and Peru (Cohen et al. 2000; ILO 2007; chapters by Mitullah and Brown and Lyons, this volume). Others are sub-regional in scope, such as the Cross-Border Traders Association, examined in the chapter by Nchito and Hansen. Transcontinental networks have also emerged in recent years. One such network, StreetNet International, is composed of some thirty member organizations engaged in organizing vendors in Africa, Latin America and Asia. Another example is Women in Informal Employment: Globalizing and Organizing (WIEGO), an international activist, research and policy network, whose members include organizations of informal 'workers'. These networks create opportunities for associations from different countries to share experiences and promote solidarity among themselves.

A new discourse has also emerged during the last few years that places the rights of people in the informal economy at its core. This discourse is evident among a growing number of local organizations and in the agendas of the above-mentioned international networks. It has also gained considerable international currency with the adoption by the ILO of the 'decent work' agenda at its International Labour Conference in 2002 (ILO 2002a, 2002b). Some elements of this general discourse can be discerned (Cohen et al. 2000; WIEGO n.d.;

Horn 2003; Gallin 2004). For example, it is an assertive discourse according to which people making a living in the informal economy are seen to be making a substantial contribution to their national economies. Consequently, from this perspective, informal income activities should be recognized by governments. First, governments should allow informals to have a say in planning and policy-making. Second, they should decriminalize informal activities and afford them legal status, thereby granting informal operators the right to earn a living, to be free from harassment, etc. Organized people in the informal economy increasingly refer to themselves, or are referred to, as 'workers', claiming that they should be legally recognized as such, be entitled to basic workers' rights and enjoy legal protection (Lund and Skinner 1999: 30–34; ILO 2002a, 2002b). There is increasing emphasis on the importance of collective organizing and representation in the struggle to achieve and protect the above rights, as well as for ensuring representation of the concerns of informal workers in the relevant forums (Horn 2003; ILO 2002a, 2002b). Accordingly, the recognition of informal workers' organizations and of their right to organize is considered to be crucial.

There are thus internationalizing discourses that for the first time stress the rights of informal people and the central importance of collective organizing for achieving those rights. Such discourses are novel and significant in various ways. They challenge the hegemonic views of informality held by political elites in many developing countries as a marginal and insignificant economic sphere (see the chapter by Brown and Lyons, this volume). They also contest governments' discursive references to the illegality of informal livelihoods, so often used to justify forceful acts against disadvantaged groups in the informal economy. The increasing reference to people in the informal economy as 'workers' is also forcing a reformulation of the notion of 'worker', contesting the exclusive proprietorship of this term by the traditional 'working class'.

To be sure, there are considerable obstacles to collective organizing in the informal economy (ILO 2002a), as several of the contributions in this volume acknowledge (see particularly the chapters by Meagher, Mitullah and Jimu). Lack of material resources, of leadership skills and of political connections are among the problems often encountered by vulnerable groups in their attempts to organize. Migrants, poor women, the disabled, the aged, youth and children, often found in the poorest layers of the informal economy, seem to face particular constraints in organizing and are often excluded from many ongoing initiatives. In addition, many organizations continue to be very limited in size and scope, isolated or restricted to particular communities or economic niches, with limited ability for political intervention, even at the locality level (Cohen et al. 2000; Mitlin 2004). But the picture is now more diverse, making it worthwhile to study those instances where disadvantaged groups have been able to organize in spite of these limitations. Among organized informal actors, the degree of success certainly varies widely, as the chapters in this book make evident. In some cases, political and economic marginality and a range of external and internal constraints hinder informal economy associations from developing a political voice (chapters by Meagher and Brown and Lyons, this volume). In other cases, associations have been able to secure certain rights, to establish a dialogue with the authorities or to have their interests represented in policy-making and implementation (chapters by Mitullah and Nchito and Hansen, this volume; Cohen et al. 2000). Some have argued that the ability to organize collectively plays a central role in such achievements (Amis 2004; Mitullah, this volume; Setšabi 2006). The new generation of organized actors expressing the concerns of the vulnerable must, however, be understood in the context of a much wider range of organized interests and actors to be found today in the informal economy.

Differentiation in the informal economy and associational dynamics

Contemporary informal economies are heterogeneous and highly differenti-ated. They are traversed by hierarchies, divisions and inequalities often struc-tured along lines of income level, gender, age, ethnicity and race, whose specific contours are time- and place-specific. Contemporary dynamics appear to have an impact on those divisions and on the social composition of informal economies in many contexts. This section provides some illustrations of how such changes are reshaping associational patterns and dynamics and the implications for the collective identities of informal actors.

Marked economic differentiation has become a feature of many informal economies today (Alsayyad 2004; Bayat 2004; Hansen and Vaa 2004: 11). These economies can no longer be considered to be the exclusive domain of the 'working poor' and the vulnerable. Rather than representing a level field, they contain today considerable income differences. As mentioned, they also contain a multiplicity of relations of employment and dependence in which individuals are differently positioned (as employers, employees, apprentices, suppliers, commissioned workers, etc.). Indeed, today a great variety of groups operate in the informal economy with varying degrees of economic capacity, as stated above. Groups commanding resources, contacts and skills have ven-tured into the informal economy and have sometimes been in a position to benefit and even thrive in the context of economic liberalization and crisis. These groups may also organize themselves to pursue their own interests. For example, employers in the informal economy are creating their own organiza-tions or joining existing employer associations, as is the case in Kenya and Ghana (ILO 2007). Cross-border traders, many with sizeable businesses, also organize into associations, as for example in Zambia and Mozambique (War on Want et al. 2006; chapter by Nchito and Hansen, this volume). Leading figures in hierarchical business networks are often represented in organizations such as chambers of commerce, which often enjoy access to the state, as in Senegal and Guinea-Bissau (chapter by Brown and Lyons, this volume; Lourenço-Lindell 2002). Some of these are thus well-resourced associations, standing in contrast to associations with overwhelmingly poor members.

Actors with advantageous positions in the informal economy may organize to maintain and further those positions. This raises the question of how better-resourced associations relate to organizations representing the concerns of poorer workers in the informal economy in particular contexts – do they ignore them, work against them or work with them? In addition, disadvantaged people may find themselves in dependent relations with those better-off actors (who may be their employers, suppliers, etc.). This may have implications for their ability to organize and voice their concerns – not least given the high levels of precariousness that tend to characterize their work and livelihoods. Importantly, however, the 'poor' or the 'vulnerable' in the informal economy are by no means a unified category with the same interests and inclinations.

The great economic differentiation that characterizes informal economies today is not simply expressed in organizational forms that are divided along lines of economic capacity. A proportion of informal economy organizations in Africa integrate people of different economic standing – both in terms of income and position in employment relations. This can be found, for example, among some trader associations, such as the largest one in Mozambique, described in Lindell (2008a), encompassing both poor and better-off members, as well as among associations in the transport sector – as in the case of the Ghana Private Road Transport Union, which includes both vehicle owners and hired drivers (Adu-Amankwah 1999). This 'multi-class' composition can be found both in many membership-based associations of more recent origin and in hierarchical networks (both male and female) with a longer history (see chapters by Prag, Brown and Lyons and Scheld, this volume), as further discussed below.[10] Better-off individuals (in terms of income, education, contacts, etc.) tend to have easier access to positions of leadership.[11] This requires attentiveness to the power relations within associations and to the issue of whose interests such associations serve – particularly where they claim to represent and defend the interests of poor members. But one should also contemplate the possibility that, in some instances, such 'multi-class' associations may also hold potential for overcoming some of the notable constraints that often deter poorer groups from organizing on their own.

The above patterns and developments contradict decades of writing that associated the informal economy exclusively with the poor and the dispossessed. They make evident that 'the political subjectivities of informals should not be seen in terms of a singular class subject, [...] sharing the same class interest' (Lindell 2010a). In addition, many individuals in the informal economy diversify their livelihoods by moving across several social and economic fields and thus may simultaneously occupy different class positions in different economic spheres. The 'multi-class' composition of some associations suggests that the collective identities they give rise to are not anchored in a singular, unified, coherent class subjectivity. It also suggests that the contours and agendas of collective organizations of informal workers cannot be mechanically read from their specific structural positions in society (ibid.). Rather, the challenge is to examine the tensions and possibilities that emerge from already existing collective forms that bridge multiple (class) locations.

As stated above, divisions and hierarchies in the informal economy are also shaped by relations of gender, ethnicity and race, themselves also being reconfigured. Economic liberalization and neoliberal policies set in motion certain trends that have changed the conditions of women's participation in the informal economy in many places. A documented trend in a wide variety of settings is that women tend to be over-represented at the lowest income levels and that many are experiencing worsening conditions (Chen et al. 2002; ILO 2002a: 31–2; Lourenço-Lindell 2002: 157–8). At the same time, there is evidence that economic differentiation is increasing among women and women's associations may also reflect these economic cleavages (as the chapters by Nchito and Hansen and by Prag indicate). Women, especially those at the lower end of the informal economy, appear to be particularly vulnerable to the hostility of governments (partly by virtue of the often exposed locations of their work) and to being discriminated against in consultation processes (Cohen et al. 2000; Clark 2010). Well-positioned women in affluent networks, however, are sometimes able to exercise informal influence on political elites (see chapter by Prag, this volume).

Self-employed women in many contexts have long elaborated networks and associations, such as those that continue to regulate relations in the markets in Ghana and Benin and to provide traders with a number of important services (chapters by Prag and by Brown and Lyons, this volume). In the last decades, women's associations have multiplied in many places (Cohen et al. 2000; Horn 2002; Lund and Skinner 1999). At the same time, dual-sex groups are also increasing in number. The extent to which women participate in the leadership of and exercise influence within such associations is therefore a pertinent question (Lund and Skinner 1999: 33; chapter by Prag, this volume). A related development of significance is the visible growth in the participation of men in the informal economy in a context of large-scale retrenchments and declining access to wage jobs. In contexts where women have long traditions in trading, such as in West Africa, men sometimes appear to be penetrating economic spheres and niches that used to be dominated by women (Clark 2010; chapter by Prag, this volume). As Prag reports, market women in Cotonou are not only facing economic competition from men. Men are also creating dual-sex unions that compete with women's long-existing associations as well as marginalizing women from leadership positions. The market women, however, also devise strategies to deal with these developments.

Indeed, some organizing forms in the informal economy, rather than being recent creations in response to contemporary economic and political processes, are informed by historically evolved social relations, cultures and forms of belonging (Meagher 2009; Lourenço-Lindell 2002; Roitman 1990). Several of the contributions here address such forms of organizing and their historical and cultural embeddedness (see in particular the chapters by Brown and Lyons, Meagher, Boampong, Prag and Scheld). Such forms range from 'traditional' worker gangs integrated into the contemporary practices of labour agencies for the recruitment of casual labour (Boampong's chapter) to a variety of networks and associations structured around ethnic, religious and kinship-related identities. While some of these associations and networks seem to have been debilitated by contemporary developments (Meagher's chapter), others have come to command the growth sectors in some countries and to engage in dense international connections through import-export activities (Lourenço-Lindell 2002; Diouf 2000; Meagher 1995). These latter networks, hierarchical in structure, often make extensive use of informal contracts and 'unregulated' work – though other kinds of regulating norms are at work (Lourenço-Lindell 2002; Meagher 1995). Drawing on idioms of religion, ethnicity and kinship, these networks tend to be 'particularistic' and exclusionary in character. For example, as reported in the chapter by Brown and Lyons, Muslim brotherhoods in Senegal often refuse admission to migrants and youth.

The above divisions, boundaries and hierarchies in the informal economy are, however, not fixed or permanent, even if they are resilient. Tightly drawn boundaries must be actively maintained, but may also be contested and put to the test by wider societal processes. For example, the growing number of Chinese entrepreneurs in the informal economy of Dakar who compete with pre-existing trader networks is prompting a variety of organized expressions and is reconfiguring alliances and oppositions in civil society, as described by Scheld. More generally, at a time when economic survival necessitates intensified mobility within and between countries and armed conflicts increase the numbers of refugees crossing national borders, ethnic-regional and sociocultural competition is reportedly increasing and is often accompanied by manifestations of xenophobia (Olukoshi 2005; Nyamnjoh 2006). Such manifestations are also evident in the informal economy in some contexts and sometimes find collectively organized expression (Amis 2004). Local reactions to the increasing presence of Chinese entrepreneurs are only the latest in a series of boundaries that have been drawn and redrawn over time between 'insiders' and 'outsiders' in the informal economy.

In contrast, other forms of association gather individuals from very different cultural and social backgrounds and in some cases from different countries. The regional association of cross-border traders described in the chapter by Nchito and Hansen, for example, functions as a network to facilitate participation by foreign members in local markets and fosters tolerance between members from different countries. On a larger scale, the emerging global networks of organized informal workers mentioned earlier also attempt to build identities that are inclusive rather than particularistic.

As has been described in this section, various axes of power and differentiation – along lines of income, gender, ethnic belonging, etc. – are at work in informal economies. Informal economies can thus be best understood in terms of multiple fields of power that intersect and interact to shape configurations of advantage and disadvantage in specific contexts. People in the informal economy thus simultaneously experience several kinds of injustice and contradictions and thus 'occupy multiple, rather than single, subject positions' (Lindell 2010a). For example, the women members in the dual-sex association at the Cotonou market mentioned above have to deal with both patriarchal relations within the association and with the exigencies of the government (chapter by Prag, this volume). Informal actors can be said to bear multiple and fragmented identities – rather than single and coherent ones – that may sometimes be difficult to reconcile.

Given the complex and multiple subjectivities of informal actors, as well as the heterogeneous composition of many of their associations (as manifested in the above-mentioned 'multi-class', dual-sex, multi-ethnic, multinational associations), one may ask what kinds of collective identities are possible or whether unity of purpose can be achieved. I have discussed the complexities involved in the formation of the subjectivities and collective identities of informals at greater length elsewhere (Lindell 2010a). Here, it is worth stressing that 'interests' and 'unity' within associations are not to be taken as given or unproblematic, but rather as actively constructed. This negotiated and contested naming of grievances results in frames that may be enacted through particular discursive practices. Such frames are thus evolving, flexible, often strategic and targeted at various audiences.

In the same light, the collective identities of organized informal workers are not pre-given or stable, but are rather continuously constructed and reconstructed through multiple struggles and relations and in response to wider societal change. In this process of collective identity formation, informal actors may engage in the construction of boundaries and of categories of difference. This is illustrated by the examples above pertaining to the exclusionary nature of some associations and the processes of Othering that have accompanied the penetration of Chinese traders in Dakar. But collective identity construction may also transgress existing boundaries and create new categories of sameness and novel forms of identification. New common ground may thus be created where it was previously non-existent. This is exemplified in the regional trader's organization and the global grassroots networks mentioned above, as well as the emerging relations with trade unions discussed later in this chapter. Indeed, the collective identities of informals are shaped by interactions with various other actors in society. This includes relations with other organized groups as well as with dominating power. This chapter now turns to a discussion of the latter, as such relations constitute a key theme in this collection and are a core concern in Part One.

Relations with dominating power

Contemporary informal economies are governed by a variety of dispersed actors and institutions operating beyond the state (Lindell 2008a; Roitman 2004; Lourenço-Lindell 2002; Meagher 2009). These governing actors range from those with a highly localized reach to those operating on an international scale. One may speak of a multilevel governance involving elements of regulation at various and changing spatial scales. This makes for a complex multilayered politics and for multiple arenas of political engagement. In spite of the myriad regulatory powers that compete with the state, the state emerges in many of the chapters in this collection as an important centre of power – even if not the only one. This section, therefore, discusses how we can understand the relations between informal actors and the state; some of these reflections can, however, also apply to their relations with a number of other governance actors. The nature of these relations is a matter of contention in the literature on informality.

Previous work has shown how, in a range of contexts in Africa and beyond, the state is a major source of anxiety for many people in the informal economy (Amis 2004; Brown 2006a; Roy 2004a; Clark 1988). Crackdowns, evictions and confiscations imposed by state agents on groups of informals appear to be intensifying in many African cities in the context of neoliberal urbanization (Hansen 2004; Lindell and Kamete, forthcoming; Potts 2008). Thus, a number of informal economy organizations appear to have been created primarily to address the major threat posed by the state (Lindell 2008a; War on Want et al. 2006). These recurrent tensions have led a number of influential thinkers to view the politics of informality in terms of a natural, clear-cut and binary opposition between informal actors and the state. This view has its roots in a deeply entrenched understanding of activities in the informal sphere as state-free, 'non-state' or 'against-the-state'. Thus, informal actors have usually been described as evading state regulations, disengaging from the state, resisting state power or gradually forcing it into retreat.[12] They are seen as being necessarily autonomous from and opposed to state power. While such accounts have helped to highlight the agency of people in the informal economy, they have often constructed informals as a relatively homogeneous and undifferentiated group – the familiar category of the 'working poor' – sharing a common structural position, relentlessly pushing against the same oppressive power, as if driven by a common intent or a singular identity. These images are at odds with the highly differentiated nature of today's informal economies and with the more complex understandings of the identities of informals discussed above. For the political identities and behaviour of organized informal actors towards the state cannot be reduced to one of sharp opposition.

A different strand of work rejects the above notions of informal actors as being anti-state or autonomous from it. Such work emphasizes that 'unregulated' economies are central to the contemporary reconstitution of state power (Roitman 2004). Actors in such economies, while seemingly operating beyond the reach of the state, do not escape the political logics of the state and its webs of domination. They are drawn into vertical clientelist networks of personalistic power relations that reach into the legal institutions of the state and through which the state extends its power into society. In this perspective, bankrupt states increasingly engage in rent-seeking practices in 'unregulated' markets, particularly in criminal networks handling drugs, smuggled arms, etc. The growth of such 'unregulated' economies, driven by the needs of predatory states, is seen as leading to the emergence of 'shadow states' and to the so-called criminalization of the state (Bayart et al. 1999; Reno 2000). In these accounts, such vertical economic-political networks hamper the development of civil society, whose organizations necessarily fall prey to the same clientelist logic (see Gay 2006 for a critique; see Meagher's chapter, this volume, and 2009, for a discussion). While these perspectives have shed light on the entangled relations that may exist between informal and state actors, the prospects for ordinary informal actors to break from the logics of dominating power appear very limited as, in this model, there are seldom autonomous spaces from which to express grievances. There are other forms of political engagement and other kinds of association, linkage and alliance in which regular people in the informal economy engage and which cannot be captured by the vertical clientelist and criminal network model.

The relations between informal actors and the state cannot be reduced to either unequivocal antagonism or to hybrid clientelist networks. Reified views of such relations tend to essentialize both the state and the political inclinations of informals and their organizations. The political behaviour of both is more varied and complex. State actors may use various modes of power that range from seduction to coercion, from indirect techniques to overt sanctions (Allen 2004). First, the state may try to infiltrate or co-opt associations of informal workers – and indeed, starved of resources and influence, many associations are very vulnerable to political capture (see Meagher's chapter, this volume). The state may use associations in the informal economy or even create new ones in order to use them as an infrastructure for the exercise of its power or for the implementation of neoliberal rationalities. Through various forms of governmentality, the state may attempt to make informal actors legible to itself

and governable. But, as mentioned above, the state may also use forceful measures and frontal aggression towards what it regards as unruly and destabilizing
groups of informal workers. Clean-up campaigns and militarized operations to
empty city streets of vendors, for example, are becoming increasingly common
in cities in Africa and beyond, not infrequently in anticipation of the hosting
of some international event (Hansen 2004; Lindell and Kamete, forthcoming;
Potts 2008; Roy 2004a). These and other interventions are often legitimized by
state discourses that marginalize and criminalize certain categories of informal
workers. For example, urban street vendors and marketers are often blamed for
a variety of evils, ranging from city decay, street congestion and theft to cholera
outbreaks (see Brown and Lyons's chapter, this volume). These criminalizing
and pathologizing discourses that represent certain categories of informals as
threats to public order, public health, public security, etc., also constitute a
mechanism of power – although, as discussed earlier, organizations of informal
workers are also articulating their counter-discourses.

Even if the regulatory capacity of the state has been eroded, the state also
makes its influence felt among groups of informals through the arbitrariness of
its practices and interventions. Rather than being merely the prime law enforcer,
the state may also suspend the law and resort to the 'state of exception', which
itself can be seen as a technique of power.[13] This may partly explain why, for
example, existing labour laws are not enforced; long-forgotten regulations are
suddenly evoked to justify an eviction (Lindell and Kamete, forthcoming); or
how many associations of informal workers, while legal, continue to be treated
by the state as illegal (Brown 2006a; War on Want et al. 2006; Lindell 2008a;
Brown and Lyons's chapter, this volume). Through the arbitrariness of its practices, the state both renders itself illegible to informals and fosters a sense of
uncertainty and risk that makes it difficult for them to make long-term plans
or to consolidate their positions.[14]

The various – and apparently contradictory – modalities of power used by
the state may coexist and be combined.[15] They may also change over time and
be deployed selectively upon particular groups of informals. The state may act
differently towards different groups in the informal economy – although such
relations are always temporal, as stated below. It may harass some groups and
protect or be an accomplice of others (Lindell 2008a). More generally, the realization that the state is not a unified and coherent oppressive power also opens
up the possibility of alliances between disadvantaged groups in the informal
economy and progressive state actors.

Informal workers and their associations too are not bound to one particular type of political behaviour and may rather make use of various modes of
influence, depending on the particular context and the opportunities available
to different groups. Some of these associations engage in networking with
political elites and sometimes achieve some influence through such channels

(see chapters by Brown and Lyons and Prag, this volume). While many would argue that such relations ultimately reproduce wider power structures in society, popular participants are not necessarily powerless. Even where associations have been created by the imperatives of dominating power, they sometimes escape initial dominant rationalities and acquire dynamics of their own.[16] But these forms of political exchange suggest that common claims that civil society necessarily brings about a transition from clientelism to citizenship – among informal workers or more generally – should be taken with caution (see Gay 2006 for a discussion).

Other associations, as discussed earlier in this chapter, openly challenge the state by contesting unfavourable policies and hostile practices. They may strive for inclusion in formal processes of urban governance (see Brown and Lyons's chapter for a discussion). They may also construct alternative discourses to the state's criminalizing and marginalizing representations, thereby engaging in a symbolic politics of contestation. Thus, organized informal actors engage with political elites in varied and complex ways. Not infrequently, they combine and use multiple and contradictory modes of engagement with political elites, and may attempt to exert influence on the state through both formal and informal avenues that in practice may be difficult to separate (Fernández-Kelly 2006; Pieterse 2008; Lindell 2008a; see also the chapters in Part One). Sometimes, they frontally oppose some state actors while playing along with others and are occasionally able to advance their positions by exploiting inconsistencies and contradictions within the state (see empirical examples in Cross 1998a; Pieterse 2008; Lindell 2008a). This may include taking advantage of divisions and tensions between local and central levels of the state, at a time when relations between these are being reconfigured.[17] In the current context of multiparty politics, where the large crowds in the informal economy are often regarded as 'vote banks', association leaders may sometimes gain some leverage by playing off politicians against each other, as documented by Gay in Brazil (2006). However, particularly in cities where ruling parties have lost local elections to the opposition, intensified political competition may deepen urban tensions and generate unrest among informal workers, as is the case with marketers in Kampala at the time of writing.

A nuanced understanding of the nature of relations between informal actors and the state requires a socially differentiated analysis of these relations that considers the configurations of gender, class, ethnic and racial dimensions of state power in particular contexts, as these often constitute axes of power and differentiation at work in informal economies. The marked social and economic differentiation that characterizes contemporary informal economies and the highly diverse landscape of organized actors in them warrant an examination of the different and varied ways in which different groups and interests in the informal economy experience and relate to the state.

The political subjectivities of informal actors and their associations are not to be assumed, but empirically investigated. I concur with Kate Meagher (2009) that the political character of networks and associations in the informal economy is shaped by the specific contexts in which they exist. The nature of the relations between informals' associations and the state cannot therefore be universalized or predicted. One can rather expect great variations between different societies – which are also evident throughout this book – as well as within societies. The contours of such relations are also temporal, reflecting the specific historical trajectories of states and civil societies in particular contexts. For example, Clark (2010) describes how relationships between traders and governing powers in Ghana alternated through history between complicity and antagonism. Others have shown how periods of state tolerance and sympathy for informal vendors gave way to periods of intolerance and repression, as happened in Zimbabwe, Zambia and Malawi.[18]

The ways in which associations of informal workers relate to the state, their political practices and discourses and their collective identities are also shaped by their relations with other non-state actors, both those in their proximity and those afar, as discussed in the next two sections.

Organizing across the formal–informal 'divide'[19]

As stated earlier, there is an increasingly diverse landscape of organized initiatives in the informal economy. This makes it pertinent to consider relations between different organized actors in the study of the politics of informality, both the tensions that may emerge from their encounters and the new political opportunities that may be created out of intersections and alliances. Such relations can be of many different kinds and involve a variety of actors. This section discusses one particular set of relations, those emerging between informal workers and trade unions. This is also the central theme in Part Two of this book.

Trade unions in some countries increasingly attempt to reach out to informal and casual workers.[20] This development ought to be understood in the context of the decline in membership that trade unions are experiencing in many parts of the world in the context of global economic change and labour market de-regulation (Gallin 2001; Bieler et al. 2008). The intensified informalization and casualization of work that have accompanied these processes have resulted in growing numbers of people making a living outside the state-regulated wage sector, where trade unions have their main constituencies. In an effort to halt membership losses, retain influence and bring about 'trade union renewal', some trade unions have adopted strategies of mobilization in the informal economy. There are great variations between and within countries regarding the extent and nature of trade union involvement in the informal economy (see Lindell 2008b for an overview of these relations in Africa). In some cases, trade unions directly recruit 'informal workers' into their membership ranks, while in other cases they establish relationships with existing self-organized initiatives in the informal economy. This collection critically assesses current experiences of organizing across the formal–informal 'divide', especially in the African context.

Some of the emerging literature addressing these developments reflects the entrenched perception that collective organizing is an exclusive capacity of formal wage workers, whereby other categories of workers (the self-employed, casual workers, etc.) are deemed incapable of self-organizing. Organizing the 'unorganized' then becomes the mission of trade unions (see, for example, Moody 2005). The danger implicit in such a view is that people in the informal economy may be seen as passive targets awaiting the rescuing hand of trade unions. Alternatively – and as we repeatedly insist in this introduction – we should look upon people in the informal economy as *actors*, capable of various initiatives, including organizing themselves, despite the many obstacles they often face. Attempts at organizing across the formal–informal 'divide' should be assessed not merely from the vantage point of 'trade union renewal', but also from the perspective of informal actors. The latter, just like trade unions, have their own reasons to engage in, disengage from or avoid close relationships with trade unions.

The idea that trade unions should engage more closely with people in the informal economy has gained international currency in several circles in recent years, including in some international activist networks and some international labour organizations.[21] Trade unions figure as key actors in the ILO's campaign for creating decent work in the informal economy – and they do this, it is worth noting, alongside employers' organizations (see ILO 2002a). The rationale behind this position is that trade unions should engage with *all* kinds of workers irrespective of *where* they work (in the factories, the sweatshops, the streets, etc.). The vision is to 'transform unions into a social movement of *working people*' (ILO 2002a: 84, my emphasis). Proponents in the academic community have come to espouse similar views under the label of 'social movement unionism' or 'new social unionism' (Waterman 1999; Moody 2005; see also the chapter by Jordhus-Lier, this volume). The latter views emphasize the importance of trade unions entering alliances with other popular social forces and reaching out to the 'unorganized' groups of self-employed and casual workers. The result will be a broadened 'working class' struggle (Moody 2005).

But the emerging close relationships between trade unions and informals and their organizations raise a number of issues that warrant reflection. First, people making a living in the informal economy experience types of constraints and contradictions that differ from those faced by workers in the regulated wage sector – some would even claim that they have 'opposing interests'. The two are often seen as embedded in different kinds of social relations of production (see the chapter by Andrae and Beckman, this volume) and therefore as occupying different structural locations. The question that arises is whether such different interests can be bridged and reconciled. Second, given that the informal economy encompasses a huge diversity of work situations and myriad types of employment relationships, it can also be asked whether trade unions can represent such a heterogeneous constituency, which includes, as noted above, employers in the informal economy. Third, where trade unions encounter self-organizing initiatives in the informal economy, one wonders how they relate to such initiatives and what opportunities as well as tensions may emerge from such an encounter.

On the basis of the above and other concerns, many disavow trade union organizing in the informal economy – which some of the contributions in Part Two also do, although conceding the possibility of collaboration and alliance between autonomous organizations. As will become evident, the four contributions in Part Two look differently upon the possibilities and challenges involved. While the above are legitimate concerns, there is some scope for conceptual flexibility. One may understand 'interests' as constructed and negotiated meanings of injustice, rather than objective, given and fixed or 'fully determined by people's structural position in society' (Lindell 2010a), and this means that common ground can be created where it is least expected – for example, between informals and trade unions. The interpenetration between formal and informal 'sectors' and the ways in which individuals and households straddle different economic and social fields in the real world also suggest that interests in the two 'sectors' may not be that opposed after all, and point to the multiple and malleable identities of informal workers. A discourse of 'sameness' is emerging internationally that construes formal and informal workers as one working people, already sharing some common ground or basic affinities. Whether the collective identities of informal workers are being reshaped through new forms of identification with workers in the formal economy remains an issue for empirical investigation.

Vulnerable groups in the informal economy may be in need of strong allies, particularly considering that their organizations often struggle with lack of recognition and political clout. And in some instances, trade unions seem to provide informals and their organizations with a platform for dialogue with other relevant actors and for widening their arenas of influence (see chapters by Boampong and Jordhus-Lier, this volume; Lindell 2008b). But such an alliance between informals and trade unions is not to be seen as natural, given or permanent. Informal workers' organizations may invest in the construction of other forms of 'sameness' and opt for other kinds of allies. For example, in Kenya organized urban informal workers have instead joined hands with the land movement in the country and articulated their joint concerns in terms of access to 'land' from which to derive a livelihood, irrespective of its rural or urban location (see the chapter by Mitullah, this volume).[22] One needs to consider, however, that associations of informal workers are sometimes severely restricted in their choices of allies. Categories of workers who tend to be stigmatized by society (sometimes street vendors, waste pickers, etc.) may in some cases find it difficult to find other organized actors who want to associate with them.

In sum, it is imprudent to generalize about the possibilities or impossibilities for alliances on the basis of structural differences or innate affinities. The construction and deconstruction of alliances needs to be understood as situated in specific spatial and temporal contexts, as do actors' preferences and their selection of allies. Accordingly, the choices of informal actors cannot be easily predicted or universalized. They are to be understood in the context of particular and shifting constellations of available potential allies, themselves with their own malleable preferences and political inclinations. The research challenge is to inquire into how 'different interests' are being bridged in practice, and into processes of construction of sameness and difference by the actors involved. Practices of building alliances and bridging across difference are not necessarily restricted to local contexts, but may also connect informal actors across international space.

International organizing

The politics of informal economies involves processes and action at wider international and global scales. Contemporary informal economies, rather than being local, indigenous or vernacular, as was once believed, are extensively internationalized and are so in multiple ways. On the one hand, informal livelihood conditions and opportunities are deeply embedded in global processes. To be sure, this embeddedness is not new in itself, but rather represents a new chapter in a longer history of internationalization, evidencing considerable continuity (see chapters by Scheld, Nchito and Hansen and Prag, this volume). But certain contemporary processes of global change are impacting local livelihoods in new ways (as discussed below). At the same time, such processes may also trigger organized responses that reach beyond national borders.

Many analyses connect contemporary informalization with processes of economic 'globalization'. In contrast, however, the politics of informals is most often described as confined to the local level (see, for example, Cross 2007 and Tripp 1997). Alternatively, informals are seen as mere victims at the receiving end of global processes. The perspective that we adopt here differs from these conceptions. First, while certainly experiencing the pressures and challenges posed by global forces, people in the informal economy are *active agents* rather than passive victims in the face of these forces and sometimes organize collectively in response to them. Second, while some of these organized responses take place at the local/national level, informal actors increasingly organize internationally, becoming international actors in their own right (Lindell 2009). Today, the collective agency of informal actors can no longer be said to be consigned to the local arena. Increasingly, rather, their politics appears to involve wider spatial scales of collective organizing.

This trend is occurring in the context of the wider contemporary internationalization of social movements and civil societies. While many global movements are initiated in the North, a variety of popular movements in the South are also transnationalizing, and many of them are focused on livelihood issues (Lindberg and Sverrisson 1997: 1–5; Soane et al. 2005). Informal economy organizations, as mentioned above, are also scaling up by building federated bodies as well as transnational networks. Member organizations of these transnational networks participate in international workshops and exchange visits organized by the networks, which activities provide participants with opportunities to relate their experiences to those of distant others (Lindell 2009). One can also discern the emergence of a loose network of international actors – including various regional and international networks, global union federations, etc. – that have informal livelihood issues as their core concern (Gallin 2004) and engage in dialogue with each other. These international connections have facilitated instances of coordinated action and campaigns regarding informal work, as, for example, at the World Social Forum held in Nairobi in 2007. Such networks are also facilitating the internationalization of discourses emphasizing the rights of people working in the informal economy.

International organizing by groups in the informal economy can be driven by a great variety of interests as well as forces. This collection illustrates only a few of these. First, changes in international political relations may set in motion processes that impact on the dynamics of local informal economies. The current intensification of the relations between African countries and China is a good example (Alves and Draper 2006; Wild and Mepham 2006). The penetration of Chinese people and goods into Africa is in some places altering the local constellation of actors, and closing and opening livelihood opportunities for different groups, as well as disturbing some social hierarchies in local informal economies. Scheld describes in her chapter the considerable tensions resulting from these developments in the informal economy of Dakar, where a range of organized actors – traders' and consumers' associations, but also a Chinese business association – make use of their international linkages as they attempt to influence these local contests.

Second, the 'global era' is also marked by the rising influence of supranational governance institutions and 'sovereignties'.[23] These are often prime drivers of economic liberalization and of the expansion of the free market, and some are involved in the production of international regulatory regimes with an impact on informal livelihoods. These institutions have contributed to turning informal economies into major distribution 'channels' of international commodities, and to increasing the exposure of informal workers to global market forces, as well as to opening opportunities for certain groups to internationalize their economic activities. While most analyses see the politics of informality exclusively in terms of relations with the state, it is just as relevant to investigate how informal economy organizations relate to such supranational governance institutions. Nchito and Hansen's contribution examines how a sub-regional association of cross-border traders lobbies a regional governing body for a deeper liberalization of regional trade. Third, groups in the informal economy may organize internationally primarily to address power relations at the local level (Lindell 2009; see also Mitullah's chapter, this volume). As mentioned earlier, many associations lack recognition, are pressed by intolerant governments and their members have to defend constantly their right to a livelihood. When under attack by local authorities, associations affiliated to international networks are often able to mobilize solidarity in their international partners (Lindell 2009). Their international experience may also enable them to articulate alternative visions for the city, thereby contesting the modernist ideals that many urban governments espouse (ibid.).

In sum, organizing by actors in the informal economy appears to be increasingly linked to various types of international and global networks. This warrants consideration of how these multiple scales of collective organizing are shaping the collective identities and discourses of informal workers. One may ask whether an increase in international interactions is giving rise to transnational identities among informal actors. However, one should be cautious about claims that such emerging transnational movements are leading to the emergence of *unified* identities across countries and regions, as Moody (2005), for example, suggests in connection with the rise of an 'international social-movement unionism'. While some groups of informal workers in different countries may share similar concerns (for example, harassment by the authorities, etc.), universalizing their experiences of injustice makes invisible the ways in which solidarity and common ground in such transnational movements have to be worked for, i.e. are constructed, through negotiation among highly diverse participants.

The ability of informals' organizations and the individuals within them to participate in transnational activist networks cannot, of course, be taken for granted. Many of them suffer variously from serious material constraints, poor access to Internet technologies and limited opportunities to travel abroad. Women may face additional constraints, not to speak of children and the elderly, many of whom earn a living in the informal economy. Cumbers et al. (2008: 189) have discussed how the majority of grassroots activists in the global South are unable to participate directly in transnational movements and are dependent upon 'imagineers', actors who are critical in furthering connectivity, in channelling information and in 'translating' the vision of the network to the grass roots. Similarly, the internationalizing activism among informal workers appears to be both differentiated and mediated (see Lindell 2010b for a thorough discussion). Even so, it is not necessarily without political significance, as suggested above. What is evident is that the ability to internationalize can no longer be seen as the exclusive prerogative of local elites. The perception of informals as a crowd necessarily 'trapped' in place is becoming increasingly difficult to sustain. Their increasing collective organizing at wider scales is of relevance for understanding the politics of informality today.

Complex landscapes of actors and the politics of informality

The above discussion of contemporary trends in collective organizing in the informal economy in Africa and beyond reveals a rapidly changing landscape of organizing initiatives and a highly dynamic associational environment, a landscape being shaped both by global processes and by local forces, histories and cultures. It brings to light a tendency towards diversification of organized actors in the informal economy, resulting in complex associational landscapes – although the level of diversification and the particular constellations of actors will vary between different places. The previous sections discuss the diversity of organized actors involved and general axes of change that can be identified: the emergence of new organized actors using a rights discourse and articulating concerns for vulnerable groups; the growing number of groups representing the interests of the non-poor in the informal economy; the multiplying initiatives of trade unions; and the increasing collective engagement in international networks. Some of these changes reflect novel patterns in collective organizing. But pre-existing patterns, many of them with deep historical roots and often structured along lines of gender, age, ethnic, religious or racial belonging, etc., are also being reworked in the face of the present challenges. Contemporary processes at work in informal economies, including changes in social composition and economic differentiation, appear to be changing the patterns and dynamics of collective organizing.

While the growing complexity of associational landscapes in the informal economy follows more general trends visible in many civil societies in Africa and beyond, its significance lies in its implications for our understanding of the politics of informality. The widening range of organized actors means that the associational environment in the informal economy should be seen as a complex political field with many collective players who may articulate different visions, rationales and interests. The way these different collective actors relate to each other is an important dimension of this politics – they may ally, compete or work against each other. These highly diverse actors may relate to relevant centres of power in very different ways. These centres include urban authorities and central state institutions, but also 'sovereignties' and loci of power located beyond the administrative reach or the territorial confines of the state. The analysis of the contemporary politics of informality thus requires a conceptual framework that takes account of the wide range of organized interests that exist today, of the various actors and governing powers that they may engage with and of the various scales of social struggle in which informal actors may participate (for conceptual discussions, see Lindell 2008a and 2010a).

These various relations, interactions and scales are implicated in the construction and reconstruction of the collective identities of informal actors. This is a networked politics that encompasses a complex web of actors and relations with shifting constellations, alliances and tensions, which are both time- and place-specific. This politics constitutes a broad field that invites situated analyses capable of accommodating the highly diverse, entangled and contingent nature of the politics of informality.

This collection does not claim to address the many sides and dimensions of this broad and complex political field. Rather, the contributions highlight certain aspects of this complexity, focusing on the particular areas of concern that were outlined in the introduction to this chapter: in short, the relations between organized informal actors and dominating power – where the state emerges from the contributions as an important actor, albeit not the only one; the emerging relations between informal actors and trade unions, to be seen as part of a wider range of possible relations between various organizing initiatives; and the international dimensions of organizing. These areas correspond with the three main thematic sections of the collection.

The contributions

The remainder of this chapter discusses the individual contributions of the authors relative to the three themes that structure the collection. As will become evident, the empirical contributions provide contrasting perspectives and findings.

The three chapters in Part One on 'The political dynamics of collective organizing' share a key concern, namely the scope for political influence by organized groups in the informal economy in the context of changes in the economic and political environment. The chapters present, however, contrasting views. The first two give a bleak picture of the prospects for contemporary informal economy organizations in terms of exercising political influence. Both claim that the development of a political voice by these organizations is hampered by political, economic, social, legal and institutional marginalization. Drawing on case studies in four cities (Dar es Salaam, Dakar, Accra and Kathmandu), the chapter by Alison Brown and Michal Lyons assesses the extent to which trader associations participate in formal processes of urban governance and succeed in extending urban citizenship to traders. The authors argue that in most of the studied cases, trader associations have been unable to maintain long-term influence in favour of their members. With the exception of the Senegalese brotherhoods, associations tend to be excluded from formal political processes and traders are often deemed 'unfit' to be citizens in the eyes of public authorities. In addition, it is argued, most associations are inward looking rather than engaging in advocacy and tend to be unrepresentative and exclusionary – of poorer traders, of migrants, etc. As a result, the authors conclude, the majority of traders' associations are 'seen but not heard'.

The chapter by Kate Meagher assesses the 'political fortunes' of producer associations in three informal manufacturing clusters in Nigeria. It argues that the autonomy and organizational capacity of these associations have generally been weakened in the context of political and economic liberalization. Deepening economic hardship has exacerbated conflicts within associations and has eroded their resource base, resulting in a weakened capacity for mobilization. In this context, association leaders also tend to resort to authoritarian leadership styles. At the same time, associations have become more dependent on the state and on NGOs for resources as well as vulnerable to political manipulation and co-option by political elites, something that effectively silences producers. The emerging trend, it is argued, is one towards political capture or exclusion rather than strengthening of political voice.

The contribution by Ebbe Prag provides a different perspective from the above two in that it attributes key political roles and political capabilities to the studied informal workers, in this case organized traders. It refers to a setting with historical traditions of women traders' associations and of female leadership in the markets. In his study of trader associations in the largest marketplace of Cotonou, Benin, Prag argues that organized market women and their leaders have been able to wield influence on public decisions affecting their livelihoods and the management of their market. The chapter discusses how female leaders exercise influence through informal channels by skilfully using political networks. While they become political brokers, it is argued, these leaders have also been able to defend the collective interests of their members. Prag depicts a situation where the political and bureaucratic elite have avoided open confrontation with the traders.

The four contributions in Part Two discuss current attempts at organizing across the formal–informal 'divide'. They assess the opportunities, challenges and difficulties involved in concrete cases where trade unions either extend their membership to individuals in the informal economy or establish a close relationship with organizations of 'informal workers'. The chapters present divergent views on the possibilities of effectively organizing across the formal–informal 'divide'. The first two chapters, by Gunilla Andrae and Björn Beckman and by Ignasio Malizani Jimu, share scepticism towards the role of trade unions in organizing in the informal economy. Andrae and Beckman discuss a current effort to merge a textile workers' union and a tailors' association in Kaduna, Nigeria. They argue that unions can neither 'integrate nor effectively organize workers in the informal economy' because of fundamental differences in social relations of production and in the nature of the contradictions at work, which warrant different forms of organization for different groups of workers. The chapter by Jimu compares organizations formed by informal workers themselves and initiatives that emerge from national trade unions in Malawi. While pointing to the many weaknesses of the former, the author also considers that organizing in the informal economy along trade union lines is rendered difficult by the variety of employment relations at work, and questions whether the interests of formal and informal constituents can be reconciled. Trade-union-based initiatives, it is argued, tend to reflect the agendas of the trade unions from which they originate. Jimu depicts a situation in which conflicts and power struggles between and within trade unions seeking to extend their work into the informal economy risk becoming a distraction from the task of addressing the real concerns of informal workers. However, both contributions contemplate a role for trade unions in supporting the self-organizing efforts of informal workers and their struggles.

The chapters by David Jordhus-Lier and Owusu Boampong provide a more positive picture of trade union involvement in the informal economy. Both address the role of trade unions in improving the conditions of casual workers and in eventually reversing the downgrading of labour resulting from casualization and flexibilization of labour. Jordhus-Lier discusses the strategies adopted by a municipal workers' union in Cape Town, South Africa, in response to the intertwined processes of privatization of municipal services and the informalization of the municipal workforce in the context of local government restructuring. Besides engaging in alliances with community organizations and social movements over service delivery issues, the union has begun to directly organize casual workers in private companies that perform former municipal tasks. Boampong discusses how the casualization of port work in Tema, Ghana, has given rise to an 'alliance' between a national trade union and local organizations of casual workers, where the latter have deep historical roots. Through affiliation to the trade union, it is argued, these organizations have been able to expand their influence on key actors and avoid labour downgrading. Jordhus-Lier and Boampong, however, also consider the difficulties and risks involved in these initiatives – for example, latent tensions between municipal workers and casual workers in Cape Town and the apparent marginalization of the smaller local organizations by the national union in Tema.

The chapters in Part Three on 'International dimensions of organizing' explicitly address cases of collective organizing by informal economy groups that reach beyond national borders. They provide a general picture of the informal economy as an internationalized social and political field. The underlying motives for organizing internationally, however, vary considerably between the cases. The first chapter by Suzanne Scheld discusses the current penetration by Chinese traders into the informal economy of Dakar, Senegal, in the context of market liberalization and changes in international politics. This is discussed as a new wave of foreign traders in a long local history of exposure to global trading communities. The author addresses the various organized responses to the 'Chinese challenge'. The picture is one of a contest and power struggle between different organized actors – consumer and trader associations as well as a Chinese business association – articulating opposing views on the Chinese issue. These opposing views have found expression in diverging discourses, where trader associations tend to resort to Othering, while the consumer associations accuse the former of xenophobia and advocate racial inclusion. In this struggle, the chapter shows, each of these actors tries to increase its influence by mobilizing support from 'transnational communities' as well as international organizations. But the rise of Chinese entrepreneurship in Dakar has triggered not only new antagonisms but also new alliances: facing a new source of competition, formerly rival trader associations bury their hatchets and combine their efforts.

Wilma Nchito and Karen Tranberg Hansen discuss the intensification of cross-border trade in Zambia in the context of economic and political change, and investigate the emergence of an international association of cross-border traders with members spread across eastern and southern Africa. The authors demonstrate how the association (its Zambian branch) interacts with regional governing bodies, such as the Common Market for Eastern and Southern Africa, lobbying primarily for flexible import regimes. It functions as a network to facilitate the mobility of traders across the region, providing access to vending space for travelling members and regulating conflicts between these and local traders. Its constituency is composed of a diverse but relatively privileged group, some of whose members are able to travel to other continents. The general picture is of an association that has achieved considerable successes. 'Courted by banks and airlines', the association has also achieved official recognition and been able to acquire land for its member traders in the heart of the capital city.

The last chapter in the collection, by Winnie Mitullah, discusses the relations between local organizations of informal workers and their transnational partners, with the focus on a national alliance of informal workers in Kenya. It is suggested that local organizations are weak as they face serious resource constraints in an environment where the majority of informal workers suffer from material insecurity. In this context, Mitullah argues, transnational organizations and networks of informal workers provide an important impetus and source of support for local organizing (in the form of financial support and capacity-building for policy dialogue and leadership). The chapter shows the importance of affiliation with such international networks and organizations to the ability of the local organization to exercise influence on local and national governments. This has earned it recognition and participation in policy processes. However, the author questions the sustainability of local organizations that are so dependent on external support. These findings are in contrast with those on the association of cross-border traders, which was not dependent on such external support, perhaps partly because of the relative economic robustness of its constituency.

From the above review, it becomes evident that this collection is not intended to generate consensus or to present one clear or singular pattern of change. Rather, the volume intends to generate academic debate by highlighting very different perspectives and exposing contrasting findings and contradictory trends. The contributions reveal a great variety and heterogeneity in patterns of collective organizing in the informal economy. Taken together, they indicate the range of contradictory dynamics and the increasing complexity of the politics of informality in Africa. Certainly, however, a focus on collectively organized informal actors does not exhaust the content and form of this politics. Some forms of injustice may not be best addressed through collective efforts. Moreover, vast numbers of people in the informal economy continue to be deprived of participation in organized initiatives. For many, individualistic forms of everyday 'resistance' continue to be the main form of politics available to them.

PART ONE

The political dynamics of collective organizing

1 | Seen but not heard: urban voice and citizenship for street traders

Alison Brown and Michal Lyons

Introduction: the informal economy of the urban South

In an age of globalization the street has become the new locus of employment for the urban poor. This chapter draws on case studies from two continents to explore the concept of *urban voice* for street traders. Over the last twenty years, many developing-country cities have seen a rapid growth in the informal economy. Street trade is particularly evident in sub-Saharan Africa and South Asia, where growth in urban populations has been accompanied by limited job creation among the poor (Cohen 2003; Carr and Chen 2002).

Precise measurement of informality is difficult, but informal employment is thought to account for around 60 per cent of all urban employment in Africa, and in India to employ over 95 per cent of non-agricultural women workers (ILO 2002a: 12–16). Street traders are the largest groups in the informal economy, after home-based workers, which together represent 10–35 per cent of the non-agricultural workforce in developing countries, in comparison with 5 per cent of the total workforce in developed countries. Women often comprise a large proportion of street vendors in developing countries (ILO 2002c), except where social restrictions prevail.

The chapter first briefly summarizes debates on the concept of *urban voice*, and its relation to *social capital*. It then explores the *associational structures* of street traders and the *institutional landscape* in which they operate. Drawing on work in Africa and Asia, the chapter then argues that the representational space afforded to street traders cannot be separated from *public discourse* on the informal economy. This discussion sets the context for a comparative study of traders' associations in four cities – Dakar, Accra, Dar es Salaam and Kathmandu – based on work undertaken separately by the authors in 2003–08.

Social capital and urban voice Urban voice is the means by which communities influence decision-making on issues that affect their lives, and draws heavily on *social capital* – the social networks based on norms, reciprocity and trust among their members (Putnam 1993; Pickvance 2003).

Social capital is recognized as a central basis of the urban economy, cultivated by the wealthy to protect and enhance their assets (Bourdieu 1984/2002) and by the poor to sustain their livelihoods and withstand adverse trends and shocks (Rakodi and Lloyd-Jones 2002). Social capital is transformed as traditional ties are adapted in urban contexts, for example through relationships that underpin changing methods of working or personal loans (Kumar and Matsusaka 2005; Lyons and Snoxell 2005a, 2005b; Buckley 1997; Phillips 2002). Critics argue that the concept has been hijacked by development agencies as a means of compensating for the neoliberal project and its lack of support for the poor (Pickvance 2003; Mayer 2003).

However, social networks and grassroots organizations are complex, facilitated by a wide range of factors including kinship, ethnic tribal and village groups, trade unions, NGOs, religious organizations, government agencies and political parties (Mitlin 2001). These are supported by a rich panoply of associational activities, for example: professional societies; trade unions; chambers of commerce; choirs; youth clubs; developmental charities; churches and religious groups; ethnic associations; welfare groups; credit associations; burial societies and many more (Tostensen et al. 2001: 17) based on networks and ties, which often go unrecognized by the state.

Global trends of democratization and decentralization have opened up new political space in which the urban poor can voice their needs, but their success depends on the institutions they can access and their ability to organize (Devas 2005). Formal processes of participation established by governments have tended to be ineffective or purloined by elites, and the extent to which the urban poor are heard depends largely on their organizing skills, and use of citizenship or participatory rights conferred by the state (Friedman 2006).

Traders' associational structures Traders' associations and organizations are rooted in tradition and the culture of the urban landscape in which they exist. For market and street traders, social capital – whether formally established as an association, or informal social networks – enables them to manage an intrinsically competitive environment and to negotiate with local government and other powerful actors (Lyons and Snoxell 2005a). Social capital allows traders to move from austerity to take advantage of new opportunities opened up by economic liberalization (Lourenço-Lindell 2002: 228).

The role of social capital in supporting traders' activities, together with the inevitability of informal sector livelihoods, is well recognized by agencies such as the International Labour Organization (ILO) (Carr and Chen 2002), and informal workers' organizations are seen as key players in the pro-poor policy debate – unions, cooperatives, associations or other representative groups (Chen et al. 2002). Yet, at urban as well as at national level, micro-enterprises rarely influence decision-making to their advantage against established interests unless they are organized (Rakodi 2003).

Trader and market associations fall into two groups – formal associations recognized by the authorities, and informal kinship, religious or other social networks. Both may provide a means for civic engagement with institutions and local authorities, but often focus on self-help and fail to maintain long-term influence (Brown 2006b). However, research suggests that many traders do not belong to any organization, and several studies suggest that organization densities among traders are low. Where traders' associations do exist they focus on financial concerns, product-specific issues or lobbying and advocacy (Skinner 2008).

For workers, the most powerful form of associations have traditionally been *trade unions*, but in developing cities these are often not well established because of the lack of formal work; *trade associations* are another form of employment representation but tend to prioritize the interests of members to the exclusion of others; other *grassroots organizations* in poor communities may be far from inclusive (Devas 2005).

Trade unions or political party affiliation sometimes connect traders with broad political interests, but unions' influence is usually only strong at times of crisis or during elections. More usually, the influence of workers' associations is indirect and unlikely to provide leverage with local decision-makers (Devas 2004). In rare cases, traders' organizations have developed significant negotiating power – for example the international alliance of street vendors' organizations StreetNet, set up in the early 1990s (Lyons 2005; Brown 2006a: 210; StreetNet 2009). Thus the status of traders' associations, and their capacity to look outwards, depends on their objectives and internal organization, but also on relations with other urban actors.

Urban governance and institutions

The governance and institutional landscape within which traders operate has a profound effect on their representational space and the extent to which they can exercise urban voice. Two trends have been evident in recent years in promoting more effective urban governance, with significantly different impacts for traders. On one hand, neoliberal philosophies have encouraged the withdrawal of urban governments from direct service provision, moving to privatization of essential services. Within this view of the 'corporate city', the informal economy has little place, and urban governments in both North and South are often hostile to street traders (e.g. Smith 1986; UN-Habitat 2007). Devas (2004) concluded that small, informal businesses have very little influence over decisions made by coalitions of public authorities and large private sector interests in Third World cities.

In contrast, there have been genuine attempts to empower the poor and engage new constituencies in pro-poor local government reform, and 'honest, efficient and effective government has moved to the top of the international policy agenda' (Ackerman 2004: 447; Isaac and Franke 2000). Development theorists argue for institutionalized participation, to foster partnerships, achieve progressive transformation and enhance pro-poor policies (Hickey and Mohan 2005; Devas 2004; Rakodi 2003), but problems occur because of the weakness of key partners, or institutional delays, leading to antagonism rather than co-operation (Devas 2004: 73, 115). Organizing poses huge problems for the poor, because of their limited time and resources, lack of leadership skills, conflicting interests, and unresponsive political systems (ibid.: 190).

One of the most successful experiments in participatory governance is participatory budgeting (PB), first introduced in Porto Alegre, Brazil, some twenty years ago. PB takes place on an annual cycle, which combines elected authorities with citizens' councils. Participants not only make decisions but are also responsible for decision-ranking the proposed projects (Novy and Leubolt 2005). The process initially focused on poor, relatively stable city-centre neighbourhoods, but later drew in the middle classes, although migrants were still excluded (Navarro 2005; Anderson 2003). Even so, 'voice' is generally exercised by experienced associations, and authorities remain reluctant to recognize urban social movements (Hickey and Mohan 2005). Nevertheless, the success of participatory budgeting in Porto Alegre, Belo Horizonte and elsewhere (Souza 2001) has led to legislative reform that enshrines participation.

Devas (2004) concluded that participatory governance was best supported by the cumulative building of grassroots structures, and establishing processes which give a sense of purpose and power through regular participatory decision-making, e.g. annual budget allocations and annual policy reviews. Facets which affect success in participatory governance include: commitment, legal/institutional support, and the regularity of participatory processes.

NGOs and community-based organizations (CBOs) can also play valuable roles in articulating the interests of the urban poor. NGOs have had notable successes in securing national programmes that benefit the poor, although they are sometimes seen as 'opportunistic and self-serving' (Devas 2004: 191). CBOs can create rallying points, but may be hampered by conflicting interests, or exhaustion of the leaders, who themselves struggle with poverty (Devas 2005). There may also be intrinsic problems with reliance on NGOs or CBOs which may undermine effective government (Putzel 1997), or lead to forced compromises because of the need to demonstrate results (Rogerson and Nel 2005). A critical problem is that most participatory programmes focus on the involvement of *residents.* There has been *no parallel effort to engage workers in the informal economy in urban political processes* – thus street traders are excluded from public debate in areas where they have a major impact on services and management.

Street trading in public discourse The influence of traders' associations is also affected by the social and cultural milieu in which they operate. Public discourse is often hostile to street traders, vilifying those working in the informal economy.

Street traders often live in a legal vacuum outside and beyond the law (Goldie 2002), with the negation of their identity partly rooted in popular attitudes.

Informalization is perceived as a sea-change in urban living, yet large-scale changes are always a major burden because they encroach on the normal, creating stress and readjustment of fragile identities (Hermochova 1997: 110). The rapid growth in street trade is acutely visible (Keith 1995: 310), challenging established urban social relations (Dudrah 2003: 343), resulting in fear and resentment.

Expressions of fear and popular concern in Durban are vividly illustrated by Popke and Ballard (2004) in their analysis of local newspaper reports, highlighting the expressions of anxiety that form part of residents' interpretive landscape, arguing that the arrival of street traders has been the most commonly articulated cause of the city's decline. The use of space for street trading challenges accepted notions of order (Cresswell, in ibid.), with frequent calls to 'bring pavement trading under control' and for traders 'to be sited in a designated part of town' (ibid.: 105).

A similar fear is reflected in debates on migration (Balbo and Marconi 2005). Migrants to Johannesburg's inner city are seen as alien, and perpetrators of disorder and crime (Kalati and Manor, in Reis and Moore 2005: 162). Johannesburg's elites have distanced themselves from the 'invasion' of the city's Central Business District (CBD) by 'hordes of desperate poor' (De Swaan, in ibid.: 191), resulting in an elite exodus to the suburbs, spatial segregation and expansion of the private security industry (e.g. Landau 2005; Kalati and Manor, in Reis and Moore 2005).

Thus, public discourse on street traders, particularly when associated with migration, sees them as 'other', an economic burden, a cause of crime and pollution, and not fit to be citizens, creating an inherent prejudice against those that try to be heard.

Methods

The chapter draws on three studies, two DfID-funded studies undertaken separately by the authors, which combine fieldwork from Senegal, Ghana, Tanzania and Nepal. Using the sustainable livelihoods framework, the studies collected data on the livelihood strategies of street traders in Dakar, Accra, Dar es Salaam and Kathmandu (Lyons and Snoxell, 2005a, 2005b; Brown 2006a). All three studies were based on extensive semi-structured interviews with traders, and key informant interviews with municipality staff, market officials, association leaders, NGOs and other relevant actors.

The four cities are chosen as exemplars of rapid urbanization and a burgeoning street economy, but with contrasting religious, social and associational traditions. With some variation, all four countries are very poor. Each has encountered the impacts of structural adjustment and economic liberalization,

TABLE 1.1 2006 Human Development Index (HDI) ratings, UNDP

	HDI		Life expectancy at birth		Adult literacy rate		Combined school enrolment*		GDP per capita	
	ranking*	value	ranking*	(years)	ranking*	% aged 15+	ranking*	(%)	ranking*	PPP $US
Ghana	136	0.532	132	57.0	111	57.9	151	47.2	123	2,240
Nepal	138	0.527	129	62.1	118	48.6	137	57	147	1,490
Senegal	156	0.46	136	56	121	39.3	159	38.1	144	1,713
Tanzania	162	0.43	157	45.9	97	69.4	150	47.8	170	674

Note: * Ranking of 177 countries for which records available

Source: hdr.undp.org/en/statistics/

and their major urban centres have grappled with the informal economy for the last thirty years.

Manifestations of 'urban voice'

Attempts by street traders to purchase a platform for legitimacy to claim their rights as urban citizens are manifest in ways which are a product of both history and culture and a response to current crises or need. This section explores the experience of the authors in four cities in the light of the discussion above. Table 1.1 illustrates comparative data for the countries in which the cities are located – all are in the lowest third of countries for which data is available both in terms of the Human Development Index (HDI) and income per capita, although interestingly all have relatively high adult literacy rates compared to their HDI, particularly Tanzania.

Dakar – brotherhoods and the colonial legacy Senegal is a francophone country with a predominantly Muslim population (96 per cent). Trade networks in Dakar are dominated by the brotherhoods, ethnic and religious trade associations which underpin both formal and informal commerce.

One of the most influential of the associations is the Mouride brotherhood, a religious group founded in the nineteenth century. Mourides developed economic power by growing peanuts, becoming incorporated into the colonial French economy, while preserving and evolving Wolof values (Diouf 2000: 683). Mouridism attracted every level of society, including freed slaves, merchants and craftsmen, creating a merchant tradition. The Mourides moved to the cities in three waves, after the First and Second World Wars and in large numbers during the droughts of the 1970s, where many became merchants (ibid.: 692).

Members of the Mouride Brotherhood dominate market associations in Dakar (Lyons and Snoxell 2005a). Brotherhood membership provides a crucial introduction to customers and suppliers in the marketplace. Trading is predominantly carried out by men, but women who work as traders also socialize through women's prayer circles, or *Dairas*. Members of the other major brotherhoods in Senegal, notably the Tijanes and Alayes, are also heavily engaged in trade.

There are also many registered trader associations in Dakar. UNACOIS is one of the oldest, created in 1990 in response to traders' frustrations with a state-controlled monopoly over rice. It now has 100,000 members and has strong ties to the government, playing a consultative role to the government's economic council (Scheld 2007).

Dakar Chamber of Commerce is an exclusive membership club for powerful wholesalers, the *grands commerçants*, who act as spokesmen for the traders. The *grands commerçants* carry out negotiations with the municipality, and discuss important issues such as the setting of trading tolls, the (re)location of markets, the density of stalls and trading. Other important players in Dakar are the

Lebanese merchants who, until independence in 1961, were the main importers of manufactured goods to Senegal, although they are now being displaced, for example by Chinese merchants (ibid.).

The role of associations remains controversial and confrontational. During 2002/03 there was renewed debate about moving Sandaga market in Dakar. The *grands commerçants* put forward a proposal to reorganize the market in a way that would tie hawkers to particular wholesalers, by designating trading tables as the property of particular wholesalers, with only their goods to be displayed there. This disenfranchised any non-member wholesalers and made sure that hawkers had no freedom to change supplier (Lyons and Snoxell 2005a). In November 2007, hawkers and street traders rioted in response to moves by the mayor of Dakar to evict them, but the president quashed the eviction, and helped to set up a national federation of street traders. An unusual feature of Senegalese market associations is that both formal and informal traders are embraced by these networks (ibid.). However, migrant traders and non-Muslims are entirely excluded from the strong bonds of brotherhoods.

Accra – product associations and women's leadership Accra is well known for its product associations, which exist in markets and are highly specialized. Each type of vegetable, product and craft has its own association, and some associations are also buying cooperatives. The associations are generally single-sex, often also single-ethnicity, chaired by a hereditary 'queen'. They have a powerful welfare function, occasionally a savings and loan function, and are closely involved with day-to-day management of market life (King 2006). Queens' authority can be absolute, although some associations are more democratically run than others.

A second tier of management is provided by the semi-formal market committee, in which the interests of traders are promoted by their queen (or chairman if it's a man, e.g. in electronics or transport). All association leaders are members of the committee, which settles boundary disputes or issues over dumping of waste, and negotiates with utility companies or municipality departments. In Accra there is also a Metropolitan Market Committee of chairmen from all the market committees in the city, which meets only biannually, but is effective during election time.

Traders' associations are influential in negotiations over planning and development, particularly in central-city markets, where there are severe development pressures. For example, the New Makola Market in Accra was established on the outskirts of the city centre, after the original Makola Market burnt down in dubious circumstances, while the Medina Market was formally designated on a central site after the traders had 'squatted' on an adjacent site for a year, and their committee had taken their case to the Metropolitan Market Committee (Lyons and Snoxell 2005a).

Market queens and chairmen owe allegiance to tribal chiefs, who have formal representation on municipal councils and are widely respected (Brown 2006a: 63). Also of interest is the predominance of strong matrilineal family structures among some Ghanaian ethnic groups. Women frequently live apart from their husbands and are economically independent (King 2006: 105), and many trades are dominated by women traders.

Ghanaian traders are predominantly Christian. Financial and trading matters are generally kept separate from the church (Lyons and Snoxell 2005b). The small numbers of Muslim traders in the two markets studied in Accra showed similar associational structures to those of Senegal, for example the butchers in New Makola Market. Product associations are also quite inflexible, and there are many traders who do not join product associations because they find membership subscriptions too high, while some trades, e.g. household goods, have no association and traders prefer to deal directly as individuals with market or municipal authorities.

Dar es Salaam – fluctuating fortunes In Dar es Salaam, attitudes towards the informal economy have fluctuated. The economic crisis of the 1980s (Evans and Ngalewa 2003: 249; Bigsten and Danielson 2001: 19) forced initial accommodation of the informal sector, facilitated by three key factors. First, the 1983 Human Resources Deployment Act required every able-bodied person to work, and established the *nguvu kazi* itinerant trader licence; this restrictive legislation was subtly 'reinterpreted', effectively conferring a 'right to work' on citizens (Tripp 1997: 187).

Second, the Sustainable Dar es Salaam Project (SDP), a strategic planning project supported by UNDP and UN-Habitat, heralded a participatory approach to city planning, and the city consultation in 1992 defined 'petty trading' as one of nine critical urban issues (Rutsch 2001). Third, the near-bankruptcy and suspension of the city council in 1996 led to restructuring of local government (Brown 2006b: 71; Brown and Nnkya 2006).

The SDP's Working Group on Petty Trading sought to strengthen trader associations as a channel for dialogue with the authorities. By 1997 about 240 self-help groups representing 16,000 traders had been formed (DCC 1999) and two umbrella groups were established – VIBINDO (Association of Small Businesses), and KIWAKU (an association of clothes sellers). VIBINDO achieved considerable status, representing about three hundred associations with a combined membership of 40,000 people (Msoka 2007). *Guidelines for Petty Traders* were published in 1997 (Nnkya 2006).

From the late 1990s, several landmark reports were published on the informal economy. The *Roadmap Study* (ILO et al. 2002) demonstrated the prohibitive costs and complexity of business registration, and sought to absorb the informal economy into the mainstream. The message of formalization was fully articulated following the visit of Hernando de Soto to Tanzania in 2005 and the subsequent ILD report (ILD 2005a, 2005b).

Since 2003 legislation has progressively marginalized traders in Dar es Salaam. In 2003 the *nguvu kazi* was cancelled, effectively de-legalizing trade in public space. The Finance Act, 2004 confirmed the requirement for all businesses to be registered and licensed. Although small businesses retained exemption from the licence fee, the ancillary financial and other costs remained prohibitive (ILD 2005a).

These pressures for formalization coincided with growing international emphasis on increasing local tax revenue and the evaluation of Tanzania's second Poverty Reduction Strategy Paper (PRSP) had shown disappointing performance (IMF 2006), as well as a growing local emphasis on Western-city ideals of city planning.

In March 2006 the prime minister's office issued an order to major municipalities to evict petty traders from the streets. Temporarily suspended owing to public outcry, the order was reinstated some months later. The evictions were carried out in the first six months of 2007 by municipalities, and hundreds of thousands of traders were affected (prosecutions alone are estimated at over 200,000 during February–July 2007), with damage to goods and kiosks, fines, confiscations and loss of trading time through jail sentences causing severe hardship (Lyons and Msoka 2007).

Although informal networks are a crucial element of coping strategies in Tanzania, their fluidity produces a situation of near invisibility (Simone 2001, in Baker et al. 2002). In the recent round of evictions they have failed to provide any significant influence for their members. Both before and during the evictions, VIBINDO made repeated representations on behalf of traders. However, where tolerance of informal trade has been eroded it is hard to represent people whose operations are illegal.

Kathmandu – traditional legacies of association Nepal has a long tradition of informal trade, and many villages have *haat bazaar* (weekly markets) selling rural produce (Sthapit 1998). Street trading is now common in all the larger cities, but there is little data on the size of the street economy, although in urban areas self-employment in 1998 was estimated at 57 per cent (NSAC 1998). Major causes of poverty include the unequal distribution of land, slow agricultural development, rapid urbanization, and an increase in the 'black' economy (Lohani 1997).

The Kathmandu valley is the main focus of urbanization, with a population of around 1.5 million in the 2001 census (HMG CBS 2002). The valley's main cities of Kathmandu, Lalitpur and Bhaktapur are growing rapidly as the marginalized hill economies and civil unrest fuel rural-to-urban migration (Karki 2004). Street trading has a strong seasonal character (Shrestha 2006), and cross-border migration to and from India is also significant. In the dense urban cores of Kathmandu and Lalitupur, several locations have a succession of different markets from day to night.

Traditionally, trading and public space were managed by a unique Newari institution, the *Ghuthi* trust, traditional societies that oversaw the performance of festival rights and maintenance of community facilities, but loss of land and revenue to urban development has undermined their historic role (ibid.). Today, municipalities have the main responsibility for managing markets, and a 1999 Act enables them to provide market facilities and to collect market revenues. Street traders outside markets are not included in the legislation.

The troubled political situation has considerably undermined street trading. Street riots and strikes have been common since the assassination of King Birendra in 2001. Maoist rebels in the countryside stepped up civil action; in 2002 a state of emergency was declared and parliament was dissolved. In 2003, the president of the Nepal Street Vendors' Union (NEST) was arrested following the government's ban on peaceful protest (StreetNet 2003). In 2005 King Gyanendra assumed direct rule, but after massive street protests in 2006 and 2007, he was forced to back down, and Nepal became a republic in May 2008 (BBC 2009).

The modern organizational structure of street traders is relatively weak. The most influential advocate of rights for the poor is Bhrikuti Mandap, a national NGO providing social welfare benefits for the poor, partly through property income. The Bhrikuti Mandap Small Traders Association runs a market of about 1,400 traders set up in Ratna Park east of Kathmandu Durbar about fifteen years ago, after traders were evicted from the city bus stand. The association collects rents (although traders complain that little is reinvested) and taxes some bulk deliveries to the markets (Shrestha 2006). Other markets are also privatized, for example at Basantapur near Kathmandu Durbar, where a broker manages the night market. Prera Construction was contracted to build six flyovers, and to lease the space beneath for markets for fifteen years; in fact, only one overpass was built while all six areas were leased (ibid.).

Localized traders' associations seem to have little influence in protecting their members. For example, at Dharahara, near the city's main bus and *tempo* stands (minibus stops), a trade association lobbies the city council for licences and improved services, but police harassment persists. The association at Anamnagar, an early morning vegetable market, did not prevent its abolition. Recent street unrest has further undermined tolerance of traders, particularly in the central areas.

Four contrasting traditions

Traders' associations in Dakar, Accra, Dar es Salaam and Kathmandu exhibit very different traditions of 'urban voice', embedded in local social, cultural and political traditions, but increasingly responding to a complex and rapidly changing environment. The associations are subject to huge pressures of national and international migration and changing patterns of trade in a context of globalization, are in a dynamic relationship with local government and chambers of trade, and are affected by political and personality struggles.

Dakar represents an unusual case, where the brotherhoods have emerged as a representation of Islamic faith and as a means of protecting traditional culture within a colonial context. Brotherhoods are influential in Muslim communities throughout West Africa but perhaps most evident in Senegal. The brotherhoods have supported both national and international trade expansion – particularly the Senegalese diaspora to Europe – and have informal but influential links to local government. They exclude new migrants and the poor, and there is evidence that they have been bypassed in emerging international trade (Lyons and Brown 2007).

Accra's trade associations also have strong historic and cultural links, based on product associations, but these are limited in remit as they are generally bound to particular localities. The product associations have not fully evolved to meet modern challenges, and many traders in Ghana see no value in joining these associations. Only where umbrella organizations have been formed representing a powerful voting lobby are the traders' associations able to have wider influence.

In Dar es Salaam associations have been unable to defend traders against a current political dynamic to banish street traders, based on 'modernist' conceptions of city planning. Over the first six months of 2007 widespread evictions caused severe hardship for traders with profound negative impacts on poverty. Where alternative trading sites have been offered most have been in peripheral locations which are not viable for trading. Trading has been undermined by a raft of legislation, including the removal of licences for itinerant traders.

In Kathmandu, seven years of political unrest, and increased police and military presence, have made the street highly unsafe. The Nepal Union of Street Vendors is affiliated with the national trade union movement but is still relatively new, and trade unions were repressed by the authorities during the political demonstrations of 2006 and 2007. As a result street trading is highly insecure, and many traders are forced to carry very little stock and only what can be moved extremely quickly – trading either from plastic sheets or cardboard stands. Word of a police patrol can clear a trading street within thirty seconds.

The case studies confirm that for successful bargaining, trader social capital must have collective, as well as individual, value. Social capital is normally viewed only as an individual asset which traders use to support their day-to-day trading (e.g. Coleman 1988; Woolcock 1998).

Formal, registered associations appear to have more power than informal kinship or other networks, but the criteria for membership often exclude very poor traders, and there is no guarantee of the extent to which associations are representative. Umbrella organizations also appear to have more power than individual associations, but lack the capacity to influence senior politicians or the media, particularly at times of political crisis. Associations must cross the boundary from welfare to advocacy, but also need legitimation from outside to sustain their influence. Here StreetNet, the international association of street vendors' associations, has been very influential in creating a global platform for knowledge exchange and capacity-building to strengthen street traders' associations' awareness of their rights.

None of the case studies demonstrated an effective legal or institutional framework for inclusion of informal sector workers, or a consistent attempt by local governments to institutionalize their participation. In all four cities, municipal officials spoke disparagingly of traders and their organizations, both in service departments such as planning, and departments responsible for market management. Local politicians were sometimes sympathetic to the problems of space and management, but in both Dar es Salaam and Dakar, where senior national politicians became involved in negotiations over space, their determination to 'tidy up' the city led to a heavy-handed approach.

An interesting move by some trader associations is recourse to the courts. Here associations are trying to use existing legal frameworks to their advantage, with mixed success. In Dar es Salaam the associations sought to fight the eviction orders issued by the government but, although they achieved a temporary stay, their efforts were eventually unsuccessful. Traders elsewhere, however, have been more successful in furthering their voice through the courts (StreetNet 2009).

Exclusion of poor traders from the established associational structure was a feature of all the case studies. For example, in Accra membership in associations is predicated on a trading space in a formal market, but only a minority of traders can obtain such places. As Popke and Ballard (2004) identify, it is in the undesignated trading areas that most friction with other urban users is experienced, and these which most clearly need further management.

The case studies indicate that street traders' voice is most effective where they organize, particularly where associations are formal with wide membership, and umbrella organizations are formed, although critics argue that the emphasis on formalization arises from a 'modernist' agenda, and stifles the core attribute of informality (Cross and Morales 2007b: 7). Whatever the structure of organizations they are still likely to exclude the most vulnerable, who are seen but not heard. Clearly, however, the representational space for traders cannot be separated from wider discourse on the informal economy, and the political and institutional landscape in which they operate. Only in a context of institutional, legal and regulatory reform can traders effectively be heard.

2 | The politics of vulnerability: exit, voice and capture in three Nigerian informal manufacturing clusters

Kate Meagher

Introduction: from exit to voice?

It was not long ago that the informal economy was deemed incapable of political organization. In Third World contexts, scholars portrayed the informal economy as an individualistic, inchoate mass that expressed its interests through political and economic disengagement rather than through organized political action. At best, the tactics of informal actors were analysed in terms of Scott's 'weapons of the weak', based on evasion and non-compliance (MacGaffey 1994); at worst, informal sector discontent brought with it the threat of spontaneous mob violence (Gutkind 1973; Bayat 1997a). Theirs was a politics of 'exit' and brute protest rather than one of articulate political expression.

Rapid economic informalization and the rise of civil society have ushered in new perspectives on the politics of informality in developing countries, as represented in contemporary research on Latin America (Cross 1998a; Fernández-Kelly and Shefner 2006), Africa (Tripp 1997; Tostensen et al. 2001) and Asia (de Neve 2004). In African societies, dramatic expansion of informal economies combined with rapid political liberalization has produced a flowering of popular associations among informal actors, opening up new possibilities for political expression. In a recent article, Aili-Mari Tripp (2001: 10) notes that:

> Many informal market associations, credit associations, trade organizations, cooperatives, farming and marketing groups, ethnically based development associations, and other societies emerged in the 1980s and 1990s to assist the growing informal sector and give it a political voice, especially at the local level.

While the proliferation of popular associations within the informal economy has been celebrated by some as a decisive shift from a politics of exit to one of collective voice, others have been more cautious in their assessments. Even in the era of civil society and political openness, underlying problems of poverty, internal divisions and vulnerability to elite capture continue to constrain the capacity of informal associations to defend popular economic interests. Given the prevalence of diversification, straddling and increased middle-class entry into the informal economy, Jennifer Widner (1991) argues that prospects for effective collective organization among informal actors are undermined by diverse 'livelihood portfolios' and pervasive mistrust among members, leading to a fragmentation rather than a coalescence of economic interests and political strategies. Where informal economy associations exist, Tostensen et al. (2001: 23) point out that they tend to be weak and suffer from limited resources, restricting their capacity for agency, especially in times of intense economic stress. In an insightful study of informal traders' associations in Johannesburg, Thulare (2004: 17) shows how persistent problems of political powerlessness, legal marginality, weak structures of accountability, and disaffected membership leave informal associations vulnerable to opportunistic leadership and state manipulation:

> [...] while there may be a temptation to see the associational life of the informally employed as something mysterious, way beyond the control of governments, this research shows that [...] governments retain a capacity to shape the organizations of the poor. It is also clear that [...] informal powerholders do seem to retain the capacity to ensure that government intervention does not disturb their power.

Despite concerns about the failings of informal associations, Thulare notes the existence of 'germs of democratic practice and culture' in emerging informal organizations, suggesting an underlying potential for voice despite the problems of marginality. By contrast, Rene Lemarchand (1988) and Bill Reno (1995) contend that civil organization within the informal economy has little to do with either exit or voice, but leads inevitably to a politics of elite capture in which popular economic interests are inevitably submerged beneath an 'elite project of absorbing and manipulating societal networks' (ibid.: 19). Focusing on the increasing prominence of political connections, extortion rackets and vigilante groups within the informal economy, Reno (2002) argues that the inescapable realities of elite capture transform informal associations into agents of state predation and violence.

While the rise of informal economic associations in Africa has certainly moved informal actors beyond the politics of exit, the question to be addressed here is whether they provide an effective mechanism for political voice. Enthusiastic assessments of informal organizational agency tend to gloss over the very real problems of effective political organization within the informal economy, particularly in the stressful economic conditions of structural adjustment. Questions need to be raised about how the evasive strategies of the marginalized have been so quickly transformed into a capacity for political opposition. Despite their growing numerical dominance in urban Africa, informal economic actors continue to suffer from problems of institutional exclusion, internal divisions and the precarious legal status of their enterprises. How do these handicaps affect the organizational capacity of informal actors? Are some categories of informal actors able to organize more effectively than others? Are more established and active associations better able to resist capture, or do they tend to attract more concerted attention from elites intent on dividing or hijacking them? Underlying all of these questions is the issue of whether economic and political liberalization have provided an enabling environment for associational development within the informal economy, or have further weakened the autonomy and organizational capacity of informal associations.

These questions will be addressed through a study of small-producers' associations in three informal manufacturing clusters in the town of Aba, a commercial centre in the Igbo cultural area of south-eastern Nigeria. Specializing in the production of garments, shoes and cosmetics, respectively, these three clusters represent ideal cases for the development of dynamic informal sector associations. To begin with, the Igbo ethnic group is noted for its informal commercial success as well as for high levels of participation in civil associations, including home-town unions, credit societies, social clubs and traders' and producers' associations (Forrest 1994; Isichei 1976). Second, indigenous Igbo institutions of occupational specialization, together with the greater capital and skill requirements of informal manufacturing, have combined to favour specialization over diversification in all three clusters. In the Aba clusters, 86 per cent of shoe producers and 73 per cent of garment producers had no other line of business, including subsistence farming or petty trade. Cosmetics producers tended to be somewhat more diversified, but many divided their time only between cosmetics production and cosmetics trading. This minimizes the fragmenting effects of diversified livelihoods, creating what Widner identifies as ideal conditions for associational commitment within the informal economy.

Third, informal associations in all three clusters developed independently of state initiatives, and in two out of the three cases were formed before the adoption of Nigeria's structural adjustment programme in 1986, suggesting a measure of institutional embeddedness and autonomy within these associations. These extremely supportive conditions for informal collective organization are by no means typical of African informal economies, but serve to highlight the kinds of constraints on the development of informal political voice, even in highly favourable organizational contexts. The material presented here is based on fieldwork conducted in Aba between October 1999 and September 2000, with return visits in 2001 and 2005. Focusing on the specific conditions of the emergence of these three associations, their internal organization and their external linkages, this chapter will examine the potential for as well as the challenges to the development of political voice within informal economic conditions in contemporary Africa.

Associational origins

The town of Aba is famous across Nigeria for the vitality of its informal small-scale manufacturing activities. Since the early 1990s, the term 'Aba-made' has emerged as a colloquial Nigerian expression for cheap local manufactures. The shoe and garment clusters represent two of the largest and most dynamic informal manufacturing clusters in the town, while the cosmetics cluster is smaller and more recent, but has been growing rapidly. Amid the faltering of the formal economy, all three clusters have drawn on complex informal supply, production and marketing networks to support their rapid expansion (Meagher 2006). Moving beyond a dependence on local consumers, the shoe and garment clusters have developed marketing networks that export their products informally as far as Senegal, the Democratic Republic of Congo and South Africa. Informal cosmetics firms have more limited distribution networks, but routinely supply consumers and salons across south-eastern Nigeria, and sell to traders with much wider distribution networks. While they all developed in the same town, the dynamic performance of these three clusters rests on quite varied institutional histories. Each of the three clusters was founded by different migrant Igbo sub-communities, with different degrees of wealth and formal sector connections, and their associations emerged at importantly different historical conjunctures.[1] Each cluster also has a very different gender composition, with shoes remaining an almost exclusively male activity, owing to the trade's unsavoury social reputation and arduous physical requirements, while garments has a mixed-gender composition, and cosmetics is characterized by a predominance of women.

Despite important historical, institutional and social differences, these three clusters have two critical factors in common: their extremely small scale of operation and their pervasive informality. All three clusters average fewer than five workers per firm, with a high proportion of one-person businesses (Forrest 1994; Meagher 2006). Moreover, the overwhelming majority of firms in these clusters are informal according to a variety of criteria. If informality is defined as 'operation outside the regulatory framework of the state' (Castells and Portes 1989), the bulk of these firms are not only unregistered, but evade key taxes (though they do pay a range of local government taxes), contravene basic labour and factory legislation, and operate in areas not zoned for industrial activity. As of 2000, 80 per cent of garment firms and over 99 per cent of shoe firms in the Aba clusters were unregistered, and even the registered firms were in violation of basic factory, labour and zoning regulations. In the case of the cosmetics cluster, while a significant proportion of the firms were registered, they all evaded the standards requirements of the National Agency for Food and Drug Administration and Control (NAFDAC), a standards agency formed in the early 1990s. Failure to obtain NAFDAC clearance, which small producers are unable to afford, put firms in the cosmetics cluster decisively on the wrong side of the law, leaving them particularly vulnerable to police harassment, arrest and seizure of goods.

The shoe cluster The first of these three informal manufacturing clusters to form an association was the shoe cluster. Informal shoe production had emerged in Aba in the 1950s, pioneered by migrants from the Mbaise-Igbo – an extremely poor, land-scarce community in central Igboland. Informal shoe production started out in Aba as a 'poor man's business' owing to its extremely low capital requirements. Mbaise migrants operated inside the market, sharing rudimentary tools for the production of cheap sandals from scrap materials. In the early 1970s, informal shoe production expanded and diversified into the production of 'fashion shoes' amid an influx of better-trained shoe producers from small and medium formal sector firms attempting to restart their businesses after the Nigerian civil war. These better-trained producers hailed from a wider range of Igbo communities, and also included some of the better-established Mbaise producers. Resenting the constrained and unconducive conditions of operating inside the market, these more successful informal producers formed an association in the early 1970s called the 'Omenka Shoe Manufacturers' Union' to lobby the government for a better location with proper production facilities, including electricity and space to operate machines.

In 1977, following a devastating fire in the market, the informal shoe cluster was moved to the newly constructed Ariaria International Market on the edge of town, but was housed in a similarly cramped area known as AME, located inside the new market. Rejecting these arrangements, the more established shoe producers moved to a residential area at the edge of the market, where rented buildings afforded more spacious shops and freedom from market opening and closing times. This area of the shoe cluster, known as Powerline, became the new home of the informal shoe producers' association, which continued to lobby for better facilities. Their struggle for a more conducive site was caught between the threat of eviction by the state, owing to their contravention of zoning laws, and opposition by powerful private landlords, who were enjoying high commercial rents on the residential properties occupied by the shoe firms.

Between the mid-1970s and the mid-1990s, the shoe cluster was fragmented into six separate zones, each represented by a separate association, owing to the construction of additional, but still seriously inadequate, production facilities. These included Shoe Plaza, constructed at the edge of the market in 1986, and the vast Umuehilegbu in 1993 (affectionately known as Bakassi, because unwilling shoe producers had to be chased by police into occupying its cramped stalls, lacking in access to electricity, water or reasonable proximity to input suppliers). Two other production zones – Imo Avenue and Ogu Avenue – emerged as dissatisfied informal producers occupied additional residential or better-serviced areas in order to operate their businesses effectively. Jurisdictional tussles between the Ariaria market administration and newly formed local government areas outside the market reinforced the associational fragmentation, as each administration jealously guarded control of its share of revenue from the rapidly expanding shoe cluster. Each new production area was forced to form a different association, depending on whether it was located inside or outside the market, and, if outside the market, which of the contiguous local government boundaries it fell into. While most of these associations operated informally through the 1980s, efforts at state-level registration were triggered after 1993, when the original Omenka shoemakers' association was moved from Powerline to Umuehilegbu and formally registered as the 'Umuehilegbu Industrial Shoe Makers Union' in an attempt to make it the 'official' union of the informal shoe cluster.

Struggles for control of rents and resources generated by informal shoe production reflect its rapid growth and comparative profitability. Despite increased income potential and the shift to 'modern' shoes, however, informal shoe production remains marked by its lowly origins. Levels of education and middle-class entry in the activity are very low. As of the year 2000, only 13 per cent of producers had secondary-school education and only 18 per cent had middle-class backgrounds, since school leavers treated informal shoe production as an activity of last resort. Arduous and risky working conditions (including the use of volatile adhesives in unventilated stalls near an open flame) and a rough social environment precluded the entry of women, perpetuating the all-male character of the activity.

The garment cluster Although Aba's informal garment cluster arose in the 1930s, pre-dating the shoe cluster, an enduring association did not emerge in the garment cluster until 1984. A number of local tailors' associations had come and gone, but these were all neighbourhood cooperative groups, none of them achieving any form of cluster-wide status, and none was in operation by the time of the study in 1999/2000. Informal garment production involved tailors, who used domestic sewing machines, and mass-producers, who used second-hand industrial sewing machinery, making it a much more highly mechanized and capital-intensive activity than informal shoe production. Informal garment production was pioneered by migrants from the Bende area in eastern Igboland, an agriculturally and commercially successful area. Relatively prosperous communal origins and comparatively high levels of mechanization fostered an orientation towards advancement through education and industrial skills. For an informal activity, levels of education in the garment cluster were extremely high. Sixty-five per cent of producers had completed secondary school, and some had post-secondary education, including university degrees. More than a quarter of producers had middle-class backgrounds, and nearly half of them were women. The first garment producers' association, known as the Aba Garment Manufacturers' Cooperative (conventionally referred to as 'Aba Garment'), emerged among the most established, highly capitalized (and male-dominated) segment of the garment cluster, the informal mass-producers, where the dominance of the founding community remains particularly strong.

While the garment cluster enjoyed a period of rapid expansion during the 1970s, particularly after the banning of textile imports in 1976, no lasting moves were made to form an association during this period. The establishment of the garment cluster in a residential district south of the main market meant that producers had more space and better service infrastructure, including water and electricity, than activities forced to operate inside the market. It was with the onset of economic crisis that an associational response was triggered. The formation of a small garment producers' association was a reaction to mounting levels of official harassment in the context of economic crisis and Nigeria's return to military rule in 1984. On the pretext that their machines were stolen or imported without proper documentation, officials took to extracting huge bribes from garment producers. The Aba Garment Manufacturers' Cooperative formed to combat this threat by forming a collective front to deal with government. The need for protection, combined with the particularly strong communal base of informal mass-producers, contributed to the cohesion of the organization. Aba Garment was registered as a cooperative society under state law in 1989. Formal registration has strengthened the ability of informal garment producers to combat official harassment, allowing the association to take the government to court in extreme cases.[2]

The cosmetics cluster Informal cosmetics manufacturing has much more recent origins in Aba. It appears to have emerged in Aba in the wake of economic crisis in the 1980s. Unlike those of the shoe and garment clusters, the origins of the informal cosmetics sector revolve around gender rather than communal identity. Informal manufacturing of cosmetics, predominantly soap and hair and skin products, was originally a women's activity linked to artisanal soap production and the operation of local hair salons, both of which are considered women's work. In an attempt to take advantage of government incentives linked to the 'Better Life' programme run by the wife of the head of state, informal cosmetics producers formed a Women's Cooperative in 1993. No resources materialized, and the cooperative collapsed soon after. As the market for cheap, locally produced cosmetics expanded, men began entering the activity, particularly from the mid-1990s. New male producers, entering largely from cosmetics trading and formal sector cosmetics firms, tended to be better capitalized and trained than their female counterparts. Competition in the business was intensified by a simultaneous influx of smaller and more desperate producers, both male and female, as unemployment and economic hardship began to bite in Nigeria.

These pressures were further complicated by the formation of the National Agency for Food and Drug Administration and Control (NAFDAC) in 1993, a body created to combat problems of unsafe and counterfeit products in the pharmaceutical and cosmetics industries, which were posing increasing health hazards across the country. In Aba, the expansion of the informal cosmetics industry was accompanied by an increase in product counterfeiting, as well as marketing of ineffective or severely caustic products as informal producers learned through practice or experimented with new products. While NAFDAC imposed a measure of consumer protection, it effectively criminalized a segment of small producers, some of whom had registered their businesses with the state, but could not afford the significant additional costs of NAFDAC registration – an offence that became punishable by fines or imprisonment. The result was that informal cosmetics producers became subject to constant harassment from police, who were responsible for enforcing NAFDAC registration, as well as being mobilized by medium- and large-scale formal cosmetics firms to combat rampant counterfeiting by informal cosmetics producers.

Owing to intense competition, the constant threat of arrest and harassment, and the absence of any communal basis of cooperation, informal cosmetics production was characterized by secrecy and mutual suspicion rather than cooperation. Producers did not cluster geographically, and generally avoided rather than sought the attention of the state. Class and educational backgrounds varied widely, depending on whether producers had entered from informal sector trade and hair salons, or from formal sector employment. It was not until 1999 that an informal cosmetics association was formed with the objective of providing protection from official harassment, as well as controlling prices and entry. Known as Aba Small-Scale Cosmetics Manufacturers' Association (ASCOMA), the association represented a collaborative effort of better-off female and male producers. With a view to dealing more effectively with the police, however, the members of the association made two established male producers the temporary chairman and deputy chairman, which has exacerbated internal conflicts along gender lines.

Internal organization

Aba's informal manufacturing clusters have demonstrated their ability to form associations, but the real question is whether these associations have developed into organs of political voice for their members. As Callaghy (1994: 240) indicates, the proliferation of civil society groups demonstrates a *potential* for civil expression, but this outcome cannot be taken for granted. The political credentials of these collective organizations depend on their ability to mobilize participation, to develop a measure of representativeness and accountability, and to pursue collective economic interests at the level of the state. Despite highly propitious conditions for collective organization, the Aba cluster associations face a number of internal as well as external challenges. At the level of internal organization, these informal associations are confronted with the pressures of rapidly expanding constituencies, serious resource constraints and divergent interests among members. While the Aba cluster associations have made good use of a number of institutional advantages, the challenges of collective organization among the poor and powerless should not be underestimated, as the following examples will show.

Economic identity and associational conflict With regard to mobilization of members, these cluster associations have been able to draw on embedded Igbo practices of civil association and occupational solidarity to rally participation. Among the Igbo, participation in home-town associations and local occupational and trading organizations is generally not considered voluntary, creating a sense of obligation even among informal producers to consider themselves members and to show up for meetings. Norms of mandatory participation are embedded in community or occupational membership, and backed by a range of sanctioning mechanisms, including fines for non-attendance at meetings, group pressure, and ostracism in cases of persistent non-participation. The informal shoe cluster has been most successful in using communal and occupational membership to mobilize associational participation. Although the expansion of the shoe cluster during the 1980s and 1990s has diluted the proportion of the founding Mbaise community to less than 20 per cent of the cluster, a strong occupational identity has persisted. By the turn of the millennium, the shoe cluster had burgeoned to over eleven thousand firms, but 83 per cent of producers considered themselves members of one of the six zonal associations.

Norms of civil obligation and occupational identity were accompanied by an attempt to develop more 'modern' democratic structures of representation within the shoe clusters. Each of the six shoe associations had an elected executive of twelve to twenty officers, depending on the size of the production zone. Most of the executive was elected, though there were also appointed members and patrons from outside the shoe sector. Below the executive was a cadre of 'line chairmen' or 'building chairmen', who represented blocks of workshops within each of the shoe zones. The line or building representatives were also elected, though the smaller constituencies at this level meant they often stood unopposed for long periods of time. Association executives met with the line chairmen on a monthly basis, and decisions were communicated to the membership by their line chairmen. In the case of Umuehilegbu, the largest of the shoe associations, there were fifty-two line chairmen, in addition to the twenty-man executive council. Members of the different unions oversaw each other's elections, along with officials from the relevant local government and from the Aba Chamber of Commerce. Efforts were made to make elections free and fair, but they were not immune to money politics or other forms of electoral racketeering. That said, there was no evidence of inordinate communal domination in the union executives, although Mbaise producers were chairmen in three of the associations. Overall, however, the community origin of the executives was roughly proportionate to the wider communal composition of shoe producers. Despite reasonably representative structures, accountability remained a problem. Members expressed a concern over their inability to control or sanction leadership. They expressed greater confidence in their local line or building chairmen, largely because they were more privy to the activities of the latter, and therefore more able to exert some form of democratic control.

The functions of the shoe associations mainly involved the maintenance of law and order within the shoe areas, interfacing with police and local government, and social welfare assistance. All of the shoe unions settled disputes among members or with customers, enforced rules of orderly behaviour and sanitation, and saw to the provision of security within their area, usually by hiring night guards. They intervened in dealings with the police, and attempted to settle lesser problems without arrest. As one union leader put it, 'Police don't come into this market except to buy shoes.'[3] Social welfare assistance was largely restricted to contributions for burials. While short-term capital shortage and workshop fires regularly put firms out of business, the associations lacked the resources to assist members in distress, prompting an aggrieved producer to complain, 'They only help you with money when you're dead!'

Associations in the residentially situated zones also attempted some measure of quality and price regulation.[4] One union prohibited the use of substandard inputs, and seized any offending materials. Two others had patchy regulations against copying designs, but enforcement was a constant problem. While price regulation has been raised as an important issue, the inability to enforce it prevented its being adopted as a policy by any of the associations. There were also sanctions, including heavy fines, on members marketing their own shoes in other towns, in order to maintain the cluster's role as a centre for traders. What was conspicuously absent from the activities of the shoe associations was the provision of actual business services, such as credit, technical training and collective input procurement or marketing arrangements. Given the low average incomes of informal producers, subscription fees were minimal, and were largely consumed by social welfare outlays. The associations lacked the financial or institutional resources to engage in even basic business services on a scale that would begin to satisfy the needs of a membership of over ten thousand producers.

The inability of the shoe associations to offer any business services undermined their ability to maintain the loyalty of members. Despite strong participatory norms, associational commitment was weakened by a serious division of interests between survivalist and more established producers. Executives were dominated by more established or better-connected producers, concerned with regulating quality and price, while the mass of poor producers were motivated by livelihood concerns, which often included strategies of cutting quality, copying designs and price undercutting. Limited attempts by the shoe associations to impose regulations to upgrade production were largely overwhelmed by the growing numbers of small guerrilla firms intent on eking out a living by any means. This led to a process of involution in which mounting competition, cost-cutting, declining quality and price undercutting depressed prices and incomes throughout the cluster. The result was that both quality-oriented and poor producers had limited faith in the ability of the leadership to respond to their interests. These structural causes of mistrust were exacerbated by significant misgivings among the membership about the ability of association leaders to use resources for the collective good, leading one member to describe the executives as 'hungry lions'.

Divided identities and economic stress The garment and cosmetics unions were more 'professional' in their organization and outlook, but have been less successful in mobilizing participation. Part of the problem stems from a less cohesive framework of communal and occupational identity. While nearly half of the 2,500 producers in the garment cluster still hail from the founding Bende communities, the garment producers' association has been unable to overcome the division in occupational identity and interests between tailors and mass-producers, despite attempts to widen its appeal to the garment cluster as a whole. Only 7 per cent of garment producers regarded themselves as members of Aba Garment. Those outside the union explained that the association was only for mass-producers. Even among mass-producers, many declined to join because they felt the association was only for producers from the founding community. In the case of the cosmetics cluster, the lack of any cohesive communal origins, combined with sharp gender and class divisions, has led to a narrow and relatively shallow membership based exclusively on the concerns of established producers. At one meeting attended, only ten members showed up out of a membership list of forty, although the delinquent members were fined. The overall number of informal cosmetics producers was impossible to assess, owing to high levels of police harassment, mutual mistrust and geographical dispersal, but the association certainly included well under half of the total.

In the case of Aba Garment, low levels of membership were not a product of poor or undemocratic organization. The informal garment association had an elected executive of twelve members, all of whom were small garment producers operating in the cluster. Meetings of all members were held monthly, were well attended by registered members, and showed high levels of internal democracy. As in the shoe associations, the main functions revolved around protection of members from official harassment, providing burial assistance for deceased members, and assisting members with formal registration. There were attempts to create a rotating loan scheme, but these collapsed owing to insufficient resources. With annual fees and levies amounting to barely 500 naira (US$5) per member, there was little the association could do from its own resources, and in current hard times, no prospect of raising fees without reducing its already narrow membership. As in the shoe cluster, there was some attempt to regulate prices and limit copying, but this was easily evaded by producers, who simply refused to join the organization. Recognizing that effective regulation required wider participation, association officials were keen to find ways of increasing membership. Given that their objectives were dominated by the concerns of better-off producers, however, widening their appeal was complicated by the lack of resources to offer any real benefits to weaker producers.

The association of informal cosmetics producers, though small and made up of relatively educated and well-established producers, was plagued by serious divisions among members. Formally democratic structures had so far failed to create cooperative relations between the male-dominated executive and the predominantly female membership, and between the more established and the economically weaker producers. The central objectives of the association focused less on opposition to the state than on opposition to survivalist cosmetics producers. Established producers trying to build a brand reputation blamed rising numbers of small guerrilla cosmetics firms for price undercutting, counterfeiting and attracting increased official harassment. Conversely, survivalist producers saw the association as an adversary that 'just collects our money and tries to drive us out of business' through price and quality regulations. Moreover, antagonistic gender relations weakened cooperation even within the association. An agreement to set minimum prices was undercut by female members of the association, who lacked the capital to sustain the action, and resented the success of better-capitalized male interlopers. The absence of any broad framework of occupational solidarity tended to promote a trend towards authoritarian rather than democratic solutions focused on compulsion.

Civil organization in a disabling environment While the cohesiveness of underlying occupational identities has played an important role in political mobilization in the Aba clusters, any organizational advantages are rapidly being eroded by the disabling economic and political environment of liberalization. Neoliberal economic reform in Nigeria triggered skyrocketing inflation, averaging 200 per cent per year between 1985 and 1999, as well as severe unemployment, which stood at over 25 per cent in 1997 (Meagher 2006). The popular impact has been one of intense pressure on livelihoods and a surge of entry into informal economic activities. Far from increasing the organizational strength of informal associations in Aba, the rapid expansion of the informal economy under conditions of economic stress has tended to weaken the capacity of these associations for effective mobilization and representation. The rapid influx of new producers into informal manufacturing has placed a growing strain on the fragile organizational structures and the limited resources of informal associations. The environment of extreme competition has also intensified the conflict between occupational and survivalist concerns, generating increased divisions among informal operators, while at the same time absorbing associational resources in meeting social welfare instead of business needs as producers struggle to make ends meet. Among poorer producers, difficulties in affording the cost of fees and levies have further weakened participation.

In addition to internal competition for influence and resources, informal sector associations also face competition from other civil organizations. As Dorothy McCormick (1999) has indicated in other parts of Africa, cluster associations are losing out to competition from ethnic or religious associations, particularly among poor producers, who see the latter as more relevant to their social welfare needs. In Aba, the rise of pentacostal religious groups is exacerbating the problem, as many of them strongly discourage members from participating in any other associations. An attempt by one of the shoe associations to make all resident producers join the organization was met with a threat of court action by those abstaining for religious reasons. Challenges of internal divisions, resource competition and power relations, combined with mounting livelihood pressures, have tended to undermine associational cohesion in the Aba clusters, despite the apparent expansion of opportunities for political expression.

External linkages

The internal weaknesses of informal associations have led to increasing dependence on external linkages with the state, the formal sector and NGOs. Far from developing as mechanisms of disengagement and popular resistance to the state, informal associations in Aba have actively sought out links with the state and other formal organizations. Among the marginalized, there is often a trade-off between power and autonomy. In the face of rapid expansion and intensifying competition within the informal economy, access to adequate resources, services, infrastructure and regulatory authority is increasingly dependent on formal sector connections. Among Aba's informal producers' associations, awareness of this reality has since the mid-1990s been exemplified by an urgent concern with official registration. Although the clusters remained overwhelmingly informal, all of their associations were actively seeking formal registration. Since the registration of the Umuehilegbu shoe association in 1994, all of the other shoe associations have been seeking registration in order to improve their access to government and NGO assistance. The cosmetics association was actively pursuing registration from its inception in order to use state backing to impose its authority on other informal cosmetics producers. Aba Garment attempted to register at the federal level in order to lobby the federal government against the 1998 liberalization of textile imports, since the local and state governments lacked jurisdiction over trade policy. Efforts at federal registration failed owing to the lack of nationwide membership, leading the garment association to settle for state-level registration in 2003.

The scramble for registration was symptomatic of the powerlessness and institutional exclusion experienced by informal firms and by their associations.

Informal producers lacked access to the institutional support of formal private sector associations, such as the Aba Chamber of Commerce (ACCIMA) or the local branch of the Manufacturers Association (MAN) because these associations required members to be formally registered. As activities dominated by migrants to Aba operating on the wrong side of the law, they had little influence at the local government level. Among informal manufacturers, access to the kinds of resources and influence necessary to address their developmental and livelihood needs was available only through informal cliental ties, or through legally registered associations. But the handicaps of economic, legal and social marginality mean that these channels of interest representation bring with them risks of further marginalization or political capture.

Accessing formal channels Comparatively high levels of education and professional values in the garment cluster gave the informal garment association the social resources to pursue formal channels of political voice. In its efforts to represent its members, Aba Garment focused on the development of formal, transparent linkages with industrial associations rather than on cliental relations with local officials. The president of Aba Garment explained that informal linkages with influential notables had not proved particularly helpful for solving their real problems, and access to influential patrons was unreliable.[5] Instead, Aba Garment joined the formal sector small-business association, NASSI, through which they gained assistance with organizing official registration, as well as information about trade fairs and limited financial support. They hoped in future to join higher-level business associations in order to obtain links with larger companies for contracts. Their efforts at federal-level registration revealed an interest in influencing policy, rather than simply lobbying for favours. The garment association also expressed an interest in pursuing links with the national textile workers' union (NUTGTWN) and the Nigeria Labour Congress (NLC) regarding their common opposition to Asian textile imports.[6] Marginalized within local structures of power and influence, the informal garment association concentrated on building ties with national institutions with a mandate for industrial development. While this strategy allowed Aba Garment to circumvent negligent and corrupt local forces, it also threw a comparatively small and weak group of informal producers into the open waters of formal industrial organization, where their lack of political and economic influence left them severely handicapped.

Indeed, little came of their various efforts at institutional access until they were included in a United Nations Industrial Development Organization (UNIDO) informal sector development programme in 2003. The UNIDO programme delivered little in the way of useful resources – routine managerial and technical training workshops, and an unrealized promise of credit – but the association executives found that working with UNIDO allowed them to gain the 'ear of the state' through easier access to relevant officials. Sadly, as garment markets collapsed under intense import competition, efforts to seize the new opportunities for political influence and economic advancement appeared to have made the leadership of Aba Garment even more remote from the wider constituency of the informal garment producers than they had previously been.

Moreover, opportunistic forces of elite capture were not far behind. Potential access to NGO resources attracted the rise of a new association in the garment cluster, called the 'Association of Tailors and Fashion Designers'. Founded by two 'entrepreneurial tailors' of middle-class origins, the new association focused on capturing resources within the garment cluster now that it appeared to have greater state and NGO attention. The new association did not seem to conduct meetings with members; indeed, some of the so-called members interviewed did not seem to realize that they were members. The leadership also had little knowledge of the collective interests and concerns of the garment cluster, and seemed to devote most of its organizational energies to lobbying the local and state governments for unspecified 'assistance' and contracts. The only activity of the new association so far has been the procurement of a government contract to collect the sanitation tax from tailors across the state, which it carried out by setting inflated rates for non-members and threatening to seize their equipment if they did not pay.

Cliental incorporation and political capture The shoe and cosmetics associations, while showing significant occupational commitment, turned to more local cliental connections in their efforts to represent cluster interests. The criminalized status of informal cosmetics producers, owing to their lack of NAFDAC registration, made formal institutional channels impossible. The central strategy of the associational leadership was to formally register the association so that they could obtain recognition from the District Police Officer (DPO) in Aba. Once formally recognized, they intended to pay the police to arrest cosmetics producers outside the association, thereby forcing them to join, while providing protection from harassment for their own members. The legal precariousness of such a strategy, as well as its authoritarian character, does not bode well for the development of political voice or organizational autonomy in the informal cosmetics cluster. Moreover, the election of male leaders in an effort to maximize their negotiating power with the police led to ongoing gender conflicts between better-capitalized male producers and established female producers with a longer history in the business.

In the shoe cluster, access to formal channels of political representation was blocked less by legal marginalization than by the social marginality of producers. Lowly occupational status, limited education and disadvantaged class origins, even among the leadership, deprived informal shoe producers of the social power to form effective formal sector linkages. Associational leadership generally shied away from links with formal private sector associations or participation in formal business events, such as trade fairs. Instead, associational linkages reflected a strategy of collusion and cliental ties with local notables, and local and state government officials. The association leadership was implicated in collusion with local government officials over tax collection, electricity supply and allocation of workshops in the shoe production zones, all of which were characterized by kickbacks and dubious arrangements between association executives and local government as well as state officials. In the 1999 gubernatorial election, the associations were used to mobilize votes through promises of improved electricity supply.

Attempts to form links with international NGOs have also been impeded by social marginality as well as by ongoing organizational fragmentation and leadership struggles among the shoe associations. Informal sector development programmes led by the United Nations Development Programme (UNDP) in 1996 and by UNIDO in 2003 required the formation of a single umbrella association in order to facilitate interaction with the shoe cluster. Not only did this disrupt existing patterns of collective organization in the shoe cluster, creating new bodies detached from their popular base, but it attracted the predatory attention of state officials and better-connected notables who claimed to represent shoe producers. These groups have repeatedly managed to absorb the bulk of the resources intended for the shoe cluster. Once the donor programmes end, the new 'joint' shoe associations fall dormant, having brought little in the way of new resources into the cluster, but leaving a legacy of associational disruption and increased popular mistrust of the machinations of their leadership. On the whole, NGO interventions, driven largely by international agendas and the pressure to show results, have tended to weaken rather than strengthen the capacity of the shoe associations to represent the interests of the informal shoe clusters.

Part of the problem lies in the inclination of the leaders in the shoe associations to cliental and collusive ties with officials and more powerful organizations, in response to the constraints of social, legal and economic disadvantages. This has made the shoe associations particularly vulnerable to political capture, creating a situation in which their activities can be mobilized in the service of interests antagonistic to informal economic advancement and popular democracy. The dangers of this scenario are most starkly illustrated in the case of the Bakassi Boys vigilante group, which was formed by Aba's informal shoemakers in 1998. Run jointly by the informal shoe associations, the Bakassi Boys constituted a popular, though brutal, force for the restoration of security in a town in which police corruption and rampant criminality had become a serious threat to business activities, as well as to physical safety (Ukiwo 2002; Meagher 2007). The success and widespread popularity of the Bakassi Boys brought the shoe associations considerable state attention, but in ways that channelled efforts and resources into the development of the vigilante group, further starving the shoe clusters of resources and attention. Once the vigilante group was well established, Igbo state governors seized control from the shoe producers, turning the vigilante group into a source of murder and mayhem across south-eastern Nigeria in the run-up to the 2003 elections (with a further revival in the run-up to the 2007 elections). By intensifying disorder and insecurity in Aba, the Bakassi Boys ended up acting against the economic interests of the very shoe producers who created them.

Popular exclusion and the exit option Amid the flurry of associational activity in all of the three clusters, the majority of informal producers felt unrepresented and powerless in the face of decaying infrastructure, scarcity of good-quality materials, and crippling competition from imports and local firms. In both the shoe and the garment clusters, the majority of producers had not heard of the UNIDO programme even after it had been in operation for over a year. Nor had increased access to the state translated into any tangible improvements at the level of popular livelihoods. Most felt that association leaders were more intent on representing their own interests than those of their constituency. Indeed, in both the shoe and cosmetics clusters, many producers regarded the cluster associations as the 'enemy', since they were more focused on harassing members and cornering benefits than on providing accountable representation. As one shoe producer exclaimed, 'They just want to eat.'

Rather than experiencing the activities of cluster associations as increasing their political voice, most of the producers interviewed seemed to feel as excluded and silenced as ever. As an established producer of men's suits put it, 'I have no way to express my interests politically [...] But it's not that I'm happy.' A poor woman tailor expressed similar sentiments, saying that all associations disappoint them, so it didn't really matter which one they joined. Whether it was tailors' associations, church associations or home-town associations, no one really represented their interests. A disillusioned shoe producer explained that he had recently withdrawn from the shoe association. He went to the extent of getting his name removed from the membership list so that he would not be fined for failing to attend meetings. Clearly, for the bulk of informal operators, the era of informal political voice has not yet replaced the politics of exit.

Conclusion

This analysis of collective associations in these three Nigerian informal manufacturing clusters has highlighted some of the challenges to the development of political voice within the informal economy, especially in developing-country contexts. While the three Aba clusters represent what are in many ways ideal cultural, economic and political conditions for the development of representative and autonomous informal associations, they illustrate the real difficulties of civil organization within the informal economy. Hemmed in by lack of resources, legal marginality and powerlessness, informal associations struggle on the one hand with a mistrustful and evasive constituency, and on the other with extreme vulnerability to political capture. In addition to economic and institutional marginality, the social marginality of informal actors and their associations is often overlooked. Disadvantages of class, education and sometimes gender or communal origins constrain the ability of informal associations to forge effective linkages with formal institutions and the state. As the Aba cases reveal, organizational experiences and constraints are shaped by the specific history of a given activity. In the cosmetics cluster, gender conflicts and extreme *legal* marginality constrained effective organization, while in the shoe cluster, it was *social* marginality based on occupation, class and education which weakened associational efforts. Among garment producers, by contrast, a professional orientation and advantaged educational status were undercut by the liabilities of informality and internal occupational and communal divisions. In all three cases, women failed to gain an effective voice in the associations, despite constituting the majority in one activity and nearly half of the members in another.

Rather than increasing the political strength of informal associations through the expansion of the informal economy and the proliferation of informal organizations, these case studies have demonstrated the tendency of liberalization to further weaken and undermine the civil capacity of the informal economy. In the Aba clusters, economic hardship and intensifying competition exacerbated internal conflicts and resource constraints, undermining mutual trust and capacities for mobilization. Liberalization has also eroded the autonomy of these associations, which have become increasingly dependent on the state and NGOs for access to the resources and influence necessary to defend informal livelihoods and represent member interests. The upshot in the Aba context has been a shift towards capture or exclusion rather than voice. Starved of resources and institutional protection, even well-established associations in activities as large and dynamic as the Aba shoe cluster can be drawn into strategies of state predation, or resort to collusive and authoritarian practices, as in the case of the cosmetics cluster.

Amid the very real constraints on informal collective organizations, it is important not to lose sight of their potential. Despite their failings, the Aba cluster associations also demonstrate what Thulare referred to as 'germs of democratic practice and culture'. Institutions of occupational identity, complex structures of representation, systems of democratic leadership selection, inclusive social welfare programmes – all of these are indications of a desire as well as a capacity for collective mobilization and expression, however fragile. In an inspired article, Pat Horn (2003) reminds us that political voice is not an automatic result of collective organization within the informal economy; it is a product of decades-long struggles for internal consensus and formal recognition. These struggles are as much about learning the skills of collective mobilization, building constructive alliances and avoiding the tactics of elite capture once associations have been formed, as they are about gaining the attention of the state:

> The struggles to win small victories help organizations to strengthen their capacity to work together and develop their organizational and collective bargaining skills. It helps each campaign to guard in a more informed manner against repeating the mistakes of the previous ones. It helps organizations to pre-empt the same old divisive strategies used by those who have an interest in dividing their struggles [...] (Ibid.)

An awareness of the deep susceptibility of informal economy organizations to division and capture, and an understanding of the complex interaction of community, class, gender and education that structures their cohesion, as well as their vulnerability, are part of the project of strengthening the informal organizational capacity. By focusing on the socio-political as well as the economic and legal marginality of informal associations, current trends in the International Labour Organization (ILO) for fostering strategic alliances with trade unions, progressive local governments and supportive NGOs offer a useful way forward. As the ILO (2002a: 83) report on *Decent Work and the Informal Economy* argues, established trade unions, along with other like-minded organizations, 'can provide guidance, training and other support to enhance the capacity of informal workers and their associations to develop organizational structures and management that would help them to become effective and democratic organizations'. As the experiences of the Aba clusters testify, the role of formal sector unions or NGOs in bolstering informal associational development can be problematic, and can easily lead to organizational disruption or capture if initiatives are too rapid or heavy handed. With appropriate local sensitivity, however, alliances with stronger organizations with similar interests can help to foster institutional access while guarding against the dangers of capture. It is only by addressing the inherent weaknesses as well as the strengths of informal sector organizations that the disabling politics of vulnerability can be transformed into a politics of voice.

3 | Women leaders and the sense of power: clientelism and citizenship at the Dantokpa market in Cotonou, Benin

Ebbe Prag

Introduction

Public marketplaces around the globe are arenas of political struggle where actors fight for access to and control over space, resources and political allegiance. This chapter focuses on women's market associations at the Dantokpa Market in Cotonou (Benin) and investigates how the associations and the leaders wield de facto authority over the management of the market.

More than half of the employment in the world is informal and takes place at home or in public places; in streets, railway stations and marketplaces where public authorities claim to regulate activities, but often lack legitimacy or means of regulation. Women constitute over 60 per cent of the employed in the informal sector in the developing world, and in sub-Saharan Africa 84 per cent (ILO 2002c: 7–8); figures that explain why women are potential political actors if organized.

Street vendors and hawkers occupying public space are often exposed to arbitrary harassment from public authorities or private security groups, and informal sector work means high risk in cases of accidents, illness or criminal charges. This lack of rights is the situation for more than half of the employed in the world, and women are in this regard the largest and most vulnerable group (UNIFEM 2005: 8). In West Africa female traders have traditionally been protected through membership of women's market associations. Strong leaders of patron–client networks were able to mobilize and defend the members' rights (Barnes 1986; Clark 1994). The case of Madame Chodaton is an example of this kind of association. Leaders of market women's associations in West Africa have for centuries wielded political influence on governance of the marketplaces, owing to their dominant position in trade. This chapter shows that this is still the case at the Dantokpa market in Cotonou.

Need for protection has recently spurred global networking between informal workers struggling for legal rights. StreetNet International and WIEGO (www. wiego.org) offer support to street vendors and market associations in setting up regional networks. In Gujarat in India, women textile workers in the informal sector have organized the Self-Employed Women's Association (SEWA) trade union, with 700,000 members, to protect the rights of self-employed women, and in Latin and Central America many women's associations and unions have existed since the 1920s, and new associations are presently being created (Gallin and Horn 2005; UNIFEM 2005: 75).

Following the economic crisis in developing countries in the 1980s and 1990s many well-educated men entered the informal job market when they lost their jobs owing to structural reforms. The influx of men in profitable sectors has challenged the female-dominated associations (Gallin and Horn 2005). Furthermore, some male-dominated sectors have been linked to organized smuggling and crime (Hart 2005: 9, 12). These non-transparent methods have been met with resistance from women's associations.

The women's network at Dantokpa has created organizational and political responses to the corrupt market management. Their autonomous association is the transforming tool (Tripp 2000; Prag 2004; Gallin and Horn 2005). For 'Claudine' in this chapter, political networking and lobbying are part of the game, but she avoids patronage relationships and follows a rights-based approach building on citizenship. The data from Cotonou suggests that organizations in the 'informal economy' are closely linked to the political field and agendas, which are not limited to the market space. Discussions from Latin American settings on how *clientship* relates to *citizenship* in studies of links between informal slum dwellers and politicians seem relevant to the political dynamics at Dantokpa (Taylor 2004; Taylor and Wilson 2004; Lazar 2004). Chodaton mobilizes market women as clients, but on a civil rights agenda, whereas 'Claudine' and her network seem to explore the rights-based approach of citizenship. This indicates that we should focus on social networks' institutional strength, emphasizing not only 'economic capacities' (Meagher 2005: 232) but also changing the 'political capacities' of the associations and leaders to influence the market, work and living conditions.

Female power in West African markets

West African women have a long tradition in business and politics and have influenced the management of central marketplaces in the urban centres.[1]

Women in Africa, and particularly in the southern part of West Africa, have for centuries been engaged in market and long-distance trade. They have reigned over marketplaces and trade in Yoruba-speaking south-west Nigeria, the southern part of Benin, Togo, Ghana and Côte d'Ivoire. The literature on women's market associations in this part of West Africa shows that despite colonial and post-colonial government attempts to curtail female leader's authority in the central marketplaces, this has never happened without resistance, and fieldwork data also confirms the existence of powerful female leaders and associations in Benin today.

Consequently, this chapter argues that women leaders at Dantokpa hold de facto authority (Lund 2006: 676) and are able to influence key decisions at the market thanks to the social networks and associations created over decades. Women constitute a critical mass at the market, and powerful female leaders of market associations are deeply engaged in political networking, which explains why they can reverse government decisions related to trade and the marketplace. In this regard Madame Justine Chodaton (Dantokpa) represents a continuation of the historically rooted tradition of female market patrons, such as Madame Tinubu in 1850s Ibadan, and the Ashanti market queens in Kumasi, as Clark has shown (Clark 1994).

Today, female leaders are at a crossroads and their quasi-hegemony is challenged by entrepreneurial male leaders, backed by traders in growth sectors at the market. These leaders head mixed associations and social and political networks from which women tend to be excluded. Moreover, competition from cheap Asian products erodes the power of female leaders in the influential associations of wax textile wholesalers. However, fieldwork data from Dantokpa suggests that new female leaders with an international outlook and skills are facing this challenge and reviving the tradition of women's leadership. The data also shows that organizations in the 'informal economy' are closely linked to the political field and political agendas, which are not limited to the marketplace but reach out into Beninese society more broadly.

Dantokpa market – the economic and political heart of Benin

More than 400,000 people come to the Dantokpa market every day, and the market is thereby the largest workplace in Benin. Together with the harbour in Cotonou, it is the economic centre of the country. It occupies a leading role in economic and political terms. Administratively, the state company Société de Gestion des Marchés de Cotonou (SOGEMA) – part of the Ministry of the Interior – holds *de jure* authority over the marketplaces at Dantokpa, Gbogbanou and Ganhi in Cotonou. However, since 2003 the municipality has contested state ownership with reference to the decentralization reform, which prescribes the transfer of the administration and the legal ownership to the municipality.

By any standards Dantokpa is huge; both on the national scale and from a West African perspective. The market covers 18.7 hectares and has around 22,000 officially registered traders (D. Fangbédji, FAOMAB, interview, October 2006; Paulais and Wihelm 2000: 62) and also a large number of itinerant vendors, mostly unregistered and estimated at approximately eight thousand (www.streetnet.org.za/English/gufs5.htm). Women are estimated to make up 60–80 per cent of the traders in Dantokpa; some organized in unions and in professional associations – two trade unions and around twenty professional associations. Several leaders claim that only half of these are legally founded and that the rest are splinter associations created by the SOGEMA leadership. The state-owned management company recognizes both the unions and the associations as discussion partners, and the associations have a joint representative on SOGEMA's board. The trade unions organize different groups of market vendors, but they both unionize wholesalers, semi-wholesalers, retailers and street vendors. The largest union, the Syndicat National des Vendeurs et Vendeuses et Assimilés des Marchés du Bénin (SYNAVAMAB), mainly organizes women, but also some men. The second union, the Union Syndicale des Vendeuses et Vendeurs de Pièces Détachées et Divers du Marché de Dantokpa (USYNVEPID), unites both men and women, but men make up a minority of around 40 per cent, mainly those who sell spare parts, electronics and hardware in the *divers* section. The federation of associations at Dantokpa, the Fédération Nationale des Organisations et Associations des Marchés du Bénin (FAOMAB), seeks to unite the associations around common positions, but it is divided by factional struggles between the member associations.

Economically, Dantokpa is extremely important to Benin. This explains why all governments up to now have refused to hand it over to the opposition in the municipality in Cotonou. Nobody is able to give precise figures for the daily turnover owing to the informal character of the economy. Estimates that are probably very low do exist, varying from 1.5 billion CFA francs per day to 10 billion CFA francs per day (1€ = 656 CFA francs).

After this introduction to Dantokpa there follows a summary of the history of women's market associations in Benin.

Women's market associations in a post-colonial perspective

The unstable political situation after independence in 1960 did not facilitate organization-building at the national level. The regime of Hubert Maga (1960–63) set up barriers to market women's business activities, and therefore many businesswomen traded from Nigeria and Togo. Until 1976, market associations and trading networks in Benin were functional and strong only at the local and regional level. After Mathieu Kérékou came to power, the situation changed. In 1976, he called on the local market women's associations to federate in what became the Union Nationale des Commerçantes du Bénin (UNACOBE), formally affiliated to the Organisation des Femmes Révolutionaires du Bénin (ORFB) (Heilbrunn 1997a: 12). A Yoruba woman, El Hadja Karamatou Adechokan, became the first president of the umbrella organization UNACOBE, which federated the hitherto divided local market women's associations and their autonomous local chapters in a support and information network (ibid.: 12; Codjia, interview, March 2007; Chodaton, interview, March 2008). The market women elected local leaders, often for life – a choice based on wealth, reputation for negotiation and dispute settlement skills (Clark 1994: 248ff.). The president of the federation was supposed to represent UNACOBE in negotiations with the government on trade policies, tariff and taxation issues, where market women seriously needed collective responses. However, under Adechokan's leadership results were poor in this regard, and UNACOBE's strength was particularly located in the regional chapters. It played an important role as a protective network in the mid-1980s when trans-border trade to Nigeria blossomed and nearly all traders joined local patron–client networks, which also offered access to stock and credit (Heilbrunn 1997b: 480). The military coup in Nigeria in 1984 closed the border and smuggling became dangerous and expensive, and the crisis pushed the regional branches of UNACOBE to cooperate and exchange information. When the Beninese banks went bankrupt in 1988, many traders lost their savings and the economic crisis triggered the democratic movement, in which UNACOBE's local branches participated. In the process of the reform movement in 1989, Adechokan was accused of collaboration with President Kérékou, lost influence in UNACOBE and was replaced by Augustine Codjia in 1991 (Onibon-Doubougan 2001). Three powerful businesswomen from Dantokpa and Cotonou participated in UNACOBE's leadership, Augustine Codjia, Justine Chodaton and Grace Lawani (Heilbrunn 1997b), and each of them led rival factions or political clientelist networks struggling for power in the organization. Augustine Codjia, from a prominent merchant family in Ouidah, won the presidency. Though the business association UNACOBE had a national character, market women from Dantokpa, and in particular the Dutch wax textile wholesalers, dominated the organization. After the first democratic elections in 1991, where the three women ran for parliament, but only Codjia won a seat for the Porto-Novo/Ouèmè-based Parti du renouveau démocratique, political and personal cleavages divided UNACOBE and Justine Chodaton founded her own association. Heilbrunn explains that UNACOBE primarily functioned as regionally based clientelist networks built around credit and saving associations, and that local leaders linked up with each other in alliances (1997a, 1997b). The democratic elections in 1990/91 produced new rivalries and reconfigured alliances between these regional networks.

The heritage of women's influence at Dantokpa

The next part of the chapter focuses on Madame Justine Chodaton's career as associational and political leader at Dantokpa and at national level. Her political role has been significant, and by investigating her initiatives and struggles, it becomes possible to draw a more precise picture of how the female associative environment has developed at Dantokpa and to analyse how women wield influence on daily management of the marketplace. The cases studies also show how Madame Chodaton's knowledge has been transmitted to the new generation of women, in a situation where global competition undermines her influence on the textile sector at the market.

The history of a female market leader Madame Justine Chodaton was born around 1935 in Adja Tado, western Benin, near the border with Togo, but moved to Abomey when she was twelve. Her parents were farmers, but her grandmother and mother traded, and they taught her the skill. Newly married, she moved into 'African textiles', trading in Cotonou, around 1956. She explains how she took the coal train to Lomé in Togo and continued with a second train to Accra in Ghana, where she bought textiles at the markets and brought them back to Cotonou for retailing. Her business developed successfully and, after three years, she bought land – 'two parcels and after that a car, because if you want to trade, you first need to buy the location where you want to live and do business. You need a home for a start, and after that you can buy comfort. I had fifteen thousand francs when I started in 1956.' She laughs. When John Walkden, the local agent of the Dutch textile company Vlisco, started up in Cotonou, she began buying Dutch wax from Vlisco directly and stopped travelling to Lomé and Accra.

It was a difficult period for the market women when President Hubert Maga came to power in 1960 because his regime tended to extract as much money from the market women as possible. She started to organize resistance against the president when he jailed some of the women. She explains:

> I started buying textiles from John Walkden in Cotonou. Well, when people saw that business was successful, the state at that time, the government, wanted to make things difficult for us women. None of the women performed well. Then I called a meeting, which I 'supervised', and I became chairman. And from that moment, nobody arrived at the market to make a fuss with us. (Chodaton, interview, March 2006)

It was during this tough post-independence period that Chodaton took the first steps to forming her social network among the Dutch wax textile wholesalers. Augustine Codjia created UNACOBE in 1976, and the younger Chodaton participated in this business association as local leader at Dantokpa, but under Codjia's leadership.

The union SYNAVAMAB The National Conference in 1990, the advent of the multiparty system and democratic elections exacerbated existing tensions and rivalry in UNACOBE's leadership. Justine Chodaton, Grace Lawani and Augustine Codjia competed for power in UNACOBE and for seats in parliament. UNACOBE continued under Augustine Codjia's leadership, but today it has lost momentum owing to Codjia's advanced age. Chodaton transformed her social network into a formal association, the Groupement Professionnel des Vendeurs et Vendeuses des Marchés (GPVMB), with the aim of reaching broader segments of market women throughout Benin. Later, in 1992, she created the union SYNAVAMAB, also with the aim of generating a broad social and political basis. Both organizations have served as electoral reservoirs and instruments in her political machine. Justine Chodaton has been elected three times to parliament, a fact that all observers mention in order to stress her popularity. She is the *patronne* of the SYNAVAMAB and some claim that she alone represents the organization in public. The union could be seen as the formalization of her social network in trade and politics. SYNAVAMAB held its first ordinary general assembly in May 2007 (*La Fraternité*, 14 May 2007; Chodaton, interview, August 2007). This process of formalization, registration and internal elections may help to strengthen the organization and crystallize new leaders when Chodaton retires. The board composition, however, reveals that Chodaton's family network controls the organization. SYNAVAMAB organizes market and street vendors in other markets throughout Benin, and Chodaton claims to have local chapters in thirty-four marketplaces and 2,400 members at Dantokpa (Xaba et al. 2002; Chodaton, interview, 2006).[2]

SYNAVAMAB collaborates with the second union, USYNVEPID, over different activities and services for the members – mainly women. They have a joint negotiation group and seek to improve managerial skills and competence to run projects. When asked about their views on SYNAVAMAB, the USYNVEPID officials argue that SYNAVAMAB's leadership is getting 'old and tired'. They are not actively setting up structures and taking new initiatives to control the sector of the textile sellers. Chodaton does not attend the market regularly, owing to her age, the state of her health and her seat in parliament. She works from her private house close to the market, but the union has representatives in different zones at Dantokpa. Despite that, many local sources recognize that Chodaton's influence is strong and that she is able to mobilize support from the market women because of her legitimacy as a 'socially sensible' leader.

Building social networks in trade and politics Chodaton started a trade network of retailers in the 1960s to defend business interests and to offer mutual assistance in periods of difficulty. She is the 'social' leader who distributes money to persons who have lost their assets by accident so that they can continue in business. By doing so, she has enlarged her business network and kept it strong, resistant and vital. 'Unity is important,' she explains, 'there is unity between the market women, we do not betray each other. That's how the market has grown into what it is today.' One way to build unity is to maintain a firm stand in negotiations with John Walkden. Once the company called a meeting where it announced that it would do business only with the best-selling women. Chodaton responded that either the company sold to everyone or they sold to none.

Her close links to the director of the national textile company SOBETEX in the 1960s, who offered her credit, and later to John Walkden (Vlisco) have enabled her to grant favourable credit conditions to vendors who could repay when the textile was sold. Her now deceased husband, Louis Chodaton, leader of the powerful transport union, Union Nationale des Transporteurs Routiers de Bénin, also supported her during the first elections. The support she gets from the Dutch wax textile wholesalers may seem unconditional when Charlotte Babagbeto, the president of the Vlisco women's association, says, 'Chodaton is our leader, and we do not take decisions without her consent. She is a woman to congratulate' (interview, November 2006). Babagbeto created the new association of Vlisco women in 2006, to represent her distribution network's interests in the conflict with women selling Chinese copies of Vlisco's products when they had talks with the president and the minister of commerce on this issue. However, despite the proclaimed unity with Chodaton, the new association is also an example of the increased factionalism and division among John Walkden's preferential wholesalers, who create separate associations and compete for Chodaton's succession.

The 'social' aspect of Chodaton's business and organizational management conceals hierarchical and horizontal relations of power. However, she has created a trade network where the clients under her protective umbrella support her politically and economically. As one observer puts it: 'Chodaton and her group have dictated their law on the market for years, and the women were compelled to buy Vlisco's product through her group.' Moreover, when burials or other social ceremonies took place, her broad trade network assisted the ceremonies and sold special *pagnes* (sarongs) used in the ceremony, which was a very lucrative market. Finally, Chodaton's gifts, according to other sources, were not unconditional, and credit in the form of unsold stock, which she distributed to women in trouble, had to be paid back and new credit taken in the form of commodities. Thus, poorer traders became dependent on her credit line (communication, LL, Cotonou, March 2006). This situation of inequality and dependency has been exacerbated owing to the current economic crisis in the wax sector.

Her network controlled the trade in the wax building at Dantokpa for years, setting the rules for trade in this female space. Madame Megnigbeto, trader in the wax business at the market and zone delegate, criticizes the monopoly that John Walkden's company, and their privileged wholesalers such as Chodaton, held for years. Megnigbeto is the president of the association Pagnes pour tous (Sarongs for all). She sells the cheap Chinese mark 'Hitarget' and other copies of Vlisco's designs. 'I was the first to fight John Walkden's prices,' she says forcefully, and hints at the ongoing war between Chodaton's group of women and those who sell cheap copies (interview, February 2007).

Over the years, Chodaton has developed her networks in trade and politics. She was often asked to come and reorganize market associations in Benin and abroad. Owing to her long career and associational experience, she has acquired a conflict mediating role – a symbolic role as 'market queen'. She is invited to inaugural ceremonies, to lay the first stone and pronounce protective prayers. Her role is similar to that of the Ekwe female leaders of Ibu marketplaces (Okonjo

1976: 48; Amadiume 1997) and the Iyolade female leader of the markets in the Yoruba towns (Humarau 1996: 15). Justine Chodaton, though illiterate, has been an extremely skilled organizer and leader. On the wall in her office and workroom at home hangs a picture of Jesus with the inscription 'With God All Is Possible', which could be seen as her guiding maxim.

Madame Chodaton represents the party Renaissance du Bénin (RB) in parliament. Despite her membership of the opposition party, she argues that it is crucial for the union to keep a friendly relationship with the government. 'In order to be leader of the Union, you need to be at good terms with the government' (Chodaton, communication, March 2006). Chodaton's political secretary pushes the argument farther, saying that 'it means that you should set up a relationship of concubinage' (he means a patronage relationship) with the government. Then you have 'green light everywhere'. Madame Chodaton adds in Mina (the local language): 'if you want to play games with the government, it will fuss up your business'. On the other hand, she argues that 'if the government does something very bad, the union leaders will go in large numbers [form a deputation] to talk to the government'. To illustrate her argument, she explains how she acted in a recent case where cheap Chinese textile copies of Dutch wax from Vlisco floated into Dantokpa. She mobilized the market women, who demonstrated and sent a deputation to the minister of commerce to demand government intervention and regulation of the textile market. The conflict, which set her in opposition to other market women selling the Chinese copies, seems to have weakened her financially and eroded her support at Dantokpa. Another example of her ability to manoeuvre politically is her position in the conflict between the government and the municipality of Cotonou. The dispute concerns who owns and who has the right to manage the Dantokpa market. Instead of supporting the mayor, Nicéphore Soglo, from her RB party, she accepted that the former government should continue to manage Dantokpa. Most important to her was to keep a maximum of influence and support at Dantokpa, and the party line was therefore less significant. Her argument was that times of economic crisis, when the state needs income, are not the right moment to change the management regime. Her position was probably guided by her interest in bargaining directly with the Kérékou government.

Influencing the state agency: the feminization of SOGEMA Chodaton's strategy of networking and bargaining with whatever government is in power is a good illustration of how she has been able to influence key decisions and management at Dantokpa. Her female network has managed to influence the composition of the leadership of the state agency SOGEMA. The feminization of the SOGEMA executive is interesting, because it was the market women's associations which were behind the decision that introduced female leaders, but also because it reinvented the custom of formal female leadership of the marketplaces.

SOGEMA was founded in 1983, and until the end of the 1990s the executives were all male, but around 1999/2000 the policy changed. Since then, three women have led SOGEMA. The shift in policy resulted from lobbying by the female-dominated associations, hoping that it would enhance transparency and improve governance of the Cotonou marketplaces (interviews LCA, CG, March 2006). Pressure in favour of female leadership of SOGEMA obviously came from Chodaton's wax women's association at Dantokpa. The feminization of SOGEMA's leadership shows Chodaton's political influence on the management of Dantokpa and the other markets in Cotonou.

The unions contacted President Kérékou in 1996 when he came to power following democratic elections and asked him for an audience. The unions, which predominantly represented market women, were fed up with the male executives of SOGEMA, because 'the men did not recognize the market women and were not sensitive to their particular problems, and did not know how to deal with women' (Claudine, interview, March 2006). The result of this meeting was that Kérékou asked them to form a bloc and participate jointly in the administration of SOGEMA. The associations believed that the leadership were embezzling their tax and lease payments and decided to see President Kérékou. At a second meeting, in 1999, they explained to him that they would not accept any male chief executive again, and proposed employing a woman from the administration with a degree in finance and management – a neutral person with experience. After this meeting, in April 2000, the government appointed Véronique Gbèdo Sagbo, who had served in the Trésor.[3]

Véronique Gbèdo was a financial specialist and political appointee from the party Fard Alafia, with its base in northern Benin. Her achievements were cleaning up and renovating Dantokpa, changing the management style radically, and attacking problems of counterfeit market access tickets and widespread corruption. The result was that the company's accounts came out of the red in 2001.[4] Despite this success, resistance against her grew for various reasons. First of all, the history of Dantokpa shows that it is difficult to get support from the market vendors to renovate and undertake new construction, because it necessarily involves some people being dislocated or relocated. The process inevitably produces victims and therefore also enemies. The second criticism was that she was opposed to handing over authority over the Cotonou markets to the municipality and the opposition around the Soglo family and the RB party. Altogether, Véronique Gbèdo became extremely unpopular among the market women because of her authoritarian management style, and the associations did all they could to get her sacked. However, other actors at the market stress that their relationship was very good and fruitful for a long period of time. The criticism of her management was not in any case unanimous. Both the press (*La Fraternité*, 10 February 2004) and vendors at Dantokpa credited her for the changes that she managed to implement. Nevertheless, it was the question of the transfer of assets and authority to the municipality and the Chambre de Commerce et de l'Industrie de Bénin (CCIB) which led to conflict and the split, because Gbèdo defended state control (D. Fangbédji, interview; onion sellers' association board member, interview, February 2007).

The market associations organized several protest marches and 'sit-in' actions at the ministries of the interior and justice to demand her departure from SOGEMA. They criticized her 'opaque' management of the company and her arbitrary way of tearing down stalls (*appatams*) without offering compensation to the users. Finally, the federation of market associations FAOMAB denounced the excessive increase in rent for plots and threatened not to pay taxes (Panapress, 11 August 2004; D. Fangbédji, interview, November 2006). Her management left little space for renegotiation and compromise. She was considered authoritarian, inflexible and arrogant, and at the end of her term she was drawn into a court case where a woman trader accused her of harassment (www.Fraternité-info. com, 27 April 2005). Véronique Gbèdo was probably more consistent in her management than the former executives had been. The fact that she managed to turn a deficit into a surplus during her first year and was opposed to the transfer of authority to the municipality was also a spanner in the works for politicians from the opposition.

The women's associations had the idea that a woman would be more sensitive to market women's preoccupations – like a nurturing 'mother' of the market. Chodaton later revised her view on female managers, because she was actively involved in the sacking of the first chief executive, Véronique Gbèdo Sagbo, in 2005. Gbèdo lost her position for political reasons. She was definitely not popular, but objectively Chodaton and her textile women derived great benefit from her efficiency. The following two executives were also women, which shows that the policy of 'feminization' continued until 2008, when the former RB politician Joseph Tamègnon took the position after Chodaton's intervention behind the scenes.[5]

Chodaton: citizenship expressed through clientelism Chodaton has skilfully used her position as leader at Dantokpa to access the national political arena. She has spun a broad social and political clientelist network using the women's market associations in Benin, her membership of the Chamber of Commerce (CCIB), contacts with Vlisco and its West African network, with StreetNet International and through the RB party with the political elite in Benin and abroad. Her political network has been useful in creating solutions and attracting investments, benefiting her group of textile women and the users of the markets in general. She has also influenced important decisions concerning Dantokpa (promotion of women chief executives, tax issues and access to stalls) through political manoeuvring and pressure during periods when her party was in opposition. She has not been interested in a government position but seems to have played a key role in creating alliances defending civil rights through clientelistic mobilization. At least her explicit strategy has been to avoid direct confrontation with the government and political opponents and instead to manoeuvre and negotiate to strengthen long-term business and political interests.

Having discussed Chodaton's power at Dantokpa and its foundations, the chapter will next examine women's organized responses to SOGEMA's management and male union leaders' marginalization of women and networking with the SOGEMA leadership in the *divers* section of Dantokpa.

Emerging male leaders and women's organized responses

USYNVEPID – the union of the young and energetic men USYNVEPID was created in 2001 by women and men vendors in the *divers* section of the market as an outcome of a conflict with SOGEMA over construction plans. The leadership depicts the union as active, efficient and defending its members' rights, whereas SYNAVAMAB's is described as old, tired and inactive. Unlike with SYNAVAMAB, the board members in USYNVEPID are predominantly male, although 60 per cent of the members or more are women. Only three women are on the board out of twenty-one members. The organization's office is located in the middle of the *divers* area in the chairman's shop. USYNVEPID claims to have around 7,000 members and 200 local shop stewards at Dantokpa.

A rising female leader and the women's network AXISSINON-KPAN AKON The question of power and how to conduct work in the union turned out to hide deep conflicts between men and women in UNSYNVEPID, conflicts related to questions of access to stalls, democracy and good governance of the union, and finally access to and use of external funding. An open quarrel between the general treasurer, a woman, and the male president revealed a power struggle between the majority of women and the majority male leadership. As a response to the conflict, the woman treasurer, 'Claudine', a trained union leader with many years at Dantokpa, organized a network of women to strengthen women's position inside USYNVEPID. She legitimized the creation of the autonomous women's group, arguing that the union's task primarily is to defend members' rights, whereas the women's group should solicit partners in order to start development projects. However, this was only part of the story, because it became obvious that strategic questions of power and control over resources were the deeper explanation for what looked more like a faction than a group to empower women (though this was also the prime aim).

'Claudine' – born in 1952 – is married and has five children. She started as a market woman at Dantokpa twenty-one years ago when she dropped out of education and had to make a living. She first became unionized after some years at the market, though brought up with syndicalism, her father being one of the first trade union leaders during French colonialism. Union work taught her to analyse social and political dynamics, to negotiate rights and mobilize around them. In this way her career is not unique, and shows similarities with those of other African women who have entered associational work (Prag 2004). Though she has her private business, she considers herself and the members in the union to be 'informal workers'.

'Claudine' was a central figure in the struggle with SOGEMA in 1999, when the company wanted to demolish part of the *divers* sector and to construct a modern market building. After the conflict, she played a central role in the creation of UNSYNVEPID, a process Madame Chodaton actively supported and funded. She was proposed as president of the new union, but despite her central role in the struggle, the male *Adja* ethnic network around the chairman managed to take power. Money from the *Adja* politician Bruno Amoussou was part of that process.

As treasurer on the board, 'Claudine' maintained a central position and the union delegated her as representative in a cooperative venture with the NGO StreetNet International, in which Chodaton's union SYNAVAMAB also participates. Owing to this position, she gained control over funding for education and training of the union members, enhanced her international support network and received personal training. The women around 'Claudine' know that donors appreciate to fund women's groups, and even prefer to do so. The external funding of trade union activities for which she is responsible gives her leverage to challenge the president. The way she has done that is to create the women's network AXISSINON-KPAN AKON, which the president sees as a rival faction. However, the network differs in its working practices from normal associational politics. 'Claudine' explains that they give priority to the education of the illiterate women who cannot run their businesses properly. She administers external funding for both UNSYNVEPID and the women's network strictly, because otherwise there is a danger that funds will be siphoned off for personal use. Women in the network virulently attack the tendency among some male leaders to embezzle funds. 'Union work is not personal business as some leaders practise it, but should be based on voluntary work and altruism' is their argument (Françoise/'Claudine', interviews, 2006).

Focusing on participation, education and civil rights 'Claudine's' international experience and training have helped her to develop skills as a union militant and organizer. Many ordinary market women do not know their rights and therefore the authorities easily cheat them, she argues. Today, she has much more knowledge about legal questions, and she feels more prepared to negotiate with the 'persons from the government'. She stresses the importance of following a negotiation strategy – knowing when to be tough or to seek compromise in talks with the authorities. She hopes that her knowledge can be disseminated to all market women, that 'her sisters in the market may have just a small grain of that knowledge' because 'then the "governors" will treat them better. Even if they continue to cheat them, it will be less' ('Claudine', interview, April 2006).

'Claudine' is a central actor in StreetNet's attempts to set up a local francophone network of market traders in West African countries and has participated in preparatory meetings since 2005. UNSYNVEPID and SYNAVAMAB also cooperate with Union Network International, which helps the organizations in the informal sector to improve their work through 'capacity-building'. The struggle against illiteracy is a key issue for 'Claudine', who sees literacy and education of market women as weapons to defend social rights. Training helps the organizations to gain political influence in the municipality and to solve conflicts between traders. Key issues in many of the activities 'Claudine' focuses on are related to citizenship and the social rights and obligations linked to it: the question of becoming an active citizen with the capacity to defend rights and take part in forming society. Knowledge of the legal framework is particularly important, because authorities refer to it when they take decisions. 'Claudine's' position in StreetNet has undoubtedly strengthened her politically in the internal struggle in USYNVEPID.

The market for stalls The creation of the women's network has helped to tackle not only struggles over gender inequalities in USYNVEPID, but also broader factional conflicts between associational leaders, which has to do with power and control over the market.

The proposal to introduce formal vigilance companies during the night instead of the informal guards that the vendors usually employ became publicly known in May 2007. It soon led to a major conflict between the two networks. Fangbédji, the president of ASMAB, and 'Azangli', the president of USYNVEPID, elaborated the plan with the former DG of SOGEMA, Carrena Azonhoumon, and jointly signed a 'protocol of agreement' between ASMAB and SOGEMA in November 2006 (*Protocol d'Accord*, 2006). The project gained support from the CCIB and the Ministry of the Interior.

The proposal combined a formalized twenty-four-hour vigilance service with the insurance of stalls and the possibility of micro-credit loans. Private interests in alliance with SOGEMA marketed the plan as development and modernization of the marketplace. The project was based on the premise that the rented market stalls would be sold at high prices owing to the rising demand (interview, DF, Cotonou, November 2006). Stall owners had to pay a monthly fee for membership for the vigilance service, which gave access to a micro-credit loan managed by the associations. The loans were calculated on the basis of the value of the stall (number of clients). If the stall owner failed to pay her rent to SOGEMA, or to repay the loan to the micro-credit institution, SOGEMA could annul the lease contract, and hand it over to someone else. SOGEMA reimbursed the micro-credit institution when the sales transaction was complete (ibid.). The hidden agenda of the project seemed to be the consolidation of the ASMAB leader's postion and SOGEMA's power at Dantokpa through control of the market for stalls. After the official presentation of the project, resistance from the users of the market increased. AXISSINON-KPAN AKON, SYNAVAMAB and even USYN-VEPID opposed the project, which they argued would increase the dependency of 'informal workers' (*Le Matinal*, 12 May 2007; interviews, August 2007). The credibility of the project was severely hit when Carrena Azonhoumon was dismissed from her position in March 2007 owing to investigations of systematic fraud and mismanagement of SOGEMA. However, the new chief executive, also a woman, after some hesitation and persuasion, continued the cooperation with Fangbédji from ASMAB and launched the project. This step triggered broad resistance from USYNVEPID and SYNAVAMAB. 'Claudine', together with another female member of USYNVEPID's board and two male Yoruba board members, successfully mobilized vendors from all parts of the market to reject the project. They collected money to arrange a press conference and 'Claudine' used her political network to arrange a meeting with the minister of the interior. After this consultation President Yaya Boni annulled the project (interviews, male and female board members, USYNVEPID, August 2007).

This case points at two important conclusions. The first is that 'Claudine's' political network played an extremely important part in the successful outcome of the conflict. Two well-positioned women in the administration helped her to get through to the minister and indirectly to the president (interview, August 2007). The two brokers' position and influence in the Ministry of the Interior were extremely important, because Fangbédji's network blocked their way at the lower levels. It also shows that mobilization of the vendors at the market in combination with a strong political network alliance with SYNAVAMAB (Chodaton) and male board members in USYNVEPID were decisive for the successful outcome of the conflict.

The second important point about the market mobilization is the transparent and inclusive process in the union and among the members of the associations, which openly confronted corruption and political clientelism, focusing explicitly on civil rights.

Participation and transparent leadership The women's group's autonomous status vis-à-vis the union is the result of 'Claudine's' strategic reflections on associational work and on how to improve women's leadership in a gender-mixed union. She has been inspired by Chodaton's way of organizing her networks, but her open and transparent struggle for social rights, against corruption and political clientelism, points in the direction of internal democracy and participation in the associations. Her leadership in the conflict over the corporate insurance and credit programme promoted by some male opponents and SOGEMA exemplified this still limited change. International support opens opportunities for her, and she manoeuvres in and out of 'feminist' arguments. Members of the women's network clearly gain advantages through the network organization in the form of education and training, collective strength, visibility, solidarity and the prestige of being organized. From a longer-term perspective the women's network may be the remedy for improving the *divers* women's representation in USYNVEPID. Through her actions, however, she recognizes that there are strategic gains from being a gender-mixed union, just as she acknowledges the personal benefits of union membership. The struggle between men and women in USYNVEPID had to do with democratic control over resources: funding, access rights to stalls and over members. Her political networking inside and outside Dantokpa, the alliances with Yoruba male members in the union and with SYNAVAMAB, point to an emerging female leader with new political ideals.

Conclusion

The democratization in Benin since 1992 has led to a proliferation of associations at the Dantokpa market. The multiparty system has created links of mutual dependency between the political parties and the different traders' associations at the market. Most associations have pursued their interests through contacts and exchange of favours with politicians, something that has also exacerbated rivalries between the associations. Despite the tendency towards factionalism, the Dutch wax textile wholesalers, under the leadership of Justine Chodaton, have until recently been able to control key decisions at the market.

For many years the women in the Dutch wax traders' associations and the unions have wielded de facto authority at Dantokpa because they have maintained a high degree of unity and collaborated with other associations when it was necessary to put pressure on SOGEMA and the government. Chodaton has created a strong clientelistic network in the associations and, as *patronne*, she has been able to forge a political career and act as broker between the vendors at Dantokpa and shifting governments. She has defended their rights and interests in questions regarding renting of stalls and shops, taxes and fees, but also against harassment of market women by the vigilante groups and ill-motivated termination and corrupt distribution of leases. The 'feminization' of the SOGEMA chief executive position was the result of Chodaton and other women's pressure. However, her support was not unconditional: three female chief executives were sacked when their management style ran contradictory to the interests of Chodaton's associations.

Justine Chodaton has skilfully used her political clientelist network and combined it with her position at the market. Neither the politicians nor succeeding executives of SOGEMA have been willing to openly confront the traders' associations at Dantokpa. Chodaton's influence has been based on the lucrative textile market, which has been radically transformed owing to the Chinese wax copies flooding the market. The competition has challenged her leading position, and she is also getting older and weaker and is less often present. Furthermore, the associational environment is going through a period of restructuring. One tendency is a closer collaboration between the two unions and the women's network AXISSINON-KPAN AKON, facilitated by StreetNet; another is the multiplication of small associations around politically ambitious leaders.

Other lines of business, particularly electronic equipment, music, household equipment, spare parts, etc., are growing rapidly. Organizations like USYNVEPID and FAOMAB, where men control the board, are seemingly gaining influence to the detriment of the women's associations. This chapter, however, shows that women's associations have not lost control over Dantokpa, and new leading female figures are emerging.

'Claudine's' case and her initiative to cooperate with StreetNet International expose a tendency to build a position of leadership by creating an international personal network and seeking institutional backing and funding for the union and her women's network. The women's network initiative attempts to create a critical mass of competent women, who are willing to struggle for board positions in USYNVEPID and in other gender-mixed associations. Her key role in the conflict over the vigilance service proves that she was able to activate her network and create broad alliances inside and outside Dantokpa, which stopped the initiative. 'Claudine's' competing political discourse and agency-building on the mobilization of members based on *citizenship* and rights has gained support, but is still a minority position. It stresses fairness, inclusion and women's direct participation in decision-making, whereas Chodaton's political praxis builds on mobilization on the basis of clientship (Taylor 2004).

Her way of mobilizing political support through classical patron–client relationships using different forms of patronage has proved to be extremely successful. As patron and broker, she is the 'social mama' of Dantokpa, defending the rights and interests of the market population. They trust her, because she delivers protection when necessary in the form of cash or political influence. Her blend of rights-based mobilization and personal politics is considered to be the most effective way to achieve political goals and protection in the non-transparent political arena of democratic institutions. Redistribution of patronage is immediately understandable and the most rational form of political accountability for poor, vulnerable citizens and traders in the informal sector, who interpret it as the essence of democracy and citizenship (Schaffer 1998; Banégas 1998, 2003; Prag 2004).

The data from Dantokpa suggests that organizations in the informal economy are closely linked to the political field and agendas, which are not limited to the marketplace. This indicates that we should focus on social networks' institutional strength, emphasizing not only economic capacities but also the political capacities of the associations and leaders to influence the market, work and living conditions.

PART TWO

Constructing alliances: organizing across the formal–informal 'divide'

4 | Alliances across the formal–informal divide: South African debates and Nigerian experiences

Gunilla Andrae and Björn Beckman

The problem: bridging the formal–informal divide

The centrepiece of this chapter is an account of the efforts by Nigeria's textile workers' union in Kaduna to reach out to the organized tailors. However, we wish to situate it within a wider framework of organizing across the formal–informal divide in countries where those making a living in the informal economy by far outnumber those in the formal sphere. Nigerian trade unions have played a key role in the building of wide alliances in civil society in opposition to authoritarian rule, in defence of democratic politics and the rights of organization, and in support of wider popular demands on the state to deliver basic social and economic services. Although the main partners on the side of 'civil society' are formal, middle-class-dominated organizations such as human rights groups, students' and professional associations, the chief attraction of the alliances is the potential to reach out to market women, butchers, motorcycle drivers and other popular groups located in the informal economy – that is, an economy where labour relations are only marginally regulated by the state. For the civil society groups, such alliances are essential in boosting their claims of having a popular political constituency. Unions already have a constituency in the wage-earning population but they too are anxious to use the alliances to reach out beyond the confines of the wage sector and to mobilize a 'mass base' that can protect them from being repressed or marginalized by the state.

The current discussions between the textile union and the Tailors' Association (recently renamed Tailors' Union) in Kaduna provide a distinct local experience of a union seeking to bridge the formal–informal divide. Why is it that the two parties feel that they have a joint stake in such cooperation? What is it in the current conjuncture affecting the industry that has activated the deal? Before addressing these questions we need to remind ourselves of the wider context in which this debate is taking place. The 'formal sector', according to Portes and Walton (1981), is where workers' conditions are regulated by state-backed legislation and defended by industrial unions working through collective agreements. In contrast, the 'informal sector' is characterized by more diffuse sets of labour relations involving categories ranging from own-account workers, home workers, family workers of varying stability and terms of employment, including apprentices but also wage workers whose conditions are not regulated by the state or through collective bargaining. Since the early 1990s the International Labour Organization has been concerned with probing the conditions of workers in the informal economy. Concerned with conditions of employment generally, the ILO has been disturbed that large sections of the working populations – including children – find themselves outside the protective networks of either laws or organizations. It has since played a leading role in analysing the prerequisites and responsibilities for creating 'Decent Work' for all, particularly in the informal economy (ILO 2002a, 2002d). In recent years, the calls from the participants in the World Social Forum have reinforced this focus on the formal–informal divide and the need for those who are more privileged in terms of organizational experience – that is, the unionized workers – to take the lead in extending the benefits of organization to the vast multitude. The role and responsibilities of the organized workers in the formal industry cannot, however, be taken as given.

There is a need to situate the discussion of organizing across the formal–informal divide in terms of the social relations of production and the nature of the contradictions confronted by people at the two ends of this divide. How is production itself organized? Who is employed by whom? Who has power over whom? What are the issues at stake at the different ends of the relationship? What are the frontiers of popular emancipation? It is important to root the efforts of bridging the divide in the commonalities of interest that can be clearly identified by the different groups involved. Scholars may assist in this by studying closely the relationship between forms of organization and the social relations of production. This account of the early contacts between the textile union and the tailors in Kaduna cannot claim to achieve this. While certainly pointing to the complexity of labour relations in the tailoring sector, it allows us above all to listen to the arguments on both sides. How are the commonalities of interests perceived? What are the separate and contradictory concerns involved? In the international debate, there is a tendency to gloss over these things with the help of appeals to voluntarism.

The wider problematic is debated both within the labour movement globally (see, e.g., Gallin 2001) and with particular intensity by intellectuals who are close to the 'new social movements'. It has been activated by what seems to be the deepening hegemony of a new type of transnational capitalism that has drastically undercut, or at least so it is argued, the scope for nationally directed, more humane forms of welfare capitalism (Robinson 2001). The new hegemony is assumed to have pulled the carpet from under national modes of regulating labour relations and undermined past achievements by organized wage labour. Moreover, wage labour is being 'deregulated' not only directly in new workplaces but also through informalization, outsourcing and casualization. Confronted with this combination of policies and structural change, the international labour movement is seen to be on the retreat.

Social movement activists point to the fact that in much of the world and in the South in particular only a minority of people find employment in the formal economy. While bridging the formal–informal divide may be crucial for the defence of the formal economy everywhere, it is even more vital for those who take a global view of the challenges of popular democracy. Radical activists on this side pin their hopes on emerging new global social forces, like those assembled in Nairobi under the auspices of the World Social Forum in January 2007. They are disturbed by what they see as the narrow, self-interested concerns of union leaders and the lip-service which they seem to be paying to the needs of those outside their own domain. Radical activists are convinced that the rising hegemony of global neoliberalism can only be effectively met if unionists shed their narrow preoccupations and join an emerging alliance of popular democratic forces that transcend the formal–informal divide. Or, as suggested by Devan Pillay in a recent draft paper on South African labour:

> The largest union federation, Cosatu, has made regular pronouncements about its intention to organise semi-formal workers and, more recently, informal workers, but has largely failed. Its alliance with the ruling party has also alienated it from other trade unions and new social movements engaged in working class struggles within the sphere of consumption – resulting in a fractured working class unable to assert a consistent counter-hegemonic offensive. Unless renewed efforts are made to organise all workers, the trade union movement could become increasingly defensive, and narrowly protect the interests of a relatively privileged 'labour aristocracy' in a sea of exploitation, unemployment and poverty. (Pillay 2006)

Is this what is happening? Is the failure to bridge the formal–informal divide suggesting that trade unions risk ending up as a 'labour aristocracy', catering for the interests of a privileged minority that finds itself in formal employment? This chapter does not see it that way. While arguing why alliance-building across the divide is important, it suggests that it is an illusion to believe that unions can either integrate or effectively organize the workers in the informal economy. Each segment of the population must find its own means of organizing that takes its point of departure from the contradictions that specifically apply to them.

A methodological note We visited Nigeria in February 2006 and had discussions with trade unionists in Kaduna and Abuja on the union–civil society and the formal–informal links. We also made preliminary contacts with the tailors' association in Kaduna. We returned in February 2007 to follow up these contacts and inform ourselves of the way in which tailors organize themselves and how they and the unions view the challenges of organizing across the formal–informal divide. This report thus draws on rather preliminary empirical observations in a context where we are more acquainted with the problems facing the trade unions and where we have only begun to look seriously at organizing in the informal sector. While the specific empirical focus of the chapter is new to us, it draws directly or indirectly on our earlier work. Kaduna in the north of Nigeria, once talked of as the 'Manchester of West Africa', houses the headquarters of the Nigerian textile union (NUTGTWN), and plays a central role in our study of *Union Power in the Nigerian Textile Industry* (Andrae and Beckman 1998). Beckman has followed developments in the Nigerian labour movement since the mid-1980s, and both of us have taken a special interest in its attempts to build wider alliances in 'civil society', including its recent attempts at building a Labour Party (Beckman and Lukman 2006). Both of us have also engaged as scholars with the trade unions in South Africa, especially SACTWU, the textile union, since the mid-1990s (most recently in Andrae 2006 and Beckman 2005a, b). As will be seen, organizing across the formal–informal divide in the Nigerian labour movement draws inspiration from South African debates, where this has become a major issue. We start out by referring to those debates and the structural conditions that have prompted them and which may also explain some of the differences between Nigeria and South Africa in these respects.

A South African debate: the failure of bridging

Nowhere in Africa has the new perspective on global organizing and the necessity of transcending formal (union) organizations, bridging the formal–informal divide, been discussed more intensely than in South Africa (Webster and von Holdt 2005). Although South Africa is by far the most industrialized and unionized part of the continent, the apartheid experience has also reinforced an extreme polarization of the labour market between an advanced wage-earning sector and a backward hinterland characterized by mass unemployment. The origin of this polarization is the conquest of agricultural land by the white minority and the deliberate destruction of African agriculture and animal husbandry – long before apartheid. Also unlike in much of the rest of Africa, in the post-apartheid period, public awareness is reinforced by the contestation of the statistics of unemployment, including heated debates over methods of compilation and reliability, with figures that suggest alarming rates of 35 per cent or more, and above all rates that have been growing dramatically since the early 1990s, when they were assumed to be closer to 20 per cent (Altman 2005). Unlike in much of Africa, where the vast majority of people outside wage employment survive, often precariously, as agricultural producers, traders and craftsmen, South Africans have been deprived of meaningful access to the necessary means of production. In the post-apartheid context many rely on transfers, pensions and other 'welfare' benefits. The growth in unemployment in the post-apartheid period is particularly traumatic as the vision of the anti-apartheid forces was that national liberation and democracy would facilitate a change in the other direction. This is certainly what informed the Reconstruction and Development Programme, the RDP, on which the first democratic elections of 1994 were contested by the ANC and its partners, including the trade unions. The failure of public policies to bring about such a shift is widely blamed, not least within the labour movement, on GEAR, the Growth, Employment and Redistribution strategy – that is, the reform strategy adopted by the ANC government after liberation, with the explicit aim of modernizing an apartheid economy that had been allowed to decay, make the South African economy competitive in the world market, and enhance its capacity to retain and attract foreign investment (Gelb 2005). Simultaneously, the international adjustment of the economy has exposed it to the new strategies of the capitalists to cut costs and slim production both by upgrading technology and by outsourcing and casualization, placing further constraints on the growth in formal employment. Informalization both feeds on and feeds into the growth of a reserve army of partially employed, scaling over into the wider mass of unemployed (Webster and von Holdt 2005: 3ff., especially Fig. 1.1).

The major trade unions in South Africa, including those closely allied to the ANC, have been highly critical of the failure of government policy to deal adequately with the combined threat of growing unemployment and informalization. COSATU has demanded massive public investment in support of local production as well as a stop to the privatization of public enterprises and public services in order to halt what it sees as the continuing haemorrhage of formal employment. Individual industrial unions, such as SACTWU, the clothing and textile workers' union, have developed their own programmes for countering outsourcing and casualization.

Radical critics outside the ANC camp go farther. For them, the ANC has betrayed the cause of national liberation and serves the interests of foreign capital and an emerging black business class. In this view COSATU has failed to have a significant impact, despite its progressive rhetoric. Rather than building an alternative to the neoliberal tendencies in the ANC on the basis of an alliance with the popular forces that emerged from the liberation struggle, it is seen to be locked into a suffocating alliance with the ruling party itself, subordinating and suppressing the alternative, independent voices.

The African trade union context In much of Africa the position of organized wage labour is even more precarious. It is commonly agreed that African trade unions, although quite tiny, were influential in the anti-colonial movement, belonging to a core group in society with sufficient experience and organizational competence to challenge the colonial state. This applied not least to core public sector workers in railways, ports and in transport in general (Freund 1988). As a result they were often rewarded by post-colonial governments with labour laws that offered recognition and certain favours, even if simultaneously incorporated in and subordinated to one-party structures. Whatever 'privileges' that may have been obtained, however, later disintegrated along with the capacity of the post-colonial state to cater for its assumed constituencies. Well before structural adjustment and market-oriented reforms, most of Africa's wage earners were unable to subsist on their wage incomes. To make ends meet they engaged in multiple livelihood strategies, with more than one job, straddling as individuals and households the formal–informal divide.

The deepening crisis of the African state opened the door for external interventions, further undercutting the position of formal wage labour in the economy. Currency and foreign trade liberalization pulled the carpet from under local manufacturing, removing protection against imports from low-cost producers, either directly or via the flow of second-hand goods over 'porous' borders. Public sector reforms caused the shedding of 'surplus' workers, presumably in the interests of fewer, more efficient and better-paid ones. In recent times market-oriented reforms are pushed by the expanding influence of liberal trade institutions (the World Trade Organization) and the phenomenal rise in the export of some leading Asian producers, China in particular. The expansion of production based on wage labour elsewhere has thus caused a further shift, numerically, to the disadvantage of formal wage labour in much of Africa. This tendency has been reinforced by features in the reorganization of globally exposed capitalist production, including outsourcing and casualization.

Nigerian trade unions are badly hit, not least those in the textile industry, in which we have taken a special interest (Andrae and Beckman 1998). While formal wage employment was maintained at around 60,000 for much of the 1990s, the sector has suffered a dramatic decline in recent years. As we visited the union in Kaduna in 2006, reaching out to the Tailors' Association was seen as a possible means of compensating for the haemorrhage while offering the professional services of a reputable trade union to the workers in the informal economy. Simultaneously, and despite such obvious weaknesses, trade unions attract much attention in Nigeria and elsewhere as presumably the best-organized and most credible source of popular democratic opposition both to the authoritarianism and to the 'market-oriented' reform programmes of the state and its foreign partners. This paradoxical strength adds particular weight to the concern with the alliances of the unions in wider society and their ability to reach out to the mass of unemployed and those who seek to survive in the informal economy.

Union leadership and popular forces: Nigerian experiences

The Nigeria Labour Congress (NLC) has repeatedly demonstrated its capacity, despite its organizational weaknesses, to offer leadership for popular forces outside the formal wage sector. In recent years this has been shown most graphically in the repeated contestation of government policy over the domestic pricing of petroleum products, where it has been able to mobilize wide popular support. Its undoubted clout in this respect explains why unionists in Nigeria would reject the suggestion that trade unions look after the interests only of workers in the formal sector. On the contrary, their ability to mobilize more widely has led them to believe that they have a special mission to speak for the popular classes as a whole.

The NLC was established in 1978 by a military government, which dissolved existing labour federations, banned key leaders from holding office, outlawed affiliation to international labour centres, and instituted a new, unitary national structure, based on a monopoly of representation, and compulsory deduction of membership dues by employers (Hashim 1994; Andrae and Beckman 1998). By 1990 the registered membership was roughly two million. (For the membership of the twenty largest unions, see Andrae and Beckman 1998: 305.) A set of labour reforms that was supposed to have been an effective means of enhancing government control seemed actually to have strengthened organized labour. In the view of most labour leaders the 'pact' provided cohesion, professionalism and financial strength. Although seriously weakened during the period of deepening military dictatorship in the 1990s, after the demise of General Abacha in 1998, the central labour organization was revived in 1999 with Adams Oshiomhole as president, committed to re-establishing itself as a leading political force. In particular, it demonstrated its clout in repeated campaigns against the attempts by the federal government to 'deregulate' the national petroleum market, allowing for a drastic increase in the prices of local petrol and kerosene. Deregulation of the oil sector was a key demand of the World Bank. Strikes and demonstrations over petrol prices met with wide national support. Market women, small transporters and other popular groups helped paralyse economic life in major cities.

The standing of the NLC as a social force that went beyond wage labour was enhanced by the dubious legitimacy of the political system. Although General Abacha's exit and the swift transition to civilian rule had been widely welcomed, the democratic credentials of the new government and its parliamentary institutions were weak (Beckman and Lukman 2006). The political parties that emerged were loosely assembled groupings of aspiring individual politicians, some with credible local constituencies, some with sufficient money to buy themselves into party caucuses. Very few were part of any cohesive network or committed to any policy except for a vague regional or communal agenda. Party cohesion had been further weakened by the repeated interventions and manipulations of successive military rulers. It reinforced a self-perception within the labour movement of being a major national social force while the campaigns over petrol prices reinforced its ability to build alliances and offer leadership to other social groups, outside the formal economy. An attempt to formalize this relationship was a key feature of the so-called 'Agura process', the development of an 'NLC–Civil Society Pro-Democracy Network' in the early years of the post-1999 revival, drawing on European Union funds that were channelled through the Friedrich Ebert Foundation (ibid.). In recent years, fresh attempts at institutionalization have resulted in the formation of LACSO, the Labour and Civil Society Coalition, which played a prominent role in organizing a series of public rallies all over the country in September 2005, aiming at 'a far-reaching and fundamental restructuring of [the] governance system in the country'. The new movement 'will include labour, civil society, women, students, pensioners, professional and religious bodies and the informal sector' (LACSO 2005). While successful in obliging the government to commit itself to a period without increases in petrol prices before the 2007 elections, the movement simultaneously suffered a major setback in that one of its leading activists, Chima Ubani of the Civil Liberties Organization, was killed in a road accident while returning from one of the rallies. In June 2007, a Joint Action Forum of civil society groups participated with labour in organizing the 'indefinite general strike and mass protests' that successfully confronted the fresh price and tax increases and privatizations imposed by the outgoing Obasanjo regime (NLC 2007). On both occasions, the joint actions were able to draw on middle-class professionals and civil society (NGO) activists. In both cases, popular elements, including market women and *okada* (motorcycle) drivers, were mobilized in support, giving the protests a wider democratic flavour. However, their organizational basis depended on the labour movement. The aspiration to reach out to a wider 'civil society', including the 'informal sector', resulted at best in some fragmentary and ad hoc mobilization. What was the scope for organized alliance politics outside the limited core of professional NGOs?

Organizing the tailors: the NUTGTWN experience Kaduna is a city of some three million people located on the savannah in the north of Nigeria. It is the capital of Kaduna State and has, since the 1970s, been the home of a number of large textile industries and the headquarters of the National Union of Textile Garments and Tailoring Workers of Nigeria (Andrae and Beckman 1998). In recent years, many of the industries have closed down, first in response to the sudden liberalization of trade policies in 1998, and later owing to the intensified competition from imported goods despite the reimposition of import restrictions. The development has left the national union with a drastically reduced membership, from more than 60,000 in 1998 to fewer than 40,000 in 2007. The decline has been particularly severe in Kaduna, where membership in early 2007 had fallen to some 5,000 only from an earlier strength of maybe 12,000. This poses great challenges to the union in defending its members against retrenchments, falling wages and employers taking advantage of the crisis in undermining labour rights and collective bargaining. It is also a threat to union finances, which depend on membership fees, deducted at source by the employers.

As in most parts of Nigeria, garments are made in small-scale informal tailoring establishments, of which there are probably more than 20,000 in Kaduna State. Only one small formal factory of some fifty workers departs from this basically informal orientation. We find the tailors in large clusters of workshops in the marketplaces. According to our interviewed informant, Kabiru Ibrahim, the Kaduna State secretary of the tailoring association, Kasua Bechi, the central market in Tudun Wada, is claimed to accommodate some 4,000 tailors, working in groups of up to three or four in each workshop in different forms of division of labour and cooperation. Here they are highly geared to the production of the embroidered male Hausa gowns. In Kakuri market, in the industrial area of Kaduna South, we visited a large number of tailors making more Western-style trousers and suits, as well as those sewing shirts and dresses from the local printed cloths. Other tailors work from separate workshops in the streets of the commercial districts of the city. Most entrepreneurs in all locations have one or two trainees attached and many employ wage workers; in some cases we encountered as many as six of them, but one or two seems to be more common.

Particularly in the marketplaces, some form of organization of tailors has existed for a long time to cater for common interests in relation to the market administration, and to local government authorities concerning taxation, licences and other regulations. These also seem to have functioned as mutual associations, regulating social responsibilities among members in connection with bereavement and sickness.

We were told of an association of tailors in Doka zone in the southern part of Kaduna North as being the first association in the commercial areas, formed in 1992 by one Peter Amtu, a tailor who has now been in the profession for thirty-seven years. He is also said to have pioneered the production of a constitution that has served as a model for other local chapters (Kaduna State Tailors Union, Doka Zone n.d.). In 2002 all such local market and neighbourhood groups collaborated to form an overarching organization at Kaduna State level. Registered members in 2007 numbered 3,000, with the potential of attracting at least ten times as many among active tailors. They are organized according to local government areas; apart from the chapters in Kaduna North and South, membership is documented for six outlying local government areas, mainly the more urbanized ones. Apart from the ten branches already affiliated, three are said to be ready to join.

Both the formal textile industry and the informal tailoring and garments sector are threatened by the pressure of imports, and they have common interests in defending local conditions of production – for instance, access to stable and reasonably priced supplies of electricity and water. They also both have an interest in regulating and restricting foreign imports, notably through smuggling. The Federal Government as the source of policies in these fields is the logical target of demands both for the textile union and the tailors' associations. So what sort of cooperation do we find?

Threatened by massive industrial decline, it seems that the industrial textile union has primarily identified the tailors and their associations as potential sources of new members. These are important not just to provide the necessary income required to finance the secretariat, pay staff salaries and so on, but as a source of bargaining strength. Approaching the tailors has been facilitated by the way in which these have established their own associations, forming a party to talk to, to negotiate with. Over the past three years discussions have taken place on the formation of a joint organization encompassing both the workers in the formal textile industries and the tailors. In Lagos such negotiations had already led to a merger. In Makurdi, Benue State, negotiations were ongoing, although in this case tailors have joined the trade union as individual members while having an 'executive committee' of their own, representing the tailors as a group vis-à-vis the union leadership. In Kaduna a meeting was called in the spring of 2006, where the industrial union invited representatives of the tailors for discussion of a proposed merger. What were the arguments voiced on each side? What were the benefits that they expected to derive?

The industrial union perspective

The thrust on the part of the industrial union in seeking alliance with the tailors is explicitly to expand their membership numbers, which are considered to be crucial for the upkeep of a strong union secretariat and for political clout in campaigns against the federal government in a situation where their own membership has been drastically reduced (Umaru, interview, 2007). The union leadership foresees that the demands on the state in the fields of import policies, such as counteracting smuggling, and public provision of infrastructure, such as water and electricity, in order to reduce costs of production, should be to the benefit also of the tailors. These assumptions were also voiced by union spokespersons at the general meeting held by the two parties in the spring of 2006, according to the union records from the meeting.

The union officials are keenly aware of their reputation as an influential player in federal politics, and that this is a resource that can be used to attract the tailors. But they are also aware that their ability to offer such leadership in the long run depends on the strength in numbers that the tailors are in a position to supply. Simultaneously, according to Solomon Kekere, the organizer put in charge of the union campaign, the union is particularly attracted by having the tailors as members because they seem to offer a closeness to the grass roots at the neighbourhood level. In Kekere's own understanding, the union is in position to offer protection against the harassment by local government officials over licences and taxes. This is what he feels that the tailors will appreciate the most. In our discussions with Kekere and Alhaji Umaru, the senior deputy general secretary, plans were also mentioned to attract the tailors as members by offering courses not only in union organization but in professional skills that would be particularly relevant to them. The process of merging the two organizations was slower than some tailor activists had expected. By early 2007, thirty tailors had joined the industrial union on an individual basis and some had enthusiastically participated in courses and training programmes as well as in the 9th Delegates Conference of the NLC in February 2007. They had also been active in recruiting new members among their tailoring colleagues. In a meeting in February 2007, to which the union had invited some twenty officials at different levels of the Kaduna State Tailors' Union to meet us, their chairman, Victor Bakare, announced that a decision had recently been officially taken to work towards the merger with the industrial union. In a separate meeting with the union officials and ourselves, the chairman explained his strategies to convince his members of the benefits of a merger. For instance, he was hoping that a loan for entrepreneurs that he had secured from the small- and medium-scale industry organization at the state level would serve to make the tailors more favourably disposed.

The tailors' perspective

What is there in the merger for the tailors that they cannot achieve through their own organization? To what extent is it true that they need the industrial union to protect them against harassment by the local government authorities? When taken around the Kakuri and Kasua Bechi markets in February 2007, we were shown badges issued by the tailors' organization which were glued to the sewing machines. They stated the level of fees that should be paid in accordance with the agreement reached with the local government. When listening to Kabiru Ibrahim, the secretary of the organization at the state level, we got the distinct impression that the organization had developed a potential of its own to defend its members against such harassment. By negotiating collectively with local state officials they had also been able to bring down the government charges considerably. Tailors operating outside the main marketplaces were probably more likely to be exposed to harassment and more likely to complain of maltreatment by tax and fee collectors than those working inside the markets. Many of these tailors saw the industrial union as their saviour. According to Ify Nwakwuo, an activist working energetically for the merger and our principal guide when visiting the tailors, the membership card of the industrial union had solved all their problems in this respect. Once brandished it would cause government officials to think twice, now knowing what they would be up against.

Kabiru Ibrahim mentioned that many tailors were also members of the association of small- and medium-scale entrepreneurs in Kaduna State, which had supported them with training in the past and where they could hope for financial and technical support, including the credit facility mentioned by the state chairman, above. How would their chances of drawing on such support to small entrepreneurs be affected if they decided to join the trade union? On the other hand, what could a union that is primarily geared to collective bargaining for workers offer tailors that their own entrepreneurial organization could not provide? How would it be able to cater for their composite identities? We got the impression that the hesitation in relation to the merger shown by some tailors reflected the ambiguity of their own class position, as indicated by this double affiliation option.

A key issue is thus the complex set of social categories involved in informal production. The constitution of the Doka zone Tailors' Association, while explicit on the sanctions that will apply to workers who do not perform to employers' satisfaction, talks very briefly of the need for responsible employer relations and not at all of any rights for workers. It is obvious that the association has primarily catered for the needs of the entrepreneurs and has operated in the first place as a business organization. Who will defend the interests of the wage workers and the apprentices, not to speak of the family workers? We may compare the situation with that in South Africa, where informalization has largely meant the creation of small workshops of wage workers undefended by labour legislation. Union strategy in that case has either been to try to recruit such workers to the industrial union or to make sure that such workshops are subjected to labour legislation. In the merger talks in Kaduna, the issues are different. Those who find themselves at the informal end of the merger are primarily the small entrepreneurs, mostly with employees of their own. How is the industrial union expected to relate to them? It seems out of the question, at least in the context of these merger talks, to take the interests of the apprentices, employees and family workers as the point of departure. In this case, the efforts to bridge the formal–informal divide are clearly informed by other concerns. When looking at the constitution of the Doka zone of the Tailors' Association we are, however, also struck by the prominence given to social obligations, such as contributions to families in situations of bereavement, visits to hospitalized members, etc. It seems that a strong force behind the organizing efforts of the tailors is indeed social, reflecting the need to safeguard the welfare responsibilities of this collective of small-scale entrepreneurs towards those who work for them. In operating at the grassroots level the tailors, however, perform welfare functions that are different from those of the industrial union towards the workers in the factories. How will the industrial union be able to handle the interests of tailors as small entrepreneurs and of their 'workers' alike? The question of the planned merger raises wider issues of the relationship between forms of organization and the nature of the social relations that characterize workplaces and communities. How relevant is the mode of organization generated by the industrial workplace to the tailors' workshop? How can the efforts of the industrial unions to develop an employment-related system of social welfare for its workers be extended to cover the new membership categories it aims to incorporate? Is this type of merger the best way to support both entrepreneurs and those who work for them? Might support to each party for their own organizations according to their particular positions in the employment relation be even more empowering to each?

What indeed are the responsibilities of the industrial union with its superior mode of organization and experience in terms of catering for the needs of those working in the informal economy? The organizer responsible for developing links with the informal sector in Kaduna is clearly inspired by notions of the special role of unions in this merger. The possibility of extending training to all is at the forefront of his mind. He is also thinking of what will happen to the redundant workers of the declining textile industries. Apart from being a source of new membership for the union, the informal 'sector' is also perceived as a possible source of alternative employment where the union may assist in training programmes and other forms of support for their own former members.

Union failure: a new labour aristocracy?

The experience of the textile union in Kaduna and its relations to the Tailors' Union illustrates some of the problems facing efforts to bridge the formal–informal divide. In terms of the wider debate, not least in South Africa, our provisional conclusion is to caution against premature voluntarist notions that gloss over the differences in social relations that characterize the formal and informal economies. In particular, there is a need to look closely at the way in which such differences set their own preconditions for organizing and the building of alliances. This is not an argument against taking organizing across the formal–informal divide seriously. On the contrary, there is a lot of scope for that, and the experience of the Nigeria Labour Congress in mobilizing wide support for its policy interventions, especially over the petrol price issue, suggests that trade unions may well play a strategic role in reaching out to other popular groups. However, our Kaduna story also points to the need to think in terms of a division of labour between different types of popular forms of organization, a division that takes its point of departure from the differences by which groups are constituted. Each and every one must organize on the basis of the contradictions that characterize the economic and social activities in which they are involved. Simultaneously, there is unlimited scope not just for promoting solidarity and alliances but also for supporting others to do the same! It is a position that is also supported by the commendable work of the ILO (2002a, d) in allocating responsibilities between the state and the different parties in employment and other work relations, and in considering the way in which they organize and the role of organized action in the process of moving towards 'Decent Work' for all.

In the case of trade unions, it is true that outsourcing, casualization and other modes of informalization are major threats to the achievements of the labour movement globally. The primary preoccupation, however, is to fight such processes, defend workers' rights and expand the sphere of a union-based labour regime. In fact, the Nigerian textile union is particularly proud that it has been able to successfully fight casualization within its own domain. The strength of the union lies in its ability to protect and expand collective bargaining and other labour rights associated with formal employer–employee relations, not in organizing the tailors. Whether this is being 'privileged' or a 'labour aristocracy' is neither here nor there. Those who are organized are always likely to be better off than those who are not, and not all social relations lend themselves equally to organizing. The scope is structurally determined. Recent developments in the world economy have seen an exceptional growth in wage labour, both in manufacturing and in public and private services. The main challenge to the unions is therefore to expand the frontiers of labour rights and organize these teeming millions. It does not make solidarity and alliances across the formal–informal divide less crucial. The Nigeria experience, however, seems to suggest that the capacity of trade unions in this respect depends on how effectively they can defend and organize themselves in their own turf.

Interviews, Kaduna, February 2007

Kaduna State Tailors' Union officials
Victor Bakare, Chairman
Kabiru Ibrahim, Secretary
Adekunle Bam, Financial Secretary

Doka Branch, Kaduna North officials
Peter Amtu, Chairman
Ify Nwakwuo, Treasurer

NUTGTWN (National Union of Textile, Garment and Tailoring Workers of Nigeria) officials
Alhaji Muhammed Umaru, Senior Deputy General-Secretary
Solomon Kekere, Organizing Secretary

5 | Self-organized informal workers and trade union initiatives in Malawi: organizing the informal economy

Ignasio Malizani Jimu

Introduction

The informal economy comprises economic activities that are not registered or regulated by the state or local government in contexts where similar activities are regulated (Bromley 1998; United Nations 1996). Typical informal economy activities are small scale, labour intensive, use simple technology, rely on family labour, use personal or informal sources of credit, have little to no fixed costs associated with the infrastructure of a shop (rentals, maintenance and security), do not pay taxes, and are relatively easy to establish and exit (Fidler and Webster 1996; Hart 1973; Hope 2001). In the 1970s and 1980s, debate on the informal economy assumed that the sector was temporary and likely to die out. There is now a consensus that the informal economy is an important and permanent feature of modern economies, at least in the developing countries, of which Malawi is a typical example. This change in attitude towards the informal economy is partly due to economic situations whereby economic growth has failed to generate an expanding and efficient formal or modern sector (Hope 2001). The informal economy is growing in both the poorest developing countries and many middle-income countries (Meagher 1995: 216). Debt crisis, the dismantling of the public sector, the deregulation of the labour market under the structural adjustment programmes of the International Monetary Fund (IMF) and the World Bank, and the successive economic and financial crises throughout most countries of the developing world since the 1980s have pushed millions of people out of formal employment and into the informal economy (Gallin 2002; Hope 2001). With such origins, it makes sense that much research in the past decades should have focused on the contribution of the informal economy to employment creation, distribution of wealth and economic development. That workers in the informal economy suffer from the failure of governments to come up with conducive policies, or the failure of employers in the sector to respect laws on labour relations or minimum wages, or ignorance of social legislation and rules on wages, safety and health (Debroux 2002) and mechanisms of enforcing them, received little attention. In other words, negotiation or collective bargaining for better working conditions in the informal economy remained remote from a policy-making point of view. Hence, to date very little is known about the organization of the informal economy or the politics of its external relationship with governments, political parties or with organized labour in the formal economy (Aguilar et al. 1998). It is this gap that this chapter will attempt to fill by focusing on the process, challenges and future directions of organization of the informal economy.

Existing studies on the subject point to diverse forms of organizing the informal economy. One of the ways is local mass mobilization of the informal economy workers. Cross (1998a: 21) showed that informal economy groups are capable of influencing state action by mass mobilization to 'capture' the state or specific state agencies. Bayat, in a study of *Street Politics* in post-revolution Iran, described this capacity as the 'quiet encroachment of the ordinary', involving silent, patient, protracted and pervasive advancement of ordinary people in order to survive hardships and better their lives (Bayat 1997b: 7). Such mobilization or collective action may be 'open and fleeting struggle without clear leadership, ideology or structured organization, one that produces significant gains for the actors, eventually placing them in counterpoint to the state' (ibid.: 7). As Bayat (ibid.: 8) further put it: 'unlike Gramsci's "passive revolution[aries]" disenfranchised groups do not carry out their activities as a conscious political strategy; rather they are driven by necessity to survive and live [a] dignified life'. Laguerre (1994: 32) talks of informality as characterized by way of the intentionality or personal needs of the actor, with the individual often aware of his or her unconventional action. It is in this context that self-organization in the informal economy in Malawi is to be located.

In some cases, it has been shown that the capacity to organize the informal economy is enhanced by the involvement of trade unions. Global trends suggest that trade union membership has been declining rapidly as retrenchment exercises remove thousands of workers from public sector employment. Many, if not most, of these workers shift over to the informal economy, often expanding activities that may have previously been used to subsidize the inadequate and declining wages in the public sector (Mwamadzingo 2002). Basically, trade unions are now eyeing the informal economy as a potential source of new membership to shore up their political clout and sagging numerical powers (Lund and Skinner 1999). Examples of trade union activity in the informal economy include the Textile, Clothing and Footwear Union of Australia (TCFUA), which is organizing home workers in textile, clothing and footwear sub-sectors; the Timber and Woodworkers' Union and the General Agricultural Workers' Union, both in Ghana, which are trying to organize artisans and small-scale farmers. In Uganda, the public service workers' union started organizing street vendors and other informal workers, who now represent most of its membership. In Hong Kong, the Hong Kong Confederation of Trade Unions, in July 2001, assisted in the establishment of the Hong Kong Domestic Workers' Union. In the United

Kingdom, migrant domestic workers have organized a union called Kalayaan, which works closely with the Transport and General Workers' Union. The success of these initiatives is limited in terms of scope and applicability in spatially and economically different environments. The real challenge and the fundamental difference has been that trade unions have traditionally focused on relations between employers and employees (Mwamadzingo 2002), relations which are in most cases poorly defined when applied to the informal economy.

The focus in this chapter is on the process, challenges and directions along the two paths of organizing the informal economy, namely: self-organized, i.e. created by the informal workers themselves, and trade union initiatives. Both of these will be referred to here as 'informal economy organizations' (IEOs) – that is, organizations or institutions established to manage and represent issues affecting the informal economy workers. Three informal economy organizations – namely, street vendors' associations, the Malawi Union for the Informal Sector (MUFIS) and the Commercial, Industrial and Allied Workers Union (CIAWU), in terms of their activities in the informal economy – will be used as case studies of self-organization for the first entity and trade union initiative for the last two. These cases studies reveal serious difficulties in both paths of organizing the informal economy, with few success stories. Drawing on the challenges of the organizations and the experience of a fourth organization known as the National Association of Business Women (NABW), which works mostly with medium-sized enterprises in Malawi, the chapter advocates the view that organizing the informal economy should not be seen as an end in itself but as a means towards addressing the real challenges confronting the informal economy. In this regard, this position is similar to that in the chapter by Andrae and Beckman, since the premise is the same – that the trade unions cannot effectively organize workers in the informal economy because of fundamental differences in social relations of production, but also because the informal economy encounters multifarious challenges that are unique and difficult to tackle from a narrow trade union perspective of employees negotiating with or confronting employers.

Methodologically, this chapter is based on two studies that were conducted between 2002 and 2006 in Blantyre city. The studies were qualitative in nature. The approach allowed in-depth appreciation of the formation of informal economy organizations, the manner in which informal economy workers perceived themselves, and the activities they undertook in and the expectations they had of informal economy organizations. The methods employed to collect data included were in-depth interviews, focus group discussions and a life history approach. In the first study, which focused on the growth, dynamics and politics of street vending in the town of Blantyre, interviews were conducted with the committee members of the street vendors' associations, city assembly employees and ward councillors. In the second study, which was part of a larger comparative research project on informal economy organizations in Africa (War on Want et al. 2006), interviews were conducted with the leadership of MUFIS and the street vendors' association in the town of Limbe. Interviews with the political elites provided an overall picture of the informal economy, its relationship to other activities, and the legal framework. Effort was also made to review newspaper articles dating way back to the 1960s, and postings on the Internet.

The economic and political context of organization

The formation of the first IEOs in the 1990s coincided with two major transformations, one economic and the other political. The accelerated liberalization of the economy in the 1990s inspired entrepreneurial acumen whose indirect manifestation is the proliferation of informal economy activities (Englund 2002). The transition from one-party dictatorship to multiparty democracy also catalysed the proliferation of informal economy organizations. However, from an economic point of view, for a long period of time the informal economy was in official circles characterized as essentially subsistence in orientation (Government of Malawi 2000a) and less significant in terms of employment creation. A survey of 2,022 low-income households in Blantyre and Lilongwe in the early 1990s found that 30 per cent and 22 per cent of the households respectively were involved in informal economy activities (Chilowa 1991, in Green and Baden 1994). Many of the activities were classified as casual and seasonal; and often carried on together with a range of other activities. Since it was assumed that the informal economy is difficult to measure, little attention was given to the study of the dynamics of the sector generally regarded as the abode of the poor (Government of Malawi 1995: 36). The GEMINI study of 2001 showed that between 1992 and 1999 the number of informal economy enterprise start-ups rose fivefold from 20,000 to 100,000 (Government of Malawi 2000c; Orr and Orr 2002). It is now well known that lack of employment opportunities, low wage rates in formal employment (Green and Baden 1994) and changes in political and economic climate since the mid-1990s (Englund 2002; Jimu 2003) contributed in one way or another to the proliferation of various forms of economic informality.

Public attitudes towards the informal economy, and informal trading in particular, have been negative over the years, as the following quotation shows: 'There is one practice which must be dropped [...] some young men who sell fruits and vegetables along Victoria Avenue [...] These people can be and are very disturbing, someone parking his car to do serious business is only hindered by one of these unscrupulous and irritating men.'[1] Public sentiments of this nature have to different extents legitimized repression and persecution of the informal economy. Persecution of informal traders in Blantyre and other cities was particularly pronounced during the one-party dictatorship from independence in the mid-1960s to the early 1990s. As early as 1976, President for Life

Dr Banda urged the city authorities to keep the city clean with the following words: 'we believe in cleanliness, grace and elegance', effectively repeated some twelve years later in 1988 in the following words: 'Cities were meant for civilized persons, and in that regard people should be able to differentiate life in the city from that of the village by the way you look after the city. If you should be proud of the city don't bring village life into the city' (Jimu 2005). A mayor of Blantyre city in the late 1980s described vending in the following words: 'We are disturbed by these people who are trying to spoil and detract us in our efforts to keep the city clean. The city has therefore decided to take drastic measures against all illegal vendors.'

During the 1970s and until the early 1990s, many informal economy workers, street vendors in particular, were beaten and their goods taken away without compensation. In November 1995, thirty street vendors in Limbe sought legal aid in pressing for compensation of their property worth 35,954 kwacha (close to US$300) destroyed by police and city rangers. Although Section 28(2) of Malawi's constitution, adopted in 1994 following the transition to multiparty democracy, states that 'no person shall be arbitrarily deprived of property', the city council refused to pay compensation, arguing that the city rangers and the police officers were simply enforcing the law and, moreover, the street vendors 'do not have legal business premises'.[2] In 1990, about eighty street vendors in Blantyre were charged and fined about US$6 each at prevailing exchange rates at the time, subject to undertaking one month of public works in default, because of hawking without licences, contrary to the Blantyre by-laws.[3] In some cases the matter was settled 'amicably' between the apprehended street vendor and his captor.[4] The street vendors had to devise individual strategies to buy 'their' right to trade by befriending law enforcement agents, alerting each other by whistling to escape or put up a fight to defend themselves and to protect merchandise from confiscation. At the dawn of multiparty democracy, these dynamics prompted self-organization among the street vendors, and later the trade union initiatives – for instance, by the Malawi Union for the Informal Sector and the Commercial, Industrial and Allied Workers Union – to organize the informal economy, as will be discussed below.

Self-organization in the informal economy: case study of street vendors' associations

At the time of the fieldwork, there were two street vendors' associations in the central business districts of Blantyre and Limbe. The origins of the associations can be traced to events when spontaneous mobilization of groups of vendors occurred. In January 1994, a group of fifty-one vendors converged at the civic centre to lobby the city council for trading rights. Six months later, a group of 200 vendors marched to the regional offices of the then new ruling party in the democratic dispensation to seek audience with the new state president, elected just two months before, following a general election held in the month of May. The vendors were protesting about infringement of their rights to trade.[5] Apparently the president had promised during the pre-election campaign to allow street vending when elected into office. The city council continued with its policy of persecuting street vendors, which the vendors felt to be undemocratic and inconsistent with what the president stood for. The vendors wore headgear with the inscription *malova*, meaning unemployed, to draw attention to their plight and reasons for taking up informal vending.[6] The informal vendors' quest for trading rights was initially not acknowledged by the state and non-state actors such as NGOs as a quest for economic liberty or the quest for human dignity as enshrined in the new republican constitution. The street vendors saw informal trading as a human right and worth defending just like any other human right (Jimu 2003).

The rationale offered by street vendors appears to be typical of grassroots organizations attempting to change situations regarded as undesirable (Cross 1998a; Bayat 1997b). Through collective engagement with the authorities at state and local government levels, vendors in Blantyre and Limbe eventually gained the right to trade in the streets, described metaphorically as being without limit to spatial mobility (Englund 2002). However, the right to trade in the streets was abrogated in early 2006. During the intervening years, street vendors organized various activities through the two committees, 'conjoining them into one moral community' (Englund 2000: 594), negotiating vending space allocations and managing relations among the vendors. Street vendors' associations worked hard to foster cooperation among the street vendors and build bridges and trust with the city authorities and the general public. The committees attempted to transform public opinion about street vending from regarding it as a 'wicked' way of earning a living, often linked to theft, harassment of pedestrians, unsanitary practices, etc., into a view of it as respectable entrepreneurship. The associations also provided a form of insurance among the vendors, especially in time of sickness and bereavement, a situation that the leaders of associations described as beneficial and in accord with the expectations of the majority of the vendors. The associations were also seen by the street vendors as 'democratic', partly because the vendors sitting on committees were elected. The street vendors' notion of 'democracy' stressed satisfaction of the interests of those in the association, rather than the interests of the individuals holding positions in the association. In this view, in the context of street vending associations, organizing the informal economy meant the pursuit of individual rights, which derived meaning from the pursuit of the group or cooperative rights the associations stood for (Jimu 2003).

Representation of the interests of the vendors was sometimes selective and biased. A street vendor was defined by the members of the street vendors' committees as any person selling non-farm or processed goods. The city assembly used the same definition. Restricting the label 'street vendor' to people selling non-farm and processed goods legitimized claims that street vendors were unfair competitors and saboteurs of the formal retail business (ibid.). Such a definition excluded and denied representation to women involved in street food vending. All food vendors, most of whom happened to be women, were expected to conduct trade in the produce markets,[7] yet one of the reasons that led to street vending was lack of adequate space in the produce markets (ibid.). Mobile vendors were also excluded, a situation that demonstrated a certain lack of sensitivity to the dynamics of the development of street vending in Blantyre prior to the 1990s, when the official view was that 'no business belongs to the streets and all informal traders were expected to sell their goods inside the markets not on the streets'.[8]

The advantage was that through self-organization the informal vendors compelled the city council to accept that trading could be done on streets with a semblance of orderliness. The leaders of the associations were later able to win for themselves power and privileges that could in the formal sense be exercised by the city council only. For example, the leaders assumed the 'power' to allocate vending spaces. The streets were perceived as belonging to the chairpersons of the associations, as far as the allocation of usage rights for informal vending was concerned; indicating multiple and contested 'ownership' of street spaces, one formal and legal, the other informal but not necessarily 'illegal', at least from the perspective of the informal traders. Prospective vendors were asked 'as of necessity' to pay a token of appreciation and to maintain a good rapport with the leadership of the associations, including giving gifts of money from time to time to avoid arbitrary dispossession and reallocation of vending spaces to other or prospective vendors. It appears that the leadership of associations had more room for manoeuvre because of dual responsibility as leaders of the vendors and as collaborators with the then ruling political party, the United Democratic Front. Vendors on each street constituted a branch of the ruling party, with the chairperson of the street vendors' association doubling as the area chairperson of the ruling party. It was such dual chairpersonship that later legitimized various excesses. One of the excesses was the existence of a group known as the bouncers or the 'young democrats', as they were called, after the notorious youth wing of the UDF. The bouncers often exceeded their responsibility to embrace extortion. Two middle-aged women vendors had stories to tell. The first woman vendor reported that:

> On several occasions I have lost my merchandise to city authorities and the bouncers. When the city authorities confiscate goods, there is no way of getting them back; as for the bouncers, one can bribe them or pay a fine to the chairman. These days, I hide some goods in a basket because I am afraid of losing everything to bouncers.

The second woman reported that the bouncers constituted a powerful clique:

We don't have freedom. It is as if we are still under the one-party rule. We are forced to attend political party meetings or risk a two-week ban. Some of the leaders you have met do not have businesses of their own. They live on the fines they collect from us.

One of the critical challenges facing the informal economy is access to credit. At no time have the street vendors' associations got involved in negotiations for credit except for the 'grant' the central government administered through the Blantyre City Assembly. In 2001, the government sourced some money amounting to 10 million kwacha (US$109,890) from a public trust company that was channelled through the Blantyre City Assembly in the form of loans to the street vendors. The 'loan scheme' was used as bait to enhance political patronage. Those in leadership positions and their close friends benefited considerably. Some street vendors were excluded from the loan facility because they were deemed sympathizers of opposition political parties by virtue of coming from the same districts as senior opposition politicians or districts where opposition political parties were more popular than the ruling party. The mechanism for loan repayment was poorly defined, such that the government decided to write off the loan as 'bad debt'. As one of the street vendors described it, this was 'compensation for losses street vendors suffered under the one party regime' (Jimu 2003), when the vendors' ability to trade was severely constrained, as described above in the discussion of the economic and political context.

It also appears that the street vendors' associations were limited in their ability to mobilize effectively because of some degree of co-optation and self-interest on the part of the leaders. Self-interest was specifically manifested in two notable incidents that took place between 1995 and 2002. In 1995 the city council organized an orientation trip to Zimbabwe for selected street vendors to learn how vendors in Zimbabwe operated in 'organized markets'. The delegation observed street vending activities in Harare; upon their return the delegates were instructed to report to fellow street vendors that in Harare there was no street vending. Some street vendors who participated in the trip to Harare confided to the researcher that they were silenced with money. Attempts by the city assembly to relocate street vendors into a flea market between November and December 2002 were compounded by turmoil. Some street vendors saw themselves as allies of the ruling political party and enemies of the city authorities. By choosing to align themselves with the ruling political party, the leadership of the associations simply postponed the local government's drive to relocate them. Such attachment to a ruling party had its own disadvantage, in the sense that when a new political party took over, the street vendors were caught off guard and were eventually forced to relocate in April 2006.

Trade union initiatives in the informal economy

This section focuses on organizing initiatives in existing trade unions. The purpose is to demonstrate the challenges of organizing the informal economy from a trade union perspective in a developing country and in the era of globalization, when trade unions are struggling to maintain or boost union membership from the formal economy, and hence are refocusing attention on the informal economy to shore up membership. The first part focuses on the Malawi Union for the Informal Sector (MUFIS), and the second on the Commercial, Industrial and Allied Workers Union (CIAWU).

Malawi Union for the Informal Sector The formation of the Malawi Union for the Informal Sector (MUFIS) dates back to 2001. The idea was initiated by the former president of the Malawi Congress of Trade Unions (MCTU), who felt the need to organize the informal economy, the widows and the unemployed. The *Weekend Nation* of 18/19 May 2002 carried a story entitled 'Unemployed to have union', in which it was reported that the MCTU had applied to the government to register a 'non-workers'' union to represent vendors, job seekers, pensioners and widows. This was an anomaly, since trade unions have traditionally focused on relations between employers and employees (Mwamadzingo 2002). Such a focus does not permit a simple extension of traditional trade union activities to cover informal economy issues, job seekers, pensioners and widows. The Ministry of Labour turned down MCTU's application, since it was felt that the constituency was poorly defined. From an initial prospective membership of 7,500, comprising 3,000 vendors, 3,500 widows and 1,500 pensioners who expressed interest in becoming members of MUFIS at the time the idea was introduced, MUFIS had no grassroots base when it was finally registered in mid-2004. During the first two years following registration, MUFIS was run by an interim committee of twelve members of which seven were men and five were women. By mid-2005, total membership was 1,000, of which only 200 were paid-up members. About 60 per cent of the members were women and 40 per cent were men. In terms of trades, 90 per cent of the members were market vendors, while street vendors made up 10 per cent of the total membership. The potential total membership countrywide was at the time estimated at 30,000. While most of the members were drawn from the informal economy, key positions including that of president and general secretary were occupied by trade unionists with senior positions in the MCTU. Hence, the formation of MUFIS represents a situation whereby an existing union or union federation extends its field of activity to include informal workers by creating an informal workers' union.

The motto of MUFIS is 'organizing the unorganized', while the main objective is advocacy. To this end MUFIS promises prospective members training opportunities in business management, improved access to loans and protection from harassment (War on Want et al. 2006). Although the intention is to have branches in all the districts of Malawi, at the moment the activities of MUFIS are confined to the major urban centres of Blantyre and Lilongwe. Most of the branches are in Blantyre, where MUFIS has set up committees at many of the produce markets. Each committee is made up of no fewer than ten people, both men and women. In 2005 MUFIS revealed that it had a women's desk to take care of the special needs of women, but these needs were not properly defined. Interviews with the members revealed that, just as in the case of the male members, the interests of women centred on financial empowerment through access to loans and adequate protection of business interests from harassment by local government authorities. Inclusion of women in the interim committee was a positive development, considering that the street vendors' associations discussed above excluded them. To reach out to more informal workers and women in particular, the real challenge has been lack of leverage to influence financial institutions to consider providing credit to vulnerable women and the informal economy workers as a whole on more concessionary terms. As an organization attempting to organize the informal economy with trade union roots, the credibility gap between what it stands for and what it is able to objectively offer circumscribes its prospects of success.

Donor funding has been a major determinant of activities since the members are not able to pay membership fees. Highlights of MUFIS activities prior to 2006 included recruitment and mobilization campaigns for informal economy workers and training in leadership skills and financial management for the committee members, which were all dependent on the availability of funding from War on Want, and were provided through StreetNet International (War on Want n.d.). Up to 2007, there was no genuine local desire to let informal economy workers who had joined the union take leadership of the organization in the real sense. The local authorities in Blantyre, where MUFIS has several branches, were at the beginning of 2005 unaware of the existence of MUFIS or any union for the informal economy. The central government was also taken by surprise when, in early 2006, MUFIS offered to arbitrate in the disagreement involving the Ministry of Local Government over relocation of the street vendors in Lilongwe, Malawi's capital (Chimombo 2006).

Commercial, Industrial and Allied Workers Union The Commercial, Industrial and Allied Workers Union (CIAWU), an affiliate of MCTU, announced at the beginning of 2006 that it had recruited 350 members from the informal economy and established committees of informal economy workers in southern, central and northern regions of Malawi. CIAWU later organized an orientation workshop under the auspices of a donor-funded project, 'Global equality: women in the informal economy', whose objectives were to strengthen women's capacity to become self-reliant and financially independent, to address the special needs

of retrenched or redundant workers affected by HIV/AIDS, to increase business
knowledge and access to economic opportunities for women and youths who had
been retrenched or made jobless, to increase the participation of members in
innovative income-generating activities, raising living standards and improving
the quality of life, to improve the capacity of partners to mainstream gender and
HIV/AIDS in their economic empowerment activities, and to promote information sharing and lesson learning among partners (Union Network International
2006). Notably, there is a convergence in areas of interest with MUFIS. Unlike
those of MUFIS, CIAWU's interests in organizing in the informal economy are
principally based on the desire to follow up on members withdrawing from the
formal economy owing to retrenchment, most of whom end up in the informal
economy.

Organizing the informal economy – which way?

Studies by Bayat (1997b) and Cross (1998a, 1998b) in Tehran and Mexico
City respectively showed that collective organization in the informal economy
is capable of producing significant gains for the informal economy actors, such
as access to loans, access to utilities including water and electricity or political
acceptance of the informal economy. No wonder informal economy workers in
Malawi often ask how membership of an organization will promote business
and livelihoods. Motivation is low, particularly among informal traders whose
businesses are small and unstable owing to, among other factors, lack of access
to capital. Interest in joining informal economy organizations is almost non-
existent where the risk of failure of enterprises is high, that is in situations
where entry and exit is easy and numbers high. Those seeking to organize the
informal economy workers at this level ought to come up with incentives or
focus on areas that can lead to tangible benefits and opportunities for business growth. In this light Lund and Skinner (1999) emphasized the necessity
of realizing and implementing different strategies because of the different
employment relationship and the complex and heterogeneous composition of
the informal economy.

Although a majority of informal economy workers are self-employed, there
is a big group within the informal economy that does not feature much in
discussions on organizing the informal economy, namely the informal economy
employees. So far it seems that attention has been paid to organizing business owners only, as if there are no employees. Yet employees in the informal
economy need as much protection as the entrepreneurs themselves, since
contracts in the informal economy are as informal as is the sector. Working
conditions are usually less in line with recommended labour practices in areas
like the minimum wage, an eight-hour working day, annual leave regulations,
etc. The employees in the informal economy earn a wage, salary or commission
that is unusually low. Commission is usually determined as any amount that

the seller is able to get by offering commodities at prices that are higher than those offered by the proprietor (Jimu 2003). Therefore, an informal economy organization that seeks to represent informal entrepreneurs must come to grips with how to deal with or ignore relations between employers and employees in the sector. Organizing from a union perspective is not an easy task since many informal businesses operate at very low marginal rates of profit and therefore may not be able to afford to pay membership fees to the union, or pay wages to employees that are on a par with minimum wage regulations, as unions will usually insist. High levels of unemployment mean that most informal economy employees are also at a disadvantage in the labour market, often with few other work opportunities, and are less likely to participate in organizing activities that may endanger their only opportunity to work and earn an income.

In terms of the viability of trade union intervention in the informal economy, there is a need to examine the chances of unions succeeding in organizing the informal economy, considering the realities of organizing in the global economy. It is surprising that trade unions are failing to promote the welfare of formal constituents, yet the leadership is seeking to extend the frontier of engagement to the informal economy, where relations of production are diverse and complex. How do they expect to succeed in fighting for the unorganized, those without an employer with whom to negotiate, or entrepreneurs who are already operating at low profit margins? Slogans used by trade unions such as 'the future belongs to the organized' and 'there is strength in unity' already have little meaning for formal economy employees – will they mean anything to the informal economy workers? If the presence of unions is not felt in the formal economy, will unionizing work in the informal economy? Already there are signs that unionizing the informal economy is not having the great impact it was expected to have. The situation at the moment is one of unions that have international or even global connections, but little to show on the ground by way of membership and achievements.

Insider accounts also show that the power struggles within and between unions seeking to work in the informal economy may complicate the already muddled situation of organizing the informal economy. It was reported that between CIAWU and MUFIS there have been cases of misunderstanding over who has the right to speak for various categories of informal workers and over affiliation to MCTU and StreetNet International. MUFIS' quest for affiliation with the MCTU between 2002 and 2004 was frustrated by claims of duplication of effort by the leadership of CIAWU, who were then already affiliated to MCTU. It was apparent then that the leaders of MUFIS and CIAWU could not work together, even though at some point the two organizations had offices in the same complex in downtown Blantyre. Coincidentally, MUFIS and CIAWU are keen to tackle HIV/AIDS issues in the informal economy. Since the activities of both trade unions are dependent on the availability of donor funding, the question here is whether it is the availability of donor support that is the major motivation? The paradox in this case is that HIV/AIDS prevention is an area that attracts more donor funding, and reports in the press have revealed the existence of bogus organizations intended by the founders as a means of siphoning money from donors. Organizing the informal economy also offers trade unions other opportunities, such as international travel and workshops. Such trips have in the past been a source of disagreement or division within the union movement. Conflicts of this nature may lead to a situation whereby real issues in the informal economy are not addressed.

Turning to the relationship between self-organized IEOs and trade unions, while the street vendors' associations have been in existence for over a decade, their organizational stability is compromised by lack of able leadership, lack of an enabling policy environment and financial weaknesses (War on Want et al. 2006). Also, some of the leaders have retained leadership positions in the organizations for over a decade and have sometimes resisted calls for change. This has been the case in the street vendors' associations, where for quite some time women could not hold any position. Most of the members operate at subsistence level and as a result cannot appreciate the value of paying membership fees. On the other hand, international funding agencies prefer to work with the trade unions. The self-organized groups are perceived as lacking in terms of institutional capacity to manage donor funding. Little is said about the fact that accountability is also a critical concern, even among self-organized initiatives, as reflected by the reluctance of members of the street vendors' associations in Limbe to contribute money to their organizations when they noted problems of accountability. In this way, accountability in the management of financial resources is as crucial to the success of self-organized initiatives in the informal economy as having a committed leadership.

Leadership in self-organized and trade union initiatives in the informal economy should be open to learning from success stories in organizing from other sectors and countries, as highlighted in the introduction. Properly functioning IEOs can promote the viability of the informal economy by negotiating for better relations with the formal economy, government and non-governmental organizations interested in the promotion of the informal economy; can provide management, entrepreneurial and technical skills training to members and other forms of assistance necessary for the growth of business in the informal economy (ibid.). Within Malawi, one success story from which lessons could be drawn is the National Association of Business Women (NABW), an initiative by business women who were once active in the Chitukuko Cha A Mai M'Malawi (CCAM). CCAM took a women-in-development perspective and was headed by a former official hostess of the former president, Dr Banda.

NABW was registered in December 1990 as a non-profit organization with a mission to promote the economic empowerment of women through disbursement of small loans. By 2000, membership of NABW was estimated at 14,000. The popularity of NABW is grounded in its successful attempt to overcome barriers to women in starting and developing businesses (CIPE 1998). A recent five-day business skills management training workshop for rural women organized by NABW focused on marketing and sales management, production management and entrepreneurship.[9] In contrast to MUFIS and CIAWU, which are headed by people without tangible business interests in the informal economy, the strength of NABW is that the organization is led by women entrepreneurs and it has structures down to the grassroots level. There is an NABW committee at each district level comprising ten women. At the top is a national committee of twelve members, and each member heads a sector. NABW's national activities are managed by a secretariat comprising twenty-three paid members. As shown above, self-organized informal workers do not have paid staff, mainly because they cannot afford to pay and volunteerism is generally prone to abuse. The supreme body of NABW is the general membership, which exercises its authority through the annual general meeting, at which major decisions are often made (Banda 1997). Although the NABW approach is still top-down, it remains a model of success, since it has responded well to the actual challenges women in business experience through district-level committees. Probably, all informal economy organizations seeking to be national in orientation should aim at developing structures of the kind set up by NABW. There is also a need to identify a niche area of intervention that addresses one of the core challenges confronting the informal economy, with the other interventions assuming a complementary role. Core challenges to the informal economy in the context of Malawi have been: limited access to credit; lack of business management skills and technical know-how; lack of access to appropriate technology; lack of suitable business premises; stiff competition from large firms and among informal entrepreneurs themselves; policy and legislative obstacles; severe market limitations; and lack of raw materials (Government of Malawi 1995; Jimu 2003).

Conclusion

The case studies of the street vendors' associations, Malawi Union for the Informal Sector and the Commercial, Industrial and Allied Workers Union reveal a convoluted process of organizing informal economy workers. Notably, self-organization is often spontaneous, while trade union organization is reactionary. Self-organized groups have sometimes been able to influence state action and have attained temporary victories in terms of rights to trade in ungazetted areas. They are, however, constrained by lack of organizational stability and an inability to realize that short-term gain is not always beneficial in the long run. On the other hand, trade union initiative is largely shaped by availability of donor funding. Limited advocacy and financial constraints imply that the trade unions can get involved only when there is donor funding. Conflicts and power struggles between the trade unions risk undermining the requirement to address issues in the informal economy. Given the organizational instability of grassroots organizations, trade unions provide a window of hope for the formation and stabilization of self-organized groups.

In the process of comparing two forms of organizing the informal economy, namely organizations formed by informal workers themselves and initiatives that emerge from trade unions, a number of major insights have emerged. First, just like most businesses in the informal economy, self-organized informal economy organizations are rarely registered with authorities (War on Want et al. 2006). Second, among the most important characteristics of self-organized informal economy organizations is that they function as loose cooperatives, and common objectives and activities centre on settling disputes among the members, determining new entrants and colluding in setting charges (Jimu 2003; Minde and Nakhumwa 1998), as well as strategizing on how to respond to state repression (Cross 2000). Third, there is a lot of flexibility in terms of entry and exit of members, depending on the dynamics of business. These dynamics contribute to organizational instability. On the other hand, trade union initiatives are offshoots or extensions of trade unions. Leadership positions in the union initiatives are held by officials from the originating trade union, and as a consequence, while seeking to serve the informal economy workers, they reflect the agenda of the formal labour unions, or sometimes the agenda of the donor funding programmes and personal interests of the leaders. It is true that informal traders find it difficult to take the time off from earning their living (Mwamadzingo 2002), but this case study does not support the view that they cannot afford to pay trade union dues on a regular basis, or that accountability is more difficult to enforce among the self-organized informal economy organizations than it is in trade unions involved in organizing the informal economy.

Despite the weaknesses outlined in this chapter, it is not a futile exercise to seek to organize workers in the informal economy. Drawing on experiences from Latin America, Aguilar et al. (1998) observed that organization of informal economy workers has long-term beneficial consequences even when the groups are not initially successful in pursuing the goals that led them to organize in the first place. Therefore, while this chapter has shown that self-organized informal economy groups are characterized by destabilizing competition, bias, pursuit of self-interest and individualism, leading to some leaders being easily enticed and co-opted by those they ought to be negotiating with, these experiences should be seen more as part of the learning process that may in the long run lead to more mature and stable organizations. This is where trade unions like CIAWU can play a role in facilitating the formation of stable self-organized initiatives within the informal economy. While agreeing with the fundamental differences about organizing in the formal and informal economies noted in the chapter by Andrae and Beckman, which in their words warrant different forms of organization for different groups of workers, it is possible to conceive a situation whereby unions in the formal economy can work with self-organized groups in the informal economy. The modalities or the direction of such collaboration will have to be in line with the characteristics of particular organizational contexts.

Acknowledgements

I wish to thank the leadership of the street vendors' associations and MUFIS for sharing experiences of organizing the informal economy. Thanks too to War on Want for granting permission to use in this chapter material gathered specifically for a study they commissioned. The report, entitled *Forces for Change: Informal economy organizations in Africa*, published by War on Want and collaborating partners, is available online (www.waronwant.org). Many thanks to Professor Francis Nyamnjoh and Wendy Willems of War on Want. Dr Ilda Lindell of NAI reviewed the original version of this chapter. Her insights on organizing the informal economy in Africa have significantly influenced the structure and outline as well as the arguments presented in this chapter. The weaknesses are entirely my own.

6 | Moments of resistance: the struggle against informalization in Cape Town

David Christoffer Jordhus-Lier

Introduction

While informal economies and casual labour have a long history in Africa, and have been instrumental in providing and reproducing pools of cheap labour in the interests of colonial and post-colonial capital, they have never been coordinated and legitimized at the scale that we are seeing today. Across the world, those national economies which throughout the post-war era developed a substantial formal sector of work have in the last two decades seen a process of informalization go hand in hand with industrial restructuring, economic globalization and regulatory change. This trend can be identified from the so-called 'neoliberal heartlands' of the Anglo-American world, via the young market economies of the former Eastern Bloc, to the semi-industrialized countries of the global South (Jessop 2002). It is certainly also applicable to South Africa and other African countries (COSATU 1997; Naidoo 2000; Webster 2006). But while the tendency is clear, the socio-political and economic starting points from which informalization unfolds differ radically from one context to another, and generalizations are difficult to make.

'Informality' has been the reality for millions of South African workers for a long time. In addition, the racially discriminatory legislation of apartheid meant that even if employment contracts and labour law were in place, they did not secure decent work conditions. But since the collapse of apartheid, South Africa has experienced an intensified process of informalization. To put it in Webster's (2006) terms, informalization refers to 'a process whereby new forms of non-standard employment, such as casualization (part-time, temporary and seasonal work), subcontracting and varieties of informal work such as street vendoring and homeworking are increasing'. The trajectory of the South African economy departs from those of most African countries in that it has a relatively extensive formal economy. But the formal economy is surrounded by extremely high levels of unemployment, poverty and underdevelopment, similar to those that can be found elsewhere on the continent. Moreover, the legacy of colonialism and apartheid has resulted in these class inequalities overlapping significantly with the categories of ethnicity and race.

Changes in the legislative framework since 1994 reflect both a movement *away* from the discriminatory labour laws of apartheid and a movement *towards* a so-called 'flexible labour market' (Cheadle and Clarke 2000):

> Alongside the government's commitment to economic equity and distributive justice has been the overall aim of stimulating growth and attracting foreign investment through increasing flexibility in some areas of the labour market. This is evident in the new legislation. Each law explicitly articulates a polarity with social justice at one pole and flexibility at the other.

The flexible labour regime has also made inroads into the public sector. The following text offers an analysis of the politics of municipal workers and their union – the South African Municipal Workers' Union (SAMWU) – in Cape Town. The City of Cape Town has gone through a fundamental restructuring process ever since the collapse of the apartheid regime. In the eyes of the trade union, some parts of this process have entailed informalization of work and commercialization of service delivery. The Cape Metropolitan branch of SAMWU has engaged in various forms of resistance to informalization since the mid-1990s, as the transition from apartheid to formal democracy has been accompanied by processes of neoliberalization.

The story recounted is based on two research projects the author conducted in Cape Town during the autumn of 2003 and the spring of 2007. While the first research project was specifically looking at alliances between unions and social movements in the city, my recent research has represented a shift in focus towards the union strategies directed at the local government authorities and various employers. Together, these two research projects involve seventy-five semi-structured interviews with key informants in the field, including unionized and non-unionized municipal workers, union officials, political activists and senior management in the City of Cape Town. The analysis of interview data has also been supported by document analysis of policy documents, minutes, congress resolutions and national legislation. In the following, I will first discuss some general observations about organizing strategies and informalization, as well as its particular political opportunity structures in the South African context. Against this backdrop, I will then account for how these dynamics have been played out in my case.

New incoming realities, new ways of organizing?

Informalization worsens the livelihoods and job conditions of many groups of workers. It also presents trade unions with bureaucratic and organizational challenges that have political implications. Traditionally, trade unions have been more successful in organizing permanent, full-time employees than casual workers, part-time workers and those employed by outsourced companies and subcontractors. Informalization often spells fragmentation of employer relations, high workforce turnover and the deregulation of employment standards

– which have led to union retreat. This has compelled many trade unions to revisit their strategies of organizing and political advocacy. While unions in advanced industrialized countries might perceive this as merely a threat to their relative influence, unions in developing countries with a dwindling formal sector often experience it as a threat to their existence.

Within the critical social science tradition, there is a growing interest in forms of labour politics which transcend the traditional trade union formula in order to embrace community-oriented strategies of mobilization and coalition-building. While some scholars tend to focus on the emergence of new social movements and workers' involvement in these (Waterman 1999; Munck 2004), others point to a significant transformation within the trade union movement, such as the development of the 'organizing model' in the USA (Brecher and Costello 1990; Bronfenbrenner et al. 1998; Lopez 2004). The academic treatment of these politics often stresses their *newness* – referring to '*new* social movements' and '*new* organizing strategies'. This language is also employed in the context of the global South, as indicated by the conference held at the Nordic Africa Institute in Uppsala in April 2007 entitled 'Informalizing economies and new organizing strategies in Africa'.[1] The assumption that what is analytically significant about this kind of politics is its newness is offered legitimacy by regulation theory (Lipietz 1987; Jessop 2002). Regulation theory argues that a Fordist regime of accumulation in the post-war era has been superseded by a post-Fordist one, wherein organized labour can no longer rely on bureaucratic union structures and collective bargaining agreements, and where political mobilization more often focuses on issues of identity and consumption than on the politics of production.

In the African and a development context, we often meet a stereotypical narrative telling us that the failure of the bloated developmental states established after independence has paved the way for a neoliberal era characterized by the rollback of the state and the strengthening of the private sector, civil society organizations and informal economies. Political organizations based on a Western model, such as trade unions, have been depicted as powerless onlookers to this political shift. As loosely networked movements are seen as better equipped to organize workers in the informal economy, it is suggested that trade unions are now gradually being sidelined (Waterman 2005). While this argument has some validity, it generalizes across space and time in a way which is problematic. Social movement tactics have been closely linked to union politics throughout history: the US labour movement in the nineteenth century (Brecher and Costello 1990) and the South African union movement of the 1980s (von Holdt 1992) represent good examples in this regard. Therefore, the notion of a political transformation from *old* trade union politics to *new* social movement politics is at best geographically uneven.

A counterpoint to these generalizing accounts can be found in recent work in human geography. An emerging literature of case studies focusing on worker-community politics is being produced by critical geographers, often working under the heading of 'labour geography' (see, for example, Savage 1998; Tufts 1998; Walsh 2000; Wills 2005). In each and every case, the local worker struggles found in this body of work are seen to be shaped by, and linked to, global economic processes. But at the same time particular attention is paid to the locally specific contexts in which they are played out; not only to local economic structures but also to working-class cultures, trade union traditions and the national political context. In sum, they portray worker politics and community politics as inseparable, and argue that the ways in which worker organizations and community organizations choose to cooperate (or, in many cases, refrain from doing so) are shaped by the national and sub-national scales, as well as the realities and imaginations of the world economy (Herod 1998).

Research suggests that worker organizations are getting to grips with informalization, in the USA and the UK, as well as across the global South (see, for example, Chun 2005; Agarwala 2007; Webster et al. 2008). They are doing so by opposing these changes politically, as well as through finding ways of mobilizing and organizing workers in the context of informalized work (Moody 1997). Both in an African context and beyond, we can detect a general shift away from bureaucratic formal trade unionism to more grassroots-based, less rigid organizing strategies. But these so-called 'organizing strategies' against informalization show significant national variations. The South African labour movement, which by African standards boasts a powerful membership base and a considerable level of political influence, has – at least rhetorically – acknowledged the immediacy of the threat which informalization poses to workers. This was already evident in the September Commission of 1997 – initiated by the biggest trade union federation, the Congress of South African Trade Unions (COSATU) – which identified the informal sector, as well as vulnerable workers and vulnerable sectors of the formal economy, as main targets for the organizing strategies of the trade union movement (COSATU 1997). However, the extent to which COSATU-affiliated and other unions have adopted policies which directly take up this challenge is not so clear.

SAMWU was established in 1987 through a merger of five local government unions, the biggest of these being the Cape Town Municipal Workers' Association. In contrast to most other South African unions, SAMWU still has its national headquarters in Cape Town. SAMWU is an affiliate of COSATU and is seen to be one of COSATU's most progressive unions in terms of continuing COSATU's political tradition of social movement unionism. Until recently, SAMWU was the majority union in the City of Cape Town. The membership of its rival union, the Independent Municipal and Allied Trade Union (IMATU), has in recent years surpassed that of SAMWU, both representing around ten thousand workers in the city. According to the unions, the unionization rate of the city's permanent workforce is around 90 per cent. While IMATU's relationship to the City of Cape Town and its restructuring processes has been based on collaboration, consultation and consent, SAMWU and the city authorities can look back at ten years of confrontation, negotiation and, at crucial points in the restructuring process, non-collaboration.

The story of SAMWU's political strategies in the post-apartheid era adds another contribution to our understanding of African worker organization, as the union is one of many political actors on the continent that is mobilizing against the informalization of work. I trace their politics back to the first democratic elections in 1994 and attempt to see their activities at the local scale in the Cape metropolitan area against the backdrop of the South African labour movement's strategies at the national scale. Their tactics evolve in relationship to the political processes of informalization, as they engage with them and resist them in particular places. The relative 'newness' of some of the globalization processes obliges trade unions to undergo a learning process in order to develop the capacity and knowledge to deal with these challenges. Interestingly, SAMWU has approached this new challenge in ways that can be seen as a return to their political past.

Post-apartheid unionism and the dilemmas of alliance-building

South African workers are well known for their track record of social movement politics. The trade union movement's part in the struggle that led to the collapse of the apartheid state testified to the potential strength of alliances between trade unions and political movements (Webster 1994; von Holdt 2003). South Africa's tradition of radical unionism has continued to play a central role in shaping and opposing the political economy in the new South Africa. When the African National Congress (ANC) became South Africa's first democratically elected government in 1994, it maintained a political alliance with its previous allies in the resistance movement, notably through the Tripartite Alliance between the ANC, COSATU and the South African Communist Party (SACP). Hopes were that the Alliance would sustain the social movement unionism of the resistance struggle and translate it into organized labour having considerable influence over government policy at a national level. Since the regime change in the early 1990s, however, two related political developments have fundamentally circumscribed the political strategies of organized labour and the prospects of social movement unionism at the scale of the nation-state.

First, an obstacle to a sustained strategy of social movement unionism in South Africa lies in the transformation of civil society since apartheid, and the growing gap between those aligned to the ANC on the one hand and diverse oppositional groups on the other (Bond 2000; Habib and Kotzé 2002; Oldfield and Stokke 2007). By the end of the 1990s, numerous community groups had emerged, resisting what they perceived as attacks on their livelihoods. Their political agenda revolves around the cost and quality of basic services and rights to adequate shelter and land. They respond to forced water and electricity cut-offs and to related grievances such as house evictions or lack of land distribution. These organizations, often referred to as 'social movements', are not using elections or strikes as their means of influence, but rather mass mobilization and direct action (Desai 2003). As far as the trade unions are concerned, their constituency and their set of demands are in line with the progressive political agenda the union movement claims to be fighting for. But at the same time, the unpredictable methods of many of these organizations and their confrontational political approach might destroy the image of the trade unions as responsible partners. Government officials and the media have at times portrayed the social movements as politically controversial and even branded them as criminal organizations. Moreover, state repression and frequent clashes with the police weaken their organizational ability, and hence reduce the impetus on the part of trade unions to build an alliance.

Second, the Alliance has, throughout its existence and pre-dating the 1994 elections, been an arena where struggles over class, ethnicity and other conflict lines have been played out. Organized labour was quite successful in influencing policy in the transition period, particularly through the early drafts of what became the Reconstruction and Development Programme, the ANC's 1994 election manifesto. But it soon became apparent that the multi-class character of the ANC organization and its representatives in government were susceptible to pressure from the associations, think tanks and leadership of domestic capital, and from international financial and development agencies (Bond 2000). The unveiling of the 1996 macroeconomic policy framework Growth, Employment and Redistribution (GEAR) is generally seen to mark the entry of neoliberalism in South Africa. The GEAR plan did not undergo consultation with organized labour and was proclaimed 'non-negotiable'. It was thus clear that merely being a part of the Alliance was not enough for organized labour to secure working-class interests in the new South Africa (Buhlungu 2003).

The clearest indication that government policies were heading in a direction that was at odds with the interests of the unions was the introduction of the GEAR macroeconomic package. The climate of the Alliance deteriorated at the turn of the new millennium, as GEAR signalled liberalization, commercialization of the public sector and the intended privatization of several state-owned companies – all of which the trade unions adamantly opposed. COSATU launched nationwide anti-privatization strikes in 2000, 2001 and 2002, and continued pressure from left-wing forces within (and outside) the Alliance has arguably led the government to reconsider many of their more radical neoliberal targets. Continued growth also allowed the government to significantly increase social spending, and has led observers to describe the post-2000 ANC as 'social democratic' or 'Third Way' (Harrison 2006; Fisher-French et al. 2007).

Informality, in South Africa and elsewhere, does not just happen. It should rather be understood as a set of political processes that are contested in different national and local contexts, and hence produce different outcomes from one place to another. Cost savings, rationalization and outsourcing in the public sector do not only spring out of national politics, neither do they always take a direct cue from the GEAR document. In the late 1990s metropolitan administrations in some of the bigger cities feared that they were heading towards fiscal crisis. Increased spending resulting from policies of redistribution and development, and a dramatic reduction in the subsidy from national government, put huge pressure on municipal budgets. This was the case in Cape Town, and consultants were hired to come up with solutions to the problem. It was argued that if the fragmented metropolitan administrations of the city were to merge into one 'unicity' with developmental responsibilities far exceeding their previous mandates, local government in Cape Town also had to go through a cost-cutting and rationalizing exercise.

The drive to reduce state spending has led the city authorities to reduce the numbers of permanently employed staff from 33,000 to around 19,000 within less than ten years. Interestingly, this has been achieved without any retrenchments: a moratorium placed on new appointments and promotions in 1997 and 2000 did the job by allowing natural attrition to take its toll. Parallel to reducing staff numbers, and partly as a result of this, outsourcing of service delivery and support functions has become widespread. By early 2007, the city had also hired between 4,000 and 5,000 contract staff via labour broker agencies to fill vacant positions.[2] In other words, the municipality's labour regime was undergoing neoliberal change. Neoliberalism in Cape Town has also meant that the municipal service delivery systems of the city are being refashioned as utilities, and hence run more like businesses. Cost recovery principles in basic services have had serious implications for user fees and the collection of payments; amid extreme unemployment levels and widespread poverty the inability to pay has led to cut-offs, installation of pre-paid water meters, and thousands of families finding themselves in arrears. Around 2000, community organizations which mobilized around these issues started to emerge. Numerous 'anti-eviction committees' in the townships surrounding Cape Town started protesting in the streets and resisting disconnections and evictions. Service delivery has since then remained one of the most important political issues in the city, and one which remains intensely contested.

Confronting the threat and reality of neoliberalization in Cape Town

The commercialization of service delivery, as well as the informalization of work, has clearly had a huge impact on municipal workers. Based on this acknowledgement, and in line with the union's tradition of community-oriented unionism, the political agenda of SAMWU's Cape Metropolitan branch in the post-apartheid era has encompassed different subjective perspectives: from the *worker's* point of view and from that of the *service user*, as well as through being an *organized collective*. In the following, I trace this learning process through three 'moments'. These moments are to a certain extent overlapping in time and scope, but for the purpose of the argument of this chapter I treat them as separate strategies. Thus I aim to show how a relatively 'new' challenge such as the informalization of work has been met by a mixture of new and old union tactics in a continuous process of trial and error.

'Anti-privatization' as a social movement? SAMWU had set up an anti-privatization campaign nationally by the late 1990s and had even appointed a campaign organizer to mobilize against local government privatization. Hence, the proposed restructuring plans for Cape Town and Johannesburg at the turn of the millennium actually triggered a determined effort from unions and community groups to join forces in stopping the neoliberalism they saw disguised in these plans. The Cape Metropolitan branch of SAMWU established the Local Government Transformation Forum, later to be known as the Cape Town Anti-Privatization Forum (APF), in 1999/2000. At this point the City of Cape Town was in the process of implementing policies flowing from the recommendations of the Unicity Commission. The union saw an opportunity in this process, which allegedly had a 'participatory' element, to bring in a broad front of community organizations that opposed the commercialization and privatization of municipal service delivery. The Western Cape Anti-Eviction Campaign, a network of the various 'anti-eviction committees' that had sprung up across the Cape Town area, as well as a number of developmental NGOs, union representatives, environmental groups and individual activists, attended the meetings of the Cape Town APF.

Privatization is a hotly contested issue in South Africa and the union saw a potential for mass mobilization in this forum. Its namesake in the Gauteng province, spearheaded by the Soweto Electricity Crisis Committee, did in fact become a mass movement. However, the militant activism of the Gauteng organization led the local SAMWU branch to withdraw, as it perceived it as a political threat to the party in government. While the Cape Metropolitan branch of SAMWU retained its involvement in their local forum, this experience has another important insight to offer. As a network between local organizations, the Cape Town APF had to bridge very different organizational cultures and constitutions: the formal bureaucracy of SAMWU – with congress resolutions, written mandates and a paid-up membership; via the informal networks of the 'anti-eviction committees' – whose mandate and legitimacy were often based on community meetings; to the agenda of individual activists, sympathizers and NGOs. This diversity by no means ruled out cooperation but it did raise some questions, such as: Who is representing whom? How do these groups work together? How to challenge the system?

In addition to addressing their concrete differences in terms of interests, organizational characteristics and political tactics, they were also forced to confront the hegemony of the ANC in South African civil society (Lier and Stokke 2006). The ANC's unrivalled position can be traced back to its vanguard role in the anti-apartheid struggle, and the Tripartite Alliance has further consolidated hegemony in civil society (Marais 2001). Since they came into office, the ruling power has managed to manufacture consent with the majority of the population. Workers and unionists are no exception. Trade unionists have tried to juggle their allegiance to the party in power, their political opposition to neoliberal policies and their sympathy with community opposition. In the case of the APF, this created friction between the participants, as well as within their constituencies (Lier and Stokke 2006). While the APF did play an important role as a networking forum, it gradually became less central to the political activity of the parties involved.

Social movement tactics were not new to SAMWU, as since its establishment in 1987 the union had been one of the most militant and active unions in the broad community-driven resistance movement. This time around, however, the 'enemy' was trickier to pin down. There was no white minority regime to rally against. Rather, the targets for this campaign were the contested concepts of neoliberalism and privatization championed by democratically elected politicians. In fact, the campaigning efforts of the COSATU unions helped these politicians into power three times in a row. Therefore, the evident dilemma of ANC's strong position in society and its role in the ongoing privatization policies represented a perplexing dilemma for the union.

Resisting neoliberal service delivery through issue-specific campaigns The attempt to build a united political front through the Cape Town Anti-Privatization Forum was perceived as challenging political power too directly. But the need for joint action between unions and progressive community organizations around issues of common interest has not waned. In the last few years, SAMWU representatives and other activists have launched campaigns targeted at political issues more directly concerning local communities, which shows that they have tried to learn a lesson from the APF experience. This shift in strategy should not necessarily be understood as an essential change, though, as the previous APF was also involved in struggles on the ground. But one can perhaps identify a change of short-term ambition. The rhetoric this time around is less concerned with building a counter-hegemonic force than it is about achieving pragmatic political victories. At the same time, many of the same individuals are involved, and they are still guided by ideological principles. In short, commercialization of service delivery and the casualization of municipal work are seen as effects of the same move by capital to allow market forces to play a bigger role in the operations of the local state. In the activists' view, this comes at the expense of the welfare of citizens and restricts their democratic participation.

An interesting political initiative in this regard is the 'campaign against pre-paid meters', which was initiated in 2003/04. The campaign was a coalition of union and non-union actors opposing the roll-out of pre-paid water meters in certain areas of Cape Town. Pre-paid water meters are seen to be particularly harmful to poor households, which struggle to pay for their water and which will have to face the health hazards of being disconnected from their water supply. Formally, this campaign was a COSATU initiative, and initially the main driving force behind it was two COSATU affiliates: SAMWU and the National Metalworkers Union of South Africa (NUMSA). Local SACP representatives were also involved, as well as the Bonteheuwel branch of the South African National Civics Organization – another old ANC ally. Representatives of some of the social movements were also active in the campaign meetings, such as the APF and the Vrygrond Action Committee. The breadth of this organizational representation is significant in the sense that it brings together actors from both sides of the previously mentioned civil society divide between ANC allies and their opposition.

The campaign managed to exert enough influence to stop the roll-out of water meters in several areas. They achieved this political success in part by inviting the mayor of the city to one of their community meetings, where she was confronted with evidence of the instalment of pre-paid water meters in the Cape Town communities. She consequently pledged to put a stop to the roll-out. While the city has seen the political administration shift since then, pre-paid water meters have not become widespread in Cape Town. Another point worth taking note of is that the political coalition had, through the involvement of the trade union NUMSA, a potential ace up its sleeve. NUMSA organizes workers in manufacturing plants in the Cape Town area, some of which produce water and electricity meters. If pre-paid meters were to be installed, and these were produced domestically, the campaign could potentially target the point of production by mobilizing workers at the manufacturing plant for direct action. This potential has not yet been exploited, but as long as pre-paid water meters continue to be an option for municipal authorities this is a strategy waiting to be pursued.

The relative success of the campaign in halting the roll-out of water meters encouraged the activists to move on to other issues, such as the restructuring of electricity distribution. Cape Town is seen as a test case in moving away from municipal electricity distribution to the establishment of independent utility companies, known as regional electricity distributors (REDs). According to the campaign organizers, the implementation of REDs will further commercialize electricity distribution to the detriment of the poor. The campaign was not able to effectively set the agenda on this issue, in part because the Cape Town RED1 pilot project became subject to intense contestation between political parties, as well as between local and national tiers of government and between different departments at a national scale. In addition to this, the coalition has mobilized around other issues that they have identified as constituting neoliberalism in practice. A third example is the city's drive to collect outstanding service charges by issuing so-called 'pink letters' (final disconnection warnings) to households that have run into heavy arrears. This campaign is still ongoing at the time of writing. In summary, the experience of this campaign suggests that specific campaigns around particular local issues might not only be easier to organize effectively, but may also represent a less controversial alliance to the formal political system. That being said, many of the activists seem to acknowledge that these ad hoc alliances only highlight the injustices of capitalism and treat its symptoms. In themselves they are insufficient to achieve fundamental political change.

Organizing casualized workers While the first two moments deal with service delivery issues, the third is bringing the focus back to the workplace. By the end of the 1990s, the link between the GEAR policies and their effects on employment conditions in municipal services had become clear. According to Samson's (2004) ILO report on municipal waste services, informalization in the public sector has been of an indirect kind. The strong union presence in local government has barred the employer from directly downgrading municipal jobs. Rather, casualization has been effected through *externalization*, meaning that an increasing number of tasks previously undertaken by the municipality are done by private contractors, entrepreneur development networks, poverty alleviation schemes and volunteers – all of them employing workers on contracts which are non-permanent, low-wage and often not covered by bargaining agreements or labour legislation (ibid.). In addition, the Cape Town experience tells of extensive use of labour broker staff at municipal depots and in the administration. What all these externalized workers have in common is that the relationship between them and the municipality is not formalized through individual employment contracts, but through a commercial contract between the municipality and the private firm that directly employs them.

If SAMWU is to represent all workers in this sector, it will therefore have to organize different groups of workers: employees of private firms (which often do exactly the same job as municipal employees at a lower wage); so-called entrepreneurs which are reliant upon a private firm to supply them with trucks and equipment; people employed by workfare programmes on an extremely low salary; and even 'volunteers' who are picking up garbage without receiving a wage in the hope of eventually being employed by one of the previous employers (ibid.). Municipal workers might struggle to see the short-term gains of joining forces with workers across this 'formal–informal continuum' (ibid.). But as Rees (cited in Webster 2006) argues, failure to do so will directly jeopardize their own work prospects:

Unions have not paid sufficient attention to dealing with the problem of casualization, often being more concerned with their core, permanent membership and improving their associated benefits and wages. Ironically this regulatory and organizational gap provides good incentives for employers to reduce particularly their non-wage costs by employing such forms of labour.

Until the turn of the millennium, the union concentrated its efforts on opposing government policies and influencing the new legislative frameworks around employment and local government which were in the making, as well as developing and promoting alternatives to privatization, such as the so-called 'public–public partnerships' (Pape 2001; Hall et al. 2005). But while the union's efforts to prevent privatization – both as an overall project and in the particular ways it unfolds in local communities in Cape Town – most definitely have shaped the trajectory of economic restructuring in the city, they have not stopped market mechanisms playing an ever more important role in municipal services. A certain level of privatization, commercialization and outsourcing in the public sector has indeed occurred. The abattoirs and markets were closed down, the Unicity continued the trend in some of the previous municipalities of outsourcing waste collection to private companies, and the municipality became to a large extent reliant on the private sector for cleaning and support services.

In recent years, the Cape Metropolitan Branch of SAMWU has been faced with a metropolitan structure in which outsourced services and a flexible labour regime comprise an integral part of the running of the city. The union could no longer solely rely on pre-emptive strikes. Rather it had to confront a reality in which municipal service delivery tasks were often performed by people other than municipal employees. In the recent congress resolutions of the union, one can read an explicitly stated ambition to bring these externalized workers into the fold. This will allow the union to better represent the sector, build working-class solidarity and in turn undermine the rationale for outsourcing. Since 2004, the local SAMWU branch in Cape Town has initiated several organizing efforts which directly target casual and informal workers.

One of their more successful recruitment drives has been the unionization of the Hlumani Wasteman (Pty) Ltd in Cape Town. The company is a part of the Wasteman Group, a domestic waste management company which is partly owned by the French water corporation Suez Environment. SAMWU became involved in Wasteman as the workforce had unsatisfactory experiences with previous unions – their former union had functioned simultaneously as a trade union and a labour broker (see also Boampong, this volume). Wasteman employs around five hundred workers, from whom the union claims to have signed up around three hundred new members by the beginning of 2007. Wasteman is one of the City of Cape Town's most significant contractors in solid waste management. The workers working on Wasteman refuse trucks perform a similar job to workers directly employed by the city, but for a lower wage and with poorer conditions of service. One of the reasons the employment conditions of workers in Wasteman and other private waste management firms are poor compared to those of municipal workers is that they do not fall under the scope of the South African Local Government Bargaining Council (SALGBC). The SALGBC provides higher minimum wages and better conditions of service, which has been the result of years of strong union presence in the sector. The drivers, loaders and operators employed by private firms fall under the Road Freight Bargaining Council under the present jurisdiction. Judicially, what distinguishes these two groups of workers – who perform seemingly similar tasks – is how the status of their employer matches the definition of a 'local government undertaking'. The private companies perform only *part* of the service delivery function, as opposed to the function in its *entirety*, and consequently they fall outside the scope of the SALGBC. This reduces the capacity of the union to represent and fight for the rights of its members in Wasteman. While the union and the employer have signed a recognition agreement, as SAMWU represents a majority of the Wasteman workers, the union is not allowed to negotiate wages and benefits. It does, however, have a mandate on organizational health and safety issues, which worker representatives emphasize as a major concern at Wasteman.

SAMWU is in the process of challenging the scope of the bargaining councils with regard to private waste companies performing municipal tasks. This is a process which is complex and time-consuming, and involves political scales other than that of the Cape Town Metropolitan area, such as the Department of Labour and the Commission for Conciliation, Mediation and Arbitration (CCMA). The union is in a similar dispute with the utilities companies in Johannesburg, which, at the time of writing, remains unsettled. Nevertheless, given SAMWU's majority representation in the Cape Town regional structure of Wasteman, this could be an appropriate site to challenge the principle of outsourced waste management. The SAMWU members at Wasteman are well aware of this ongoing fight, but have little room for participating actively in this struggle. Rather, they are awaiting a slow, bureaucratic process with growing frustration. A victory in the case of Wasteman could be a significant step in SAMWU's fight against the commercialization of service delivery and the casualization of municipal work, and allow the union to become a broad-based *public services union*, as opposed to a narrow *public sector union* (Foster and Scott 1998).

SAMWU's organizing efforts in externalized municipal services do not end with Wasteman. The union has also managed to unionize workers who are working for the City of Cape Town through the labour broker company Masibambane Recruitment. By April 2006, 176 workers of Masibambane were SAMWU members. Labour broker companies pose a difficult challenge for unions, however, as they employ workers who work in numerous workplaces, often for short periods of time. This makes it difficult to recruit workers and to keep them as members for long. Masibambane has a number of clients, of which around 70 per cent are in the private sector. For SAMWU, this is a real obstacle for achieving majority representation in the company. Notwithstanding SAMWU's representation in Wasteman, Masibambane and some other waste companies and labour brokers, their overall private firm membership accounts for less than 5 per cent of their membership. The general unionization rate remains very low in the externalized municipal services. In other words, if SAMWU is to undermine the rationale for outsourcing municipal services by effectively raising the conditions of these workers, it still has a long way to go.

Concluding remarks

In an African context, municipal services in the City of Cape Town might be said to give work to relatively protected, privileged and well-organized blue-collar workers. Still, the city's workforce has gradually witnessed the threat of informalization become a reality. The way in which South African municipal workers experience informalization is likely to be different from the experience of workers in other African countries, but the contrast between different workers' experiences within South Africa is also vast. This unevenness poses a challenge for unionism, as the prospect of a united working class in the immediate future requires conscious efforts to build unity across this formal–informal divide (see also Andrae and Beckman, this volume). SAMWU, which until recently was the biggest union in the metropolitan municipality, with a long tradition of movement-based politics, has in different ways tried to fight back. The three moments depicted above illustrate this. The first two of these show that the local union branch has revisited, but also revised, their repertoire from the apartheid days of using community alliances to achieve common goals. A rather different strategy from these can be found in the third moment, namely the unionization of workers in the private firms in order to improve their employment conditions and thereby reduce the incentive for the city's authorities to externalize municipal services. By way of conclusion, there are three important points to make about the relationship between informalization as a process and this third moment.

First, insofar as this organizing strategy can be seen as a new and innovative union strategy, it is important to acknowledge the close relationship between this strategy and the other two. A certain logic can be discerned between them: the first moment attempted to confront neoliberalism head-on as a political project; the second moment was aimed more specifically at the negative effects of this political project on the working class as service users; whereas the third moment represents a strategy to fight informalization in the municipal workplace and beyond. As informalization processes unfold, and are implemented, throughout Africa, trade unions and other organizations can potentially acquire in-depth knowledge and hands-on experience of the nuts and bolts of economic restructuring. By challenging it on a political, legal and technical level, they can learn how to confront and possibly reverse these processes. In other words, whereas informality should be understood as a process – informalization – the struggle against it also represents a learning process.

Second, it is precisely around the issues of casual labour that the union ought to tread carefully as far as its relationship to the wider community is concerned. In contrast to the issue of service access and affordability, issues around casual work (potentially) complicate the relationship between municipal workers and other community members. The casualization of municipal labour has given many community members who were previously unemployed the opportunity to work in short-term contract jobs. The union's fight to 're-municipalize' these functions risks facing resistance from those with a direct interest in these jobs. Samson (2004) describes a similar attitude among unionized workers, as she identifies a 'perception by many SAMWU members that these workers are "the enemy"'. To further complicate matters, community organizations and even certain trade union structures have become involved in job creation schemes which effectively undermine the creation of formal jobs in the municipality.

Third, the unprecedented levels of informalization in South Africa have triggered responses within the trade union movement that point towards the future, while at the same time borrowing from the political traditions of South African unionism from the recent past. Not only does the union try to keep its identity as a social movement alive, but experiences from the 1980s might even prove relevant in the union's attempts to unionize externalized municipal services. Von Holdt (2003) and others describe how organizers used community meetings and neighbourhood networks as recruitment grounds during the apartheid days; SAMWU might have to consider similar tactics in order to reach the thousands of workers who now do work for the City of Cape Town: through a labour broker, through a small subcontracting company, through a multinational's subsidiary or through a poverty reduction scheme. In short, the time might be right for going back into the communities.

Acknowledgements

This chapter has been made possible by the generous assistance of many people. My research in Cape Town owes much to Lance Veotte and Stanley Yisaka at the South African Municipal Workers Union, David Beretti at the City of Cape Town, and Jonathan Grossman and Sophie Oldfield at the University of Cape Town. I would also like to thank my supervisors, Neil M. Coe and Noel Castree, for constructive feedback on drafts of this chapter. In addition, I would like to thank Ilda Lindell at the Nordic Africa Institute in Uppsala for the initiative behind this project and for helpful comments on my contribution. However, any potential errors or misinterpretations in this chapter remain the author's sole responsibility.

7 | The possibilities for collective organization of informal port workers in Tema, Ghana

Owusu Boampong

Introduction

Informal employment is here to stay, and in Africa and elsewhere in the world it is noted to be expanding faster relative to formal sector employment (Gallin 2001). The expansion of the informal economy since the 1980s, among other factors, has been attributed largely to the global economic crisis and the way production is organized by domestic and international capital (ibid.). The economic crises that inflicted many developing countries and the concomitant adoption of structural adjustment programmes (SAPs) in the early 1980s saw a massive downsizing of public (formal) sector employment. Faced with the imperative of survival in the highly competitive global market, domestic and international capital adopts flexible strategies for the deployment of labour. Firms cut down on the body of permanent full-time workers with the aim of concentrating on their core activities and where possible rely on informal workers (ibid.). The strategy includes outsourcing labour arrangement practices to subcontractors and agents. The benefits of such employment strategies to firms are a reduction in labour costs, and transferring the responsibility of dealing with labour agitation as well as wages, benefits and other working conditions to either the individual worker or to the subcontractor.

The deployment of workers through agencies is emerging in Ghana. It has been reported that private and public firms are increasingly utilizing flexible labour market practices (e.g. subcontracting arrangements) which are making employment conditions more precarious (Ocran 1998). It is argued in the literature that such flexible labour deployment arrangements tend to complicate employment relationships, offering little hope for collective organization of informalized workers. This chapter attempts to enhance our understanding of these emerging forms of employment practices, and to determine whether or not they give rise to new, ingenious ways of collectively organizing 'fluid' informal workers. Using informal port workers in Tema as a case, it is argued that flexible labour practices are giving rise to new forms of collective organization of casual port workers. This new organizing strategy entails an alliance between local organizations of (or self-organized) informal workers and national trade unions. The politics surrounding this new employment arena encompass a complex web of actors, with each acquiring a different role in the process, which may have an influence on the process of negotiating the conditions of casual workers.

Informal work is defined by Breman (2004) in terms of the employment relations[1] exiting between workers and employers or the agents that recruit the workers. The setting up of an enterprise or a labour agent may comply with official rules but the nature of employment relations with employees may be informal. That is, workers are not employed on a permanent basis and as such do not appear in the books of the firms they work with. They work on the basis of mostly oral contracts – even in cases of written contracts the terms still make them informal – agreed for a specified period of time with a subcontractor. These come with little or no entitlement to social security. Informal workers are least protected by the laws of the state but often work under deplorable conditions. Informalization is therefore taken to mean the downgrading of employment conditions through the use of flexible strategies of labour deployment.

Informalization and the possibilities for organizing

Informalization is widely attributed to the restructuring of formal sector employment and the survival responses of individuals without formal jobs to earning a living. The economic crisis during the 1970s and 1980s in many developing countries, and the subsequent adoption of structural adjustment programmes to address the crisis, led to the downsizing of formal employment and sometimes a freeze on the absorption of low-skilled workers into formal employment. The economic circumstances of workers who are expelled from formal employment, as well as individuals having difficulties securing formal jobs, dictate that they undertake some economic activities outside the formal economy to earn a living. The informal economy becomes their final destination for survival (Ninsin 1991). This is not to say that informal work has no linkages with formal economic activities. It is argued that informalization is in itself a creation of capital and the state to seek answers to the contemporary economic crisis (Meagher 1995; Lourenço-Lindell 2002). Informal economic activities are intricately enmeshed with formal economy activities. This is an idea that is advanced by the informalization approach.

The informalization approach recognizes informal work as part of capital's search for flexibility in the use of labour, with the objective of evading the costs of social security and other obligations associated with labour management (Meagher 1995). Drawing on empirical evidence from Latin America, Portes and Schauffler (1993) observed a practice whereby large firms indirectly hire informal workers off the books through subcontracting strategies. Jason and Wells (2007) report on a fashionable informalization process in sub-Saharan Africa whereby employers decide to lay off their workers overnight and re-employ them through labour intermediaries. In their analysis, Jason and Wells (ibid.) identified labour subcontracting arrangements through different forms of intermediaries, including *labour brokers*, *gang leaders* and *labour subcontractors*. Labour agents, according to them, recruit and deploy workers to the working site as and when they are needed by the employer. The agents are responsible only for recruitment, which always attracts a commission. Supervision and payment of wages are undertaken directly by the employer. In addition to recruitment, *gang leaders* may take on further responsibilities, such as supervising the workers as well as managing the work on-site. In this instance, the employer may still pay the workers directly and remunerate the gang leaders separately. Labour subcontractors, described by Jason and Wells (ibid.: 5) as the 'complete form of outsourcing', are paid a lump sum for a task by a client. The subcontractor recruits, manages the work and pays the workers out of the sum received from the client. In this case the subcontractor is an entrepreneur and a risk-taker who is rewarded in the form of profit.

The literature cautions us not to regard informalization as an ahistorical process. The emerging flexibilization and organizing strategies of informal workers may exhibit new characteristics, but their current forms and their underlying processes have their roots in history. The contemporary forms of organizing informal activities are path-dependent on historical processes and practices (Roitman 1990; Lourenço-Lindell 2002). As will be shown in the empirical analysis, the current attempts at labour deployment via intermediaries, as well as the effort to collectively organize informal workers in Tema, are influenced by the historical forms of deploying casual workers. The historical forms of organizing casual workers (i.e. the gang system) are being used in today's labour practices or absorbed by today's labour agencies, which is a reflection of global trends being shaped at local level by local historical forms of socio-economic organization.

The incentive for the formal/informal interface, it is argued, is geared towards the evasion of labour regulations to reduce labour costs and maximize profits, with untold consequences on the worker. Similarly, Lourenço-Lindell (2002) has observed that merchant capital in Guinea-Bissau employs poorly regulated labour as a means of dealing with the challenges of economic liberalization and global competition. In the process, casual workers have been drawn into global commodity chains through informal arrangements. Informal work can be seen as: 'part of [the] global corporate economy and providing crucial infrastructure for the major growth sectors of the "new urban economy" [...] [which leads to] a disenfranchisement of the working class, a downgrading of labour and a worsening condition of work' (ibid.: 16).

Moreover, workers are not only downgraded by the process of informalization but also experience decollectivization. According to Portes et al. (1989), informalization undermines the power of labour to organize itself in the areas of economic bargaining, social organization and political influence. Undeclared labour and multiple intermediaries between firms and employers characteristically contribute to decollectivization of the labour process. Jason and Wells (2007: 7) have also indicated that a flexible labour deployment strategy through intermediaries tends to complicate the effort to collectively organize casual workers. As they put it: 'When workers are employed through intermediaries [...] (as broker, gang leader or labour subcontractor), it is clear that the use of an intermediary drives a wedge between the principal employer and the workers, complicating the employment relationship and raising critical issues for organization.'

A major criticism of the above perspectives on informalization is that they overly associate informal work with victimization and the downgrading of labour, and the explanations for this process are narrowed down to the imperatives of capital and state (Lourenço-Lindell 2002) and pessimism concerning any effort to collectively organize informal labour. The area that has been neglected by the informalization discourse is how informal workers could be collectivized to bring about improvements in their employment conditions. This inadequacy is traced to the belief that the informal workers are difficult to organize owing to the heterogeneous nature of their employment relations, their fluidity – i.e. the difficulties of locating and contacting informal workers (Gallin 2001) – and the short-termist nature of their employment relation. This chapter assumes a more optimistic attitude to the collective organization of informal workers and argues that labour downgrading associated with flexible labour strategies can be reversed through a strategic alliance between informal workers' unions and national trade unions.

Gallin (ibid.) has also proposed a more optimistic view of organizing informal workers. Gallin's position is that organizing informal workers is not an activity among amorphous individuals; rather it depends on the ability to reach out to groups of workers who are survival experts, dynamic and resourceful. Informal workers, like any other workers, 'will organize whenever they have a chance to do so, and they are best organized by themselves' (p. 538). Gallin (ibid.) has indicated, based on a number of empirical studies, that informal workers the world over are already organizing themselves. Two paths of organization exist. The first entails a situation wherein a national trade union extends its activities to groups of informal workers. This path is taken by national trade unions as a response to the erosion of their membership base as a result of the onslaught of trade liberalization and structural adjustment regimes (Anyemedu 2000). The second comprises new unions or proto-union associations/NGOs created out of horizontal solidarity groups of informal workers and operating independently of national trade unions. According to Gallin, wage increases, improvements in working conditions and job security for the worker can be achieved by solidarity and collective action.

As organized informal workers attempt to collectively struggle for better working conditions they have to deal with other actors having an influence on their employment conditions. Indeed, informal work, rather than being un-regulated, is in fact regulated (through various sets of rules) and by a variety of actors (Lourenço-Lindell 2002), including quasi-government regulatory agencies, national trade unions, organized informal groups or unions, agents such as labour contractors and informal workers. Some of these actors may or may not participate in negotiating and enforcing the rules governing the working conditions and the collective actions of informal workers. Informal workers are often noted to lack representation and visibility in rule-setting or in groups or associations that claim to represent their interests: 'The lack of visibility and recognition has been an obstacle to the growth of informal economy organizations and in some cases a threat to their survival. A successful organizing strategy requires securing recognition and representation at different levels [...] first for organizations that already exist' (Gallin 2001: 545). The conditions of informal workers and the rules governing their work are to be understood as resulting from the power play between these various actors involved in negotiating improvements in the working conditions of informal workers.

Struggles within the realm of informal work may also range from open protests to non-compliance (Lourenço-Lindell 2002). However, to many groups of informal workers open protest remains an unlikely option, unless such groups have strong bargaining power, are legally protected or have achieved some level of political status. Otherwise, when individual groups of informal workers stand up to their bosses they may rock the boat. In this instance, 'subtle forms of resistance may be making progress. For the majority who are walking on a tightrope, small steps may be safer than bold moves' (ibid.: 254).

In summary, arguments associating dehumanization of labour with flexible labour strategies are often oblivious to the possibilities that exist to collectively organize informalized workers in order to defend their interests. Admittedly, flexible labour strategies tend to complicate employment relations, leading to the worsening of working conditions. Nevertheless, one institutional possibility that could enable the reversal of labour downgrading is by organizing informal workers through a strategic alliance between local unions of informal workers and national trade unions. This organizational path, however, is not apolitical. The alliance is a political arena embodying a constellation of actors with varied interests and assuming different roles with implications for negotiating the working conditions of informal workers.

The analysis of the organization of informal port workers in Tema is based on the qualitative data collected in 2004 for a study on casual workers and intermediary labour agencies (Boampong 2005), followed by subsequent field visits in 2006 and 2007. All the interviews took the form of in-depth conversations with the interviewees. During these visits, the executives of five casual workers' unions were interviewed, as well as four officials of two labour hiring agencies. Thirty individual casual workers at the port were also interviewed. The selection of the casual workers was made to reflect the structure of the gang – internally differentiated as the replacement casual workers, the regular casual workers and the headmen. The headmen interviewed had more than a decade's experience as casual workers at the port. Selection along the lines of the different categories of casual workers, as well as the choice of experienced headmen for the interviews, was meant to enhance our understanding of the internal dynamics of the gang system over time.

The chapter is organized into six sections. Following this introductory section is a review of the literature on the informalization process and the discourse on possible spaces for organizing informal workers. Background information on informalization and casualization in Ghana and specifically Tema, the case study area, is presented in Section 3. The section on labour subcontractors looks at the structure of the subcontracting agencies and their effects on employment relationships. Section 5 looks at the alliance between the casual workers' unions and the Maritime and Dockworkers Union and how the alliance is enabling the unions to offset some of the negative effects of the informalization process. Section six is the conclusion.

Informalization and casualization in Ghana

This section looks at the broader context of informalization in Ghana from three historical epochs categorized as pre-1970s – comprising the colonial and the Convention Peoples Party (CPP) regimes – the 1970s, and the contemporary era, i.e. the structural adjustment regime. This historical distinction should enable us to understand how different policy environments over time have had different implications for the increasing numbers of informal workers in Ghana. Also, it seeks to avoid the pitfall of regarding informalization as an ahistorical process. The macro-analysis of informalization in Ghana in this chapter relies on the scholarly works of Ninsin (1991), Manuh (1994) and Hutchful (2002).

The emergence of informal work in Ghana is traced to the attempts by the colonial government and the immediate post-independence socialist regime to modernize Ghanaian society. The inadequacies of the educational policies of both the colonial and the CPP governments and the low capacity of the modern economy to absorb the urban labour force, according to Ninsin (1991), explain the origin of informal work in Ghana. The colonial governments promoted a primary education in which the emphasis was on training school leavers in white-collar skills. The CPP regime, in particular, undertook extensive educational reforms under its Accelerated Development Plan for Education to increase access to education to as many Ghanaians as possible at all levels of the educational ladder. The massive investments undertaken by the CPP government to expand educational infrastructure saw a tremendous increase in student enrolment in pre-tertiary schools. The educational expansion, however, was merely in terms of numbers, and not quality (ibid.). There were high drop-out rates among pre-tertiary school leavers, and even those who managed to complete their primary and secondary education had skills that were insufficient to enable them to secure scarce white-collar jobs. Again, the colonial and the post-independent economies had not been transformed enough to begin to cope with the minimum changes in the labour force (ibid.). According to Hart (1973) the high rate of formal unemployment among the urban youth in the sixties was in part the result of the influence of Western education.

The CPP government attempted to address the unemployment situation in the sixties through the creation of a public sector paramilitary organization. This effort, however, was not adequate to matching the increasing numbers of the urban labour force (ibid.). The National Liberation Council and its offshoot, the Progress Party, which succeeded the CPP from the mid-1960s till the early 1970s, embarked on a series of retrenchment exercises to reduce the size of the public sector workforce. The majority of those who were laid off between 1966 and 1970 were semi-skilled and unskilled workers in the public sector (Ninsin 1991). The justification for the retrenchment exercise was that the previous government had disproportionately increased the size of the public sector without consideration of the ability of the economy to sustain such increases. This historical analysis traces the origins of the informal economy to the high growth rate of the urban labour force relative to the rate of economic growth. The economy failed to cope with the mass of the urban labour force, leading to the emergence of an excess reserve army.

The National Redemption Council (NRC)/Supreme Military Council (SMC),[2] through its indigenization policy, nationalized a number of private enterprises in the 1970s and, according to Ninsin (ibid.), private sector employees were retrenched in the process. The NRC/SMC regime simultaneously pursued an interventionist policy similar to that of the CPP. Between 1975 and 1983, the bottom ranks of the civil service grew by 14 per cent, even while shortages of inputs were leading to redundancy of existing staff (Hutchful 2002). The economic crisis and unemployment deepened in the late 1970s and 1980s. The expulsion of labour from the formal economy continued and intensified with the implementation of structural adjustment programmes in the 1980s.

The impact of the reforms on the workers in the lower ranks of the public sector was massive (Ninsin 1991; Manuh 1994). The economic reform package implemented in the 1980s included the retrenchment of excess labour from the public service, and a freeze on new recruitment into the lower and middle grades in all areas of the public sector in order to cut the government's wage bill. The civil service retrenched 10,500 workers in 1987, 11,000 in 1988 and 12,000 in 1989. During 1988/89, of the estimated 320,000 employees in the total of 200 state-owned enterprises, at least 39,800 were retrenched. The Cocoa Board had retrenched 29,000 workers by 1988. Also, an estimated 13,000 jobs were lost in manufacturing and the electricity industry during 1982–84 (Manuh 1994). In the view of Ninsin (1991) the retrenchment exercise targeted the junior staff of the public sector, including labourers, cleaners, drivers, stewards, cooks, porters, messengers, security personnel, clerical personnel, store officers and secretarial personnel. Following the freeze on recruitment to the lower echelons of the public sector, it was projected that 'no school leavers from primary and junior secondary schools can expect formal wage or salaried employment' (Manuh 1994: 67). Some categories of workers employed in state plantations in some rural communities were also retrenched. Manuh (ibid.) mentioned, in particular, the retrenchment of casual workers[3] employed on state plantations. The General Agricultural Workers' Union (GAWU) reported a loss of 14,000 workers in the cocoa sub-sector under SAP, about 12,000 workers from the Food Production Corporation and 9,000 from the state Farms Corporation. Its membership had fallen from 150,000 to about 110,000 by 1988 (ibid.). According to Baah-Boateng (2004), the retrenchment exercise in the public service contributed about 89 per cent of the loss of about 235,000 formal economy jobs between 1985 and 1990, and under the current Public Sector Management Reform Programme (PSMRP) about 20,000 workers are expected to be laid off between 2001 and 2010, at an average of 2,000 per annum.

The series of retrenchment exercises associated with the various political regimes, the inadequacies of the educational policies and the low absorption capacity of the modern economy led to a high rate of unemployment pushing an increasing number of people into informal/casual work as a survival strategy. It is this mass of informal workers which is flexibly deployed by capital in contemporary times (Ocran 1998). The case study explores these processes, practices and the emerging collective organization strategy in the context of casual work at the port of Tema, Ghana's main industrial and port city.

Tema and casual gangs in retrospect The population of old Tema in 1937 was estimated to be a thousand inhabitants. By the close of 1959, when the construction of Tema Township and the port were in progress, the population had reached 10,000. The greater percentage of this figure was non-indigenes who had migrated to Tema either to work for the contractors as labourers or to trade with other workers (Amarteifio et al. 1966). The population distribution of the new migrants to old Tema in 1961 showed a preponderance of youthful male residents who apparently had moved to Tema to work on the construction projects. The old Tema Zongo, where the majority of the migrant workers lived, was characterized as predominantly inhabited by people from northern Ghana[4] (ibid.). Zongo is a multi-ethnic enclave common in many Ghanaian towns and cities. Each ethnic group appointed its own *Sarkin Zongo* (Zongo chief), and headmen. According to Amarteifio et al. (ibid.), until 1961 the headmen who came under the *Sarkin Zongo* wielded a lot of authority, and the major different ethnic groups that lived in Zongo tended to live close to their kinsmen. This social structure of ethnic enclaves organized around headmen crept into organizing unskilled labour (i.e. gangs), the majority of whom incidentally lived in old Tema Zongo. The site these migrant workers occupied in old Tema Zongo was demarcated for the new Tema Township development. However, the initial plan to resettle the indigenous people did not capture these migrants, so they had to be moved to Ashaiman, on the Accra–Ada road, 6 miles from Tema (ibid.). Ashaiman, which is today at the periphery of Tema, exhibits all the characteristics of a slum community: highly congested and displaying poor sanitary conditions. It also continues to serve as the source of a cheap labour supply for Tema.

Peil's (1969) study in Tema and its suburb, Ashaiman, revealed that as the major building projects were completed, and with the stagnation of the country's economy, the government and the private industries were not in a position to start new projects. This led to limited job openings, particularly for semi-skilled workers. The exception, according to Peil, was unskilled labour, which was highly utilized by the port. Her analysis indicated that unemployment was highest among middle school leavers. Peil's analysis of Tema unemployment in the late sixties complements other observations on the processes of informalization that occurred at the national level during the 1960s (Hart 1973; Ninsin 1991).

Most casual positions at Tema port, from the 1960s (Peil 1969) and until the early 2000s, were by statute required to be filled by the old Tema Labour Office, which was affiliated to the Ghana Ports and Harbours Authority (GPHA). Once recruited by the Labour Office, a casual worker was subsequently given a gang to work with. The gang consisted of the headman, the *regular casuals* and the *replacement casuals*. The regular casuals, whom the interviewees frequently referred to as *permanent casuals*, are those gang members who could regularly get a job offer and had worked at the port for quite a number of years. On the other hand, job allocations for replacement casual workers are highly irregular and unpredictable, even if their gang is offered a job. They represent a kind of buffer casual worker who, if a regular gang member fails to turn up for work, is called to replace the absentee worker. The drafting of new recruits into the gangs had to meet the approval of the headmen. New members were initially placed in the *replacement* category – their performances were monitored, sometimes for about three years, before admittance to regular membership. During this period the new entrant learned the tricks of the job under the tutelage of the headman. The criteria for progression were based on the new entrant's willingness to learn the tricks of the job and the *gang culture* – defined by the interviewed casual workers/headmen as consisting of hard work, discipline, honesty, brotherliness and above all respect for the headman. All these virtues, together with the three-year period required for regular status in the gang, ensured cohesion and restricted entry to reduce competition among the casual workers for job allocations. The gang system ensured the deployment of disciplined and hard-working casual workers for employers at the port. About twenty gang groups operated at the Tema Main Harbour. Their job involved mainly loading and unloading bagged cargo. Some of the gang members interviewed had regularly worked for the GPHA for more than fifteen years, yet they had no formal employment agreement with the authority.[5]

Similarly, gangs of casual workers are noted to be prevalent in Guinea-Bissau (Lourenço-Lindell 2002). According to Lourenço-Lindell, these groups of casual workers exhibit employment relations that are highly informal – the workers neither enjoy social security nor compensation for injuries picked up at the worksite. The gang groups are led by their headmen. These headmen, who in India are referred to as *Mukadams*, are brokers or mediators between employers and labour: 'They are the bosses of the work gangs [they ...] recruited [...] and maintain a powerful grip on the workers through their personal contacts with them (Streefkerk 2002: 142–3).

In the case of Tema, the headmen were not entrepreneurs in the sense of brokering for profit motives. Instead, they were leaders of the gang groups who by their positions as supervisors of the gangs earned higher wages than the other gang members. The headmanship position was attained through long years of working with a particular gang. The headmen were themselves casual workers whose major role was to supervise the other casual workers. They were responsible for distributing the tasks among the gang members. In addition, the headmen could recommend via the defunct Labour Office that a worker be recruited into the gang or fired. They had sole knowledge of any employment agreements between the workers and their employers and were responsible for effecting the payment of the daily wage of their gang members – no records of these were kept, and they often held meetings under trees to carry out their activities. The headmen's behaviour was not always impeccable. There were complaints that, by virtue of their sole knowledge of how much the employers paid the casual workers, the headmen could manipulate the daily wages, bonuses and allowances of their gangmen to their advantage. The concern that has been raised regarding this horizontal network of casual workers is whether they could be mentored to gain political strength in order to demand a bigger share of, or contest their exclusion from, the profits they help to create (Lourenço-Lindell 2002).

The employment relations between the casual workers and the employers have been altered following the emergence of the new labour agents at Tema port. At the same time, some of the casual workers have organized themselves into local unions and developed an alliance with the Maritime and Dockworkers Union of the Ghana Trades Union Congress. Both of these developments are discussed below.

The new labour agencies: GDLC and NFSA The Ghana Dock Labour Company (GDLC) is a private labour hire agency established in 2002 to recruit and manage casual port workers at the Tema Main Harbour. GDLC is owned by eight bodies consisting of the Ghana Ports and Harbours Authority (GPHA), the Maritime and Dockworkers Union (a majority shareholder) and six domestic and international private companies. Interestingly, the owners are at the same time the major clients of this labour hire agency. The GPHA, which regulates the port industry, chairs the board of the Ghana Dock Labour Company.

GDLC was established with the sole aim of recruiting and managing casual port workers at the Tema Main Harbour. The majority of the casual workers hired by GDLC came from the gangs of casual groups that were laid off by the GPHA. In May 2002, a number of casual workers, who formerly worked under the GPHA, embarked on a public protest to press the authority to pay them their 'severance benefits' (Ghanaian Chronicle 2002). In the wake of the demonstration, announcements were carried on local radio stations requesting individuals willing to work at the harbour to register with the GDLC. Most of the demonstrating casual workers, in fear of being deprived of their livelihood, ended up registering with the agency. The decision of the state regulatory body to lay off the casual workers, who were engaged regularly at the port for long periods of time, and the subsequent establishment of a private agency to manage such workers crudely resemble decentralized and indirect labour recruitment arrangements that have characterized public sector reforms in a number of developing countries.

The agency has a modern administrative set-up. Instead of the workers meeting under trees, the agency has constructed a big shed in which the casual workers sit and wait for job allocations. A television set is provided in the shed to kill boredom. When jobs become available, the gangs are called through loudspeakers. In spite of a modern outlook, the company has incorporated the old gang system in its operations, even though its internal dynamics have been altered. Under the agency the gang system still consists of the headman, regular and replacement casual workers. The gang is made up of either eight or thirteen casual workers, depending on whether the gang is *shore* or *on-board* respectively. GDLC has fifty-nine shore gangs and forty-five on-board gangs. In 2004 the agency could supply about 4,000 casual workers on demand during peak seasons but had about 2,500 active casual workers on its books and 150 casual workers on its replacement list. In 2006, it recruited about 1,000 new casual workers.

The National Fish Stevedore Association (NFSA) is another labour agency that has been operating at Tema port since 1999. In terms of the number of casual workers deployed, it is the second largest after GDLC in Tema. NFSA can deploy about six hundred casual workers for its operations daily. NFSA is an amalgam of seventeen contractors who hold contracts to handle frozen cargo at the Tema Fishing Harbour. Like GDLC, NFSA has adopted the gang system that has long existed at the port. Each contractor maintains a gang whose size varies depending on the volume of cargo that a contractor has to discharge. There are two categories of workers who constitute the gang; they are the core gang members and those that can be considered as an outlier to the gang. The core gang is akin to the gang group adopted and adapted by GDLC, and consists of the reliable old hands that have been working as casual workers at Tema fishing harbour for a decade. In times of shortage of men due to a high volume of cargo the headmen simply walk around and mobilize the *mango boys* (young men who sit idly under mango trees) to join them – these are the outliers. While the casual workers registered by GDLC are engaged in the loading and discharge of dry cargo (e.g. bags of rice, sugar, fertilizers) at the main harbour, NFSA operates at the fishing harbour, where the workers are mostly involved in the discharge of frozen cargo (e.g. frozen fish).

The agencies now perform the intermediary role of the headmen. The new role of the headmen, by virtue of their experience, includes training the new casual workers, who currently are frequently recruited into the gangs for short periods. The loss of the powerful supervisory role once performed by the headmen means loss of all the financial 'perks' that went with their previous role.

At Tema port, the relationship between the employers and casual workers enrolled by the agencies has become more distanced, but employers' control over the casual workers has not necessarily been reduced. The employers achieve this control through the hiring agency and the supervisors they appoint to monitor the casual workers to ensure that they work according to the required standards. The role of the supervisors on-site, if not to enforce work discipline, is not clear. The role performed by these supervisors is effectively performed by the headmen working with the agencies. Supervision at the work site, however, has become difficult because of the workers' understanding of the indirect relationship that exists between them and the employers. Peck (1996: 126) has indicated that while the flexible labour strategy favours 'some form of labour control [...] it simultaneously undermines supervision'. An employer who hires casual workers from GDLC had this to say:

> Supervision is becoming a bit difficult for us as the labour is coming from a different outfit. The casual workers we hire from the agency are insensitive to the plight of the company. For instance, previously we used to have what we called 'work to finish', that is, a situation where the workers stayed a little while and finished the small quantum of work that would have been left undone even though their twelve working hours would have elapsed – but these days as soon as they achieve their target, they leave the worksite irrespective of whatever quantity of work is left to be finished. This was not the case when we used to have our own regular casual workers.

An interviewed casual worker confirmed this impression:

> Until we were retrenched as casual workers none of us could have the urge to refuse to follow the foreman's instructions to perform certain jobs. I knew that

if I fail to clear whatever work I'm instructed to do and the foreman reports me to the operations manager, I would be in trouble. But now the casual workers know the companies hire them from dock labour so if they do not obey the instructions of the foreman or even insult him, he knows that the following day he would go to another company.

This does not suggest that the casual workers enrolled by the agency are completely out of the control of their employers. According to a headman:

Those days there were companies that when they came to look for casual workers, the workers would decline to follow them, there was nothing they could do to them. But now once the agency says you are going to work for, say, Company A, you can't protest, whether raining or shining. In those days the workers were free to choose whoever they wanted to work with. So at the end of the day it was the company that offered good working conditions that attracted the hard-working and the experienced workers.

Most of the casual workers interviewed also persistently complained about their dwindling incomes since they started working under the agencies. The general lack of formal employment for low-skilled workers in Ghana has led to the influx of workers into casual jobs. In addition to this, the ease of entry into the informal labour market has decreased the regularity of securing casual jobs in Tema. The entry into the informal labour market has become unrestricted as the screening process that new entrants had to go through under the old gang system has been removed. The agency operates an 'open-door' policy such that anybody who walks into its office to look for a casual job may immediately be given a place in the gang. This has led to the artificial creation of a large reserve of casual workers resulting in increased competition for jobs among the various categories of casual workers. Similarly, it has been observed in Bissau, Guinea-Bissau, where the conditions of casual workers are noted to be undergoing changes owing mainly to the increasing number of people embarking on casual work (Lourenço-Lindell 2002). For instance, GDLC has created 104 gang groups as compared with the twenty gangs that existed previously at Tema Main Harbour, and it is unlikely the agency will restrict entry by putting a ceiling on the number of casual workers it registers. The reason is that control over the labour process is derived from creating such excess labour, which is made possible by the teeming number of the unemployed who troop to the agency's premises to register. The statement below illustrates the sentiment expressed by a group of casual workers:

As I'm sitting here now, our gang has no allocation. You can come here and sit for the whole day without allocation. Previously we were about twenty gangs. Because of these foreigners [referring to the new casual workers that were recently enrolled by the agency, including non-Ghanaians] they have formed about forty-five gangs. The highest job allocation that one can get per week is about two. Formerly, if you wanted to work every day in the week, you could. But now they have opened their gate such that anyone who walks in looking for a job is registered immediately and [allocated] a gang. In fact, when I saw you come, I thought Ken was coming to register you as a tally clerk. [...] Here, when somebody comes today, they will give him a place. If another comes tomorrow they will register him. Because of that the number keeps on increasing and as a result it may take you about three to four days to get [an] allocation. [...] Those days we were not taking monthly salaries but at the end of the month, if nothing at all, my income altogether could be equated to someone who earns a monthly salary because I had several jobs. At my previous job, as a headman I was receiving about 60,000 cedis and the boys 40,000 cedis per day.

The health and safety issues of the casual workers interviewed are rarely catered for. The workers are barely provided with the necessary safety apparel such as helmets, gloves and safety boots, which are required to undertake the job they describe as very risky. The incidence of injuries suffered at the worksite was reported to be very high, with some of the injured workers maimed for life and two deaths reported in 2006. GDLC records showed that about 200 million cedis and 169 million cedis were paid as compensation to some of its casual workers who suffered serious injuries at the worksite in 2005 and 2006 respectively. GDLC implements the legislation on accident reporting and compensation once the Labour Department decides on the amount to be paid based on a medically determined level of incapacitation suffered by the injured worker.

The new labour agencies that have emerged in Tema resemble the description of labour subcontractors described by Jason and Wells (2007) as risk-takers and entrepreneurs operating with profit motives. The case of casual work in Tema is an evolution from gangs of casual workers led by headmen to labour subcontractors or agencies. These agencies had sought to formalize the management of casual workers and to ensure quick deployment of workers to the worksite to increase the turnaround time for loading and unloading of merchant ships. However, their operations are embedded in the old forms of organizing the gang groups. The close working interaction that existed between the gangs and their respective ultimate employers no longer exists under the agencies. At the same time the rate of securing casual jobs under the agencies has become highly irregular. The reason is that the entry barriers that were instituted by the old gang groups have been dismantled by the agencies, thus leading to increased competition for casual jobs with an impact on their incomes. The casual workers working with the agencies and those employed directly by their employers have formed local unions of casual workers with the aim of collectively protecting their interests against deplorable working conditions.

The alliance between MDU and the local unions: what are the benefits?

The casual workers under GDLC have formed a local union, which is affiliated to the Maritime and Dockworkers Union (MDU), called GDLC Non-permanent Workers of MDU. Most of the initial members of the local union, it was gathered in the field, were also members of the old gang groups (two executives of the local union still work as headmen) – in effect, the gang groups have evolved to become the local union. The mandate of the local union is to negotiate with the agency for better working conditions for its members and to support them materially in times of need. The executive positions of the union are elective ones. The union has recently built an office within the compound of the agency. The casual workers under the NFSA have also constituted themselves into a local union that is part of MDU; they refer to themselves as fish stevedores' casual workers. In addition, there are pockets of local unions of casual workers affiliated to the MDU, but unlike the GDLC and the NFSA, they are directly employed by most of the shipping companies.

The alliances between the MDU[6] and the local union of casual workers typify an organizational path whereby a national trade union reaches out to informal workers or informal workers take the initiative to develop an alliance with a national trade union. Jordhus-Lier (this volume) has made a similar observation regarding South Africa, where the Municipal Workers' Union seeks to confront labour downgrading at the workplace by reaching out to externalized workers who provide municipal services.

Each local union has one representative and one vote at the meetings of the National Executive Council, the highest decision-making body of the MDU. A central issue is whether this alliance can help to avert labour downgrading and determining the challenges involved. The following discussion looks, in particular, at the GDLC Non-permanent Workers of MDU, the largest, well-organized local union of casual workers in Tema, with active leadership that is well versed in unionism.

GDLC Non-permanent Workers of MDU derives its membership from the casual workers who register with GDLC. The elected officials of the local union are also casual workers who have been working at Tema Main Harbour for more than a decade. GDLC Non-permanent Workers of MDU holds a collective bargaining agreement which enables it to negotiate with the agency on conditions of employment for its members. The officials of the union claimed to have been indemnified under the collective bargaining agreement. The MDU has devolved the collective bargaining process to the leadership of the individual casual workers' unions. The effectiveness of the decentralization of collective bargaining, and whether or not the leadership of the casual workers' unions have the skills to negotiate with the employers, is still not clear.

There exists no written employment agreement between the workers and the agency; however, the interviewed workers showed a high level of awareness of what the agency expects from them. Again, unlike in their previous arrangements with the headmen, who were the only repository of any employment dealings with employers, the workers showed a good knowledge of the obligations of the agency towards them regarding wages and other benefits. This awareness is achieved through information transmitted through the gang and also through the effort of the local union. In particular, the GDLC local union occasionally puts on noticeboards figures for the basic daily wage, overtime rates and transport allowances to inform its members.

Some of the old casual workers who are aware of the legal provision under Labour Act 621, subsection 75(1), have consulted their lawyers to seek clarification with the agency on their behalf about their employment status with the agency under the act.[7] The biggest challenge, according to an official of the agency, is the implementation of this legal provision. The act covers temporary or casual workers, but as the official indicated, it would be difficult to bring temporary or casual workers employed through hire agencies under this act. The reason being that such workers are 'loosely in the books' of the agencies and are hired 'off the books' of the employers. In the view of this official, employers cannot be compelled to give permanent employment status to workers who are not on their books; neither can the hire agencies be compelled to do so since they do not regard themselves as offering employment to the casual workers but rather helping the workers to secure jobs.

In addition to being paid basic daily rates, some of the casual workers interviewed receive annual bonuses and transport allowances[8] – the exception being the NFSA and individual casual workers employed directly by the shipping merchants. GDLC pays the social security contributions and overtime allowances to the casual workers, in spite of the fact that there exist no written employment contracts between them. The agency workers are paid daily wages above the national minimum monthly wage.[9] These achievements are made possible through the active intervention of the local union in negotiating for improved wages and benefits. Even though the casual workers receive wages and fringe benefits that are comparable to those of some permanent employees, yet their work is based on the availability of jobs and as such is highly unstable.

Most of the casual workers interviewed had little confidence that their unions could negotiate for better wages and improvements in their working conditions. The role of the union is perceived by many of the casual workers as an avenue to seeking only material support in the face of dwindling incomes. While they admitted the practical challenges that the unions face, the interviewed officials of the local unions maintained that the conditions of the casual workers would have been worse in the absence of the local union or the mother union.

Interestingly, the MDU, which is the mother union of the casual workers, holds the majority share in, for instance, the Ghana Dock Labour Company. This raises the question of whether an alliance between local unions and the MDU can bring about improvements in the working conditions of the workers, given the conflict of interests found in the role of the MDU. However, some union officials maintained that the presence of two officers of the MDU on the board of the GDLC, by virtue of its being a shareholder, should be interpreted as a leverage point in the decision-making of the agency, and not just seen as 'aiding the exploitation of the casual workers'. The mother union seems to have been able to influence the decisions of the agency through its board membership and to mainstream the grievances of the casual workers in the decisions of the board to ensure that the interests of its members are protected. The following event, as narrated by an official of the GDLC Non-permanent Workers of MDU, illustrates how the support that the local unions enjoy from the national union has worked to protect the interests of the casual workers and to influence the decisions of a state agency:

> Recently the Internal Revenue Service (IRS) audited the books of GDLC and realised that a huge amount has gone into the wages of casual workers untaxed. They insisted the company pays the income tax arrears on the earnings of the casual workers from 2002 to 2004, which ran into about 3.7 billion cedis. Management, admitting this as an unlawful act, began to implement the IRS directive by deducting the arrears from the workers' wages. The national union called a board meeting to deliberate on the issue and in the end it was decided that the owners of the company [should bear] the income tax arrears. Following from this, the board immediately stopped management from implementing the unilateral decision to pass the tax arrears to the casual workers.

The union official continued:

> By law we are supposed to pay 15–20 per cent tax (national rate) on our earnings. The local union together with the national union waged a war on IRS and negotiated a fairer deal for our members, basing our argument on the circumstances of the casual workers. Instead of 15–20 per cent we are now paying 5 per cent and still negotiating with IRS to reduce the figure to 2 per cent or a complete waiver of taxes on the earnings of the casual workers. In fact IRS closed down the company to demand the payment of the income tax arrears. Again, the local union together with the national union and other stakeholders in the port industry prevailed on IRS to open the company's office and within two hours the office was opened. This attracted national attention and [was] hotly debated.

An article in a Ghanaian newspaper, *The Statesman*, confirmed how the MDU firmly positioned itself on the side of the casual workers in this event:

> The Maritime and Dockworkers Union has called on the Internal Revenue Service to waive the tax arrears being demanded from casual workers of the Ghana

Dock Labour Company, 'as payment of taxes on wages with retrospective effect is not feasible'. According to the Union the casual workers of GDLC were in the past exempted from paying income taxes because they were classified among the vulnerable class of workers with irregular incomes and poor conditions of service. In a resolution adopted at its 51st National Executive Council Session and signed by the General Secretary [...] the union could not understand why the 'poor workers' should be made to pay taxes on wages they had collected between 2003 and 2005 even though they started paying taxes on their wages from 2005. The resolution expressed the Union's readiness to support any action that will be embarked upon by its members 'if attempts are made to squeeze the tax arrears from our poor brothers and sisters. Our stand is based on the fact that the casual Dockers had earned slave wages and toiled at the expense of their health to make the maritime industry what it is today.' (Statesman 2007)

While the MDU used its leverage to cause the management to reverse its decision to pass on the arrears to the casual workers, it concurrently used its voice to demand that the IRS, a state institution, rescind its directive to the casual workers to pay income tax arrears on their wages.

The alliance between the local unions and the mother union is not without challenges. First, some of the small groups of casual workers complained about neglect from the mother union. In their view, the support of the national union tends to be mainly focused on addressing the grievances of the relatively large local unions. For these atomized groups resorting to strike action without the backing of the mother union remains a risky venture since their unprotected vocal leaders are often threatened with dismissal. Second, there are signs of a growing indifference to the activities of the unions owing mainly to the members' mistrust of and lack of confidence in their leadership in terms of addressing their grievances and needs. However, there was a hint that casual workers working for the Ghana Cocoa Marketing Company and unionized under the Industrial and Commercial Workers Union (ICU) were contemplating breaking away from the ICU and joining the MDU because in their view casual workers under the MDU are better off. The MDU faces competition for membership from a budding union operating independently of the Ghana Trade Union Congress, the National Union of Harbour Employees, which seeks to draw its membership from disenchanted members of the MDU.

Conclusion

This chapter has sought to understand how flexible labour strategies are giving way to new forms of collectively organizing casual workers in Tema. Flexible deployment of casual port workers in Tema is characterized by labour downgrading, but this process simultaneously and unwittingly prompts collective organizing by casual workers who are eager to seek change in their conditions of employment. Informal port workers in Tema have historically been organizing themselves, albeit in small networks in the form of labour gangs. The operations of the current labour agencies reveal more formalized management of casual workers at the port, yet the gang system that has long existed at the port provides the foundation for the modern operations of the labour agencies. Similarly, the gang groups under the agencies have been transformed into local unions of casual workers. The internal dynamics of the gangs, however, have been altered under the agencies, with varying effects on the working conditions of the workers. On one hand, informal work in Tema reflects global trends of flexibilization and informalization processes. On the other hand, these processes are shaped by local peculiarities derived from the historical context and position of the city in the global economy (Lourenço-Lindell 2002).

This new organizing strategy, entailing an alliance between local unions of casual workers and national unions, is a contested arena entailing a more complex web of actors than before, who influence the conditions of casual workers. The extent of representation of these actors, including government agencies, national trade unions and labour contractors, and the complexity of their varied interests and roles, has implications for negotiating working conditions.

The interest of the MDU in the labour agency, a profit-seeking entity, is clearly in contradiction to the role of national unions in seeking improvements in the working conditions of its members. However, this national union seems to have been able to effectively combine its profit-seeking motives with the protection of the interests of its members. Not only does it represent the concerns of the casual workers in the decisions of the private agency, it also uses its strong political voice to neutralize the adverse attitudes of state agencies towards the vulnerable casual workers. When the tax agency demanded that the casual workers pay tax arrears on their incomes it took the support of the national union to cause the state agency to rescind its decision. Such political manoeuvring is often beyond the capability of individual informal workers' unions. Through the alliance with the national union, the local union of the casual workers gained the necessary political status to influence their working conditions.

Change in the conditions of informal workers also depends on the level of involvement of the casual workers themselves or their representative groups in negotiating the conditions of employment, as well as their relative strengths or vulnerability. The smaller unions of casual workers lack visibility, and their grievances are rarely attended to by the national union, in contrast to the situation of the relatively larger unions of casual workers.

To protect the interest of the casual workers, building alliances with national unions still seems to be a viable option away from the path leading to labour downgrading, even though they often face potential exclusion. It requires of the strong groups, with which atomized informal workers' unions seek alliance, that they open up and mainstream the grievances and the concerns of the small informal groups. The challenge is how national unions, with which informal workers seek alliance, can be made to be responsive to the grievances of informal workers. What is the state of the institutional mechanisms adopted by national trade unions to mainstream and address the needs of local unions of informal workers? By answering this question we should then be able to understand the mechanisms required by national unions to become more responsive to the needs of informal workers. This question should be addressed using a much wider scope of sub-sector analysis of an alliance between informal workers' unions and national trade unions.

Acknowledgements

I wish to express my appreciation to the Department of Sociology and Human Geography of the University of Oslo, Norway, where the initial inspiration to study the informal economy was derived. Special thanks also go to Dr Ilda Lourenço-Lindell of the Nordic Africa Institute for her useful comments, which significantly shaped the focus of this chapter.

7 | Collective organization in Ghana

PART THREE

International dimensions of organizing

8 | The 'China challenge': the global dimensions of activism and the informal economy in Dakar

Suzanne Scheld

Introduction

Chinese traders are changing the dynamics of the informal economy in Dakar, Senegal. Chinese now operate 90 per cent of the shops in Gare Petersen, a small commercial centre built for Senegalese vendors who have no place to sell merchandise. In Allées du Centenaire, a neighbourhood within walking distance of Gare Petersen, Chinese merchants operate approximately two hundred new businesses. Homeowners of this former middle-class neighbourhood have added cement-block shops on to the façades of their homes. These unpainted, unadorned and dimly lit rooms are rented to Chinese merchants at high prices. From behind a barricade of showcases, the merchants sell fashion garments, shoes, handbags, toys and home decorations, among many other cheap, plastic goods from China.

Despite the rapid growth of Dakar's new 'Chinatown', commerce in Centenaire is loosely regulated. Taxes are collected from vendors; however, there are inconsistencies in the ways they are paid and the amounts that are charged. In addition, there is little oversight of street vending. The pavements are packed with Senegalese selling shoes and bags displayed on tables made of scrap wood and cardboard. Others display their merchandise on sheets spread on the ground. The number of street vendors makes it difficult to walk through Centenaire. Some question the usefulness of Senegalese street vending in the neighbourhood too. Since many of these vendors buy their merchandise from Chinese wholesalers, they create an over-abundance of similar-looking merchandise in the market. This diminishes the possibilities for Chinese and Senegalese retailers to make many sales.

Senegalese responses to the development of Chinese trading in Dakar vary. Street vendors support Chinese vending, but importers feel threatened by its growth, which is shrinking their market share. In 2008, importers who were members of the local traders' associations agreed to unify two separate associations in order to put the brakes on Chinese trading and enlarge the power of Senegalese traders in the informal economy.

Senegalese consumer protection associations are also divided. Some feel that Chinese trading liberates the informal economy by offering affordable products, which thereby enables more Senegalese to participate in the economy. Others however, criticize the quality of Chinese goods and argue that low-quality imports create dependency and disempower consumers. Consumer protection activists have not considered merging associations. In fact, differing views on Chinese trading have helped to clarify the separation of two associations that used to be one.

Chinese traders also have varying opinions about the conflict their arrival in Dakar has created. Some are sympathetic to Senegalese frustrations because they too have struggled to earn a living in a developing economy, and have experienced fierce market competition in China. Avoiding the competition, in fact, is one of the main reasons why traders leave China and trade in African countries. Others, however, embrace the principles of the free market and feel it is their right to challenge Senegalese traders wherever they are on the globe. These differing points of view, in addition to major cultural differences, contributed to a long-standing apathy towards organizing in Senegal. The murder of a Chinese trader in February 2009, however, persuaded many to put aside their differences and form a new Chinese business association in Dakar.

The merging, splitting and formation of new groups raises the question: what forces shape patterns of organizing in Dakar's informal economy? Given the arrival of Asian global traders, to what extent are groups in Dakar's informal economy relying on global resources to respond to Chinese trading? I explore this question through a case study of collective organizing in Dakar's informal economy, where it is revealed that some associations rely on international resources to stake claims to the local informal economy, while others focus on resources within Dakar. At first glance, these developments seem surprising. To begin with, it is surprising that Chinese traders are migrating to work in the informal economy of this developing city. It is also surprising to have spontaneously turned on my television in LA, to find a local Senegalese consumer activist being interviewed on CNN regarding Chinese trading in Dakar. To what extent are groups in Dakar seeking international exposure and using global connections to affect change in the informal economy?

I examine these developments in the context of the historical development of informality and collective organizing in the informal economy in Dakar. A comparison with the past suggests that the global dimensions of Dakar's informal economy are not new. Traders from the south have shaped the informal economy and its central associations for decades. The globalized strategies used by today's associations are a natural development that results from Dakar's long-standing embeddedness within globalization. The localized strategies of some Dakar associations highlight the fact that although free market trade intensifies conflicts, new possibilities for organizing can be found in the informal economy. Some groups look 'inward', or within Senegal, for these solutions. Others look 'outward', or to global resources. Collective organizing in the African informal economy is therefore not confined to the city and state, nor is it dependent upon global forces for its development. Acknowledging the mix of local and global organizing strategies in Dakar encourages researchers to revisit long-standing assumptions about informal economies and collective organizing, such as the notion that the informal economy is a bounded and provincial space. It also fosters an appreciation of collective organizing as a significant tie by which Africans shape and are shaped by globalization.

Organizing in the bounded and local informal economy

The informal economy was once conceived as a particular trait of developing countries. It is now, however, observed in cities in the North and South (Castells and Portes 1989; Rakowski 1994; Hansen and Vaa 2004; Cross 1998a; Roy and Alsayyad 2004), and acknowledged as a site of significant political organizing (Hill 2001; Gallin 2004). Although informal economies are acknowledged as being present across the globe, studies rarely examine them in relation to processes of globalization. As a result, the processes of organizing in informal economies are poorly understood.

The paucity of works exploring global dimensions to organizing in informal economies may be attributed to a long-standing assumption that the informal economy is a small and bounded 'sector' set within a broader 'formal' economic space. For example, studies that examine the struggles of street vendors see them as actors who are pushed or left out of the formal economy (Castells and Portes 1989; Cross and Morales 2007b). In these cases, the informal economy is framed as a safety net that catches small-scale economic operators who do not have the capital or social networks to operate viable businesses in the formal economy. Or, it is viewed as a reserve of labourers in need of training before joining the sophisticated and skilled workforce of the formal economy. Either way, the informal economy is a sub-space of a greater economic arena. It comes across as bounded, inferior and dependent upon the formal economy. This view diverts attention away from the intrinsic dynamism of informal economies and the possibility that their political and economic activities are fuelled by forces beyond the local.

The bounded view of informal economies, especially those in the South, is reinforced in applied studies that aim to advise governments on how to work with activists and other stakeholders. In these studies from the development field, the informal economy is approached as a space that is defined by the perimeters and authorities of a city or nation-state structure (Blunch et al. 2001; Loayza 1994). This view makes the informal economy appear as a local space that, apart from commodity chains, has a limited relationship to globalization. Ironically, many of these studies are produced by the World Bank, a supranational organization that plays a large role in shaping informality in the South. The World Bank's role in these processes is not often critically reflected upon in reports. Instead, it is framed as part of a backdrop to an ongoing play of contentious interactions among 'locals'. Framed as indirectly relevant to the informal economy, the global dimensions of informal economies are obscured in these studies. New studies are beginning to redirect attention to the ways in which supranational organizations are in fact agents of informal economies. Ilda Lindell (2009a) illuminates this in her study of StreetNet in Maputo, Mozambique. She illustrates how this supranational organization shapes and is shaped by Maputo vendors, and persuades readers that a global framework is necessary for analysing the complexity of collective organizing in African informal economies.

The relevance of globalization to understandings of organizing in informal economies is further underestimated in studies that assume that informal economy actors are a culturally homogeneous group. Studies of transnational migration have done much to reinforce this idea about informal economies of the South. First, they tend to narrow the characteristics of transmigrants in general by describing them as 'urban' or 'rural' labourers prior to transmigration. These descriptors obscure other economic contexts that may be more relevant to characterizing transnational migrants and their labour experience, such as the notion that labourers derive a particular knowledge from working and organizing in informal economies.

Second, studies tend to overemphasize how the politics of the cities of the North are enriched by the arrival of culturally diverse labourers from the South (Sassen 1998; Kasinitz et al. 2004; Marwell 2004). In this framework, the South-to-South supply of labourers is overlooked, in addition to the reality that politics in these cities is shaped by culturally diverse groups with international experiences. De-emphasizing the significance of South-to-South migrations, in effect, diverts attention away from the full range of global processes that shape informal economies of the South and their political interactions. It renders informal economies of the South as provincial places where only 'locals' interact with one another.

The picture of Dakar that I convey defies the notion that the informal economy is a bounded and culturally homogeneous place, and the idea that political organizing in Africa is a localized phenomenon. It highlights the informal economy's long-standing relationships with globalization, its cultural diversity, and the mix of global and local strategies that are taken up by associations in the informal economy. My analysis is based on ethnographic data collected during field stays in 2005, 2006 and 2009. My data includes six one-hour open-ended interviews with key leaders of Senegalese trader and consumer protection associations, and leaders of the Chinese business associations in Dakar. Thirty briefer interviews were conducted with Senegalese traders and interested individuals who are outspoken on the topic of consumerism. Fifty-three interviews were conducted with Chinese traders.

I adopted an open-ended approach to interviewing which is consistent with traditional qualitative anthropological methods. The topics of conversation included histories of organizing, perceptions of associations in Dakar and the Senegalese government, expectations of and adaptations to the informalization of Dakar, general views on globalization and economic liberalization, and views on Chinese and Senegalese traders in Dakar and abroad.

I conducted most of my key interviews in my informants' offices and in restaurants near their offices. Chinese and Senegalese traders were predominantly interviewed in their shops and in the streets. Most of the interviewes with Senegalese were tape-recorded and transcribed by trained university students in Dakar. Most Chinese participants refused to be recorded. In these cases, I took handwritten notes.

All of the interviews with Senegalese were conducted in Wolof (the lingua franca of Senegal) and French. Although I speak these languages, I was assisted during my interviews by a native speaker of Wolof. Interviews with Chinese traders were mostly conducted in Mandarin by a research assistant from China. Mandarin was not always the first language of many of these traders; however, most could communicate effectively in Mandarin. A few Chinese participants were interviewed in combinations of English and Mandarin, or French and Wolof. This occurred because some traders were fluent in these languages and wanted to accommodate the research team. In sum, the fact that fieldwork involved multiple languages and cultural expertise from various parts of the world highlights the globalized nature of Dakar's informal economy. In effect, a globalized approach to fieldwork was required in order to view the global dimensions of Dakar's informal economy.

Informalizing, nationalizing and globalizing Dakar

In order to demonstrate the mix of strategies that contemporary associations employ in Dakar's informal economy, it is necessary to draw a picture of the development of informality and political organizing over time. Within this picture, I highlight the fact that informality in Dakar did not develop in a vacuum. Local and global forces shaped its development as an economic space. It is therefore not surprising that a mixture of local and global resources shape political actions in the informal economy.

I also highlight how the informal economy in Dakar has become a highly divided and contentious space. The divisions that have developed since the colonial period contribute to the drive for today's activists to look in all directions for resources to support their organizing efforts. Thus, some associations seek to connect with an international audience, while others seek to renew relationships in Dakar as a means to strengthen their position in the informal economy.

Informality and organizing in the colonial period During the colonial period, Senegal's formal economy was largely defined by the groundnut trade and controlled by French entrepreneurs. Africans coped with two forms of domination, though, because Lebanese immigrant traders also controlled a sector of the groundnut industry. After the First World War, when a French mandate was established in the Levant, Lebanese migrated to Senegal in large numbers. They worked as *traitants* (middlemen) in the groundnut trade, transporting produce from farmers in their fields to local trading centres. They were enthusiastic about their role because many came from underdeveloped regions in the Levant. They saw Senegal as the land of opportunity since at the time it was the centre of the Federation of French West Africa, and was growing in prosperity. Their strategies for working with farmers were successful too. In addition to buying groundnuts from farmers, they sold bicycles, farm tools and other consumer goods on extended credit, which was established on an informal basis (Cruise O'Brien 1975: 100). Their knowledge of how to exploit informal networks, therefore, allowed Lebanese traders to develop a competitive edge over Africans in the groundnut economy. It also contributed to creating cultural delineations within Senegal's economies. As Lebanese had frequent contact with French trading houses in Dakar, their activities intersected with Senegal's marketing board, tax system and other regulated aspects of the groundnut economy. Africans in Dakar, in contrast, were increasingly pushed to the margins as they were relegated to performing low-paying, informal, service-sector work.

During this time, Lebanese attempted to balance a desire to excel in trade with their sympathy for colonized Africans. They sought to convey their solidarity with Africans by constructing mosques, schools and hospitals in Dakar, and by providing other forms of charity and assistance (Boumedouha 1990: 538–40). These acts helped to temper conflicts between Africans and Lebanese; however, they did not overcome all Senegalese ambivalence towards the Lebanese. In the 1920s, Senegalese who did not embrace Lebanese trading referred to it as 'the Lebanese menace' and the 'Libano-Syrian invasion'. Others who welcomed the Lebanese in Senegal, however, were compelled to combat their exclusion from Senegal. The Syndicat Coopératif Économique du Sénégal (SCES) was formed in the 1920s to challenge the negative views of the Lebanese in Senegal (Cruise O'Brien 1975: 102). Lebanese traders attempted to organize as well. In 1926, the Comité Libano-Syrien was formed to combat anti-Lebanese propaganda in Senegal. The organization, however, did not last long owing to internal conflict (ibid.: 102).

Informality and organizing after independence After independence, the Senegalese government took control of a significant portion of the formal commercial sector. This led to the spread of informality in Dakar, the creation of additional cultural hierarchies, and new conflicts that prompted groups to organize. When the French were forced to leave, Lebanese traders were better positioned than Africans to acquire French businesses. This immediately increased their access to wealth, although it did not increase their control over trade. The Senegalese government assumed full control over the groundnut trade, and sought to empower Africans by selectively relaxing certain regulations. For example, Africans who were aligned with Léopold Sédar Senghor in the presidential elections were handed free licences to work in profitable import-export networks. They were awarded business loans and means to circumvent taxes (Thioub et al. 1998: 65–7). In addition, Senghor obliged foreign businesses to accept informal Senegalese truckers to transport their groundnuts. This gave informal African transporters new opportunities in state-controlled sectors of the groundnut trade. In short, the nationalization of the groundnut economy in the 1960s reorganized economic relations in Senegal. It legitimized informal labour, and contributed to blurring the boundaries between the formal and informal economy. What is more, it introduced new divisions of power among Africans and between Africans and Lebanese (ibid.: 65–9).

These new divisions intensified conflicts and gave rise to new organizing efforts. Under the 'Senegalization' of the economy, the government did little to promote private businesses. Thus, Senegalese businessmen who were frustrated by ongoing competition with Lebanese traders and the government's laissez-faire attitude formed the Union of Senegalese Economic Groups (Union des Groupements Économiques du Sénégal; UNIGES). The government attempted to diminish the union's voice by creating a rival organization, the Federal Council of Senegalese Economic Groups (Conseil Fédéral des Groupements Economiques du Sénégal; COFEGES). Eventually, the government responded to UNIGES and gave more credit to Senegalese businessmen. As a result, Lebanese traders were forced to abandon their role in the agricultural trade and shift to urban activities such as transporting gas, groundnut shelling, real estate, fast-food restaurants and bakeries, and importing goods that Senegalese traders were not well positioned to obtain (e.g. building materials, textiles, soaps, perfumes and beauty care products) (Gellar 1982: 34; Boumedouha 1990).

Lebanese traders recognized their loss of power in Senegal and organized to protect themselves. This gave rise to the Groupement Professionnel des Commerçants et Industriels Libanais du Sénégal, an association that formed in 1969. This was yet another short-lived experiment, however (ibid.: 540). The repeated failures of Lebanese traders to organize highlight how different groups in Dakar negotiate their rights to the economy using a variety of strategies. A traditional political, occupation-based association was not a significant structure for unifying Lebanese. Informal networks within religious communities (both Islamic and Maronite Catholic) and affiliations with wealthy families involved in party politics were more effective strategies for organizing among the Lebanese during this time (ibid.).

Post-post-colonial informality and organizing In the 1970s informality in Dakar steadily spread as contraband in Senegal increased. The government did little to control contraband, and its toleration looked like an indirect strategy for giving poor traders a means to make a living during economic recession. Researchers have noted a similar pattern in other African states (MacGaffey 1987; Meagher 2003). The government's laissez-faire approach to contraband, however, may also have been a strategy to strengthen the regime's political power (Boumedouha 1990). For example, wealthy informal traders who benefited from loose border policies were thereafter obliged to renew their commitment to maintaining the status quo in Senegal (Thioub et al. 1998: 70). Either way, the state capitalized on economic shifts and strategic alliances in the informal economy to develop its power.

In the late 1980s and early 1990s, informality in Dakar spiked significantly. During this time, the World Bank began to view the rise in contraband in countries across Africa as a failure of state power (Meagher 2003). The Bank then recommended that African nations implement structural adjustment programmes (SAPs), a set of economic reforms designed to help gain control over the economy, including controlling contraband and excessive government spending, as well as other economic 'weaknesses'. SAPs required governments to downsize, open borders and implement currency devaluations. In 1983, Adbou Diouf, Senegal's second president, implemented the first round of SAP reforms. He permitted an overall downsizing of government, the opening of borders to foreign businesses, and currency devaluation. Instead of alleviating the economic recession, however, currency devaluations drove the price of rice and sugar up by 500 per cent over what it had been in 1965 (Sommerville 1991: 156). This intensified the spread of informality in Dakar because with increased expenses and no work opportunities to help people make ends meet, increasingly Dakarois sought their livelihoods in the informal economy. And, with the government's limited ability to provide basic infrastructure and amenities, Dakarois picked up the slack by creating their own systems of transportation, construction, education and waste management. The concept of eking out a living through informal labour became so central in Dakar that by the 1990s a host of street expressions in Wolof were created to refer to this lifestyle. People speak of *duggu ak gënn* (poking in and out of a hole, or peeking around in search of work), *goor goorlu* ('just try hard!'; 'be the man'), and working like a *houselman* (scratching and pecking at the ground like a chicken).

Lebanese power in Dakar further diminished in this period. This was due, in part, to the shrinking size of the community in Dakar. In fact, by the 1980s most 'Lebanese' in Dakar were actually Senegalese citizens who were either born in Senegal (thereby qualifying for citizenship), or were naturalized when the Senegalese government declared that all foreigners must become citizens or leave the country. This mandate was created in response to Lebanese traders returning to the Middle East after the civil war without paying off their debts in Senegal (Boumedouha 1990). Well-to-do Lebanese easily qualified as new Senegalese citizens because they could demonstrate a long-standing financial commitment to the state, whereas petty traders with informal accounting could not and thus were forced to leave. In effect, the move to incorporate Lebanese within the nation created new divisions among Lebanese traders, and pushed small-scale traders into the margins of the informal economy.

Changes in the global economy also contributed to Lebanese traders' loss of power in Dakar. In the 1980s, production regimes for beauty products, textiles and other goods controlled by Lebanese became more 'flexible' in the 'global factory', and the products more affordable for Senegalese traders to obtain and distribute. Eventually, with wealth accumulated through transnational migration to Europe, the USA and other places (Carter 1997; Mboup 2000; Perry 1997), Senegalese traders were able to take control of some of these markets, relegating traders of Lebanese descent to fewer areas of the economy. Scholars have closely documented how Mouride religious organizations have played an important role in giving rise to African trading in Dakar's informal economy (Ebin 1995; Diouf 1999; Perry 1997; Buggenhagen 2003). This again highlights how groups in Dakar's informal economy have not always accessed power through formal political organizing. The role of transnational migration in shifting power among traders also highlights how interactions in Dakar's informal economy are shaped by global forces.

Contemporary Dakar Today, Dakar is a prime example of the failure of neoliberal economic policies to make large improvements in the urban economy. Open pavements designed for strolling have become crowded sites of unregulated petty commerce. Contraband enters Dakar in massive quantities in suitcases at the international airport and containers at the seaport. In the city streets, larger groups of children than ever before rush out into traffic to sell goods. According to statistics, 20 to 25 per cent of households in Dakar live below the poverty line (Soumaré 2002: 262). The majority of urbanites still live in dirty and under-resourced neighbourhoods where blackouts and breaks in the water supply are frequent, and the municipality's rubbish collection is poorly organized. For many, life is difficult in Dakar. But Dakarois do not sit by passively waiting for change. Social groups seek new niches within the informal economy. For example, young women join men at traffic intersections to sell newspapers and in artisan mechanic shops to fix cars. Young men join women to fry doughnuts on street corners, and to be employed as tailors in women-owned artisan workshops. Now Chinese traders are contributing social and cultural diversity to Dakar's informal economy. The multiculturalism developing in Dakar, however, has been a new source of conflict, and not societal enrichment. This situation calls to mind research on street vending in Zambia by Karen Tranberg Hansen.

She contends that 'free market' trade is intensifying conflicts and disrupting alliances in the informal economy (Hansen 2004: 64). The informal economy has become a more contentious place than in the past. Indeed, in Dakar conflict has increased with the arrival of Chinese trading, and some groups have broken off alliances with one another owing to differing views on the situation. As I demonstrate below, however, although there are new divisions in the informal economy, new alliances are also forming. Let us now turn to examine patterns in the organizing strategies of associations in Dakar's informal economy, and their local and global dimensions.

Responses and strategies: traders, consumers and Chinese immigrants

I analyse three categories of associations that are currently organizing in response to Chinese trading in Dakar's informal economy. These include Senegalese trader associations, Senegalese consumer protection associations and Chinese business associations.

Senegalese traders' associations Before the controversy over Chinese trading developed in Dakar, there were two Senegalese traders' associations that dominated the informal economy: UNACOIS (L'Union Nationale des Commerçants et Industriels du Sénégal) and UNACOIS-DEFS (L'Union Nationale des Commerçants et Industriels pour le Développement Économique et Financier du Sénégal). UNACOIS was created in 1990 to specifically protect the *Baol-Baol* trader. *Baol-Baol* literally means in Wolof 'from the region of Baol'. This region of Senegal is not highly urbanized, and generates many small-scale Mouride traders who, despite their rural roots, are known to be savvy and street smart when it comes to business in the city.

Because the informal economy in Dakar is so large, the association easily acquired many members and rapidly became very powerful. As an example of its power, in 1996 UNACOIS organized *Opération villes mortes* (Operation dead towns), a strike which shut down Dakar and a few other towns in response to the government's proposal to apply the value-added tax to informal economy commerce (Thioub et al. 1998: 78–9). It also successfully challenged the government's monopoly over the trade of imported rice in the mid-1990s. These successes earned the association the reputation of a militant labour union, even though on paper it was defined as a 'business association'.

Over time, the association lost its radical edge. While it developed a prominent voice within Dakar's Chamber of Commerce it also deepened its ties and commitments to the government. Meanwhile, it enhanced its image as a modern business association as it focused on developing tools that would enhance credit opportunities and address insurance needs, instead of critiquing the conditions of the informal economy and the government's responsibility for its condition.

The radical image of the association was also diminished by the internal hierarchy of the association. UNACOIS comprised major Senegalese rice importers and other well-to-do transnational traders in addition to small-scale operators. Policies and projects tended to address the needs of the wealthier entrepreneurs, and not traders with limited capital.

Eventually, divisions within UNACOIS became so great that a faction of the association broke off to develop UNACOIS-DEFS. This second association purported to be more focused on the needs of the 'traditional' trader of Dakar's informal economy. For example, in 2005 the association was threatening to close down business in Sandaga, Dakar's main market. The market hall, built in 1933, is in desperate need of repair, and as the city has developed around it, it has become a major obstacle to the circulation of traffic. The government plans to knock down the market hall, which would thereby displace Sandaga traders. According to Moustapha Diop, the leader of UNACOIS-DEFS in 2005, the government was making no promise to relocate traders or to address the fact that many would lose business and have increased expenses if they had to move out of Sandaga. In the meantime, Chinese traders were rapidly moving into newly built commercial spaces in the city because they could afford the rent. In Diop's view, the only thing left to do was shut down the city in protest against the government's neglect of small-scale Senegalese traders.

UNACOIS-DEFS never implemented this action, however. Instead, in 2007 UNACOIS and UNACOIS-DEFS negotiated their reunification in a new association called UNACOIS-Jappo (In Wolof, *Jappo* means 'togetherness'). The reunion was announced in Centenaire, and this spot was strategically chosen to symbolically signal that UNACOIS-Jappo traders planned to take back Dakar. In this light, the merger of traders' associations represented the re-radicalization of organizing among Senegalese traders in Dakar's informal economy.

As an association with a dual identity (e.g. at times a militant union, at other times a conservative business association), UNACOIS has been able to attract international attention and receive support from a broad range of global organizations. It has worked with liberal groups such as StreetNet and the International Labour Organization, and conservative business groups such as the Centre for International Private Enterprises (affiliated with the US Chamber of Commerce). Its greatest source of power, however, appears to derive from Senegal and the combination of two groups' members and resources. In this light, although the informal economy is becoming more deeply embedded within globalization, it is also producing new and unexpected forms of local alliances. That said, it remains to be seen whether UNACOIS-Jappo can return to organizing union-like activities within the context of a business association. Members continue to reflect the mixture of well-to-do transnationals, small-scale transnationals and small-scale traders who never leave Senegal. Thus, resources may not be evenly distributed within the association, and new divisions may develop in turn.

Consumer protection associations The landscape of consumer protection associations in Dakar is slightly different from that of trading associations in that there are many small associations which organize in response to specific consumer/environmental issues (e.g. the quality of food and water contamination). ASCOSEN (L'Association des Consommateurs du Sénégal), however, is the most comprehensive association in Dakar. It seeks to educate consumers on a broad range of issues including problems associated with the quality of imported food and local water, and the rising cost of bread and the impact of taxes, among other issues. It is the oldest of the consumer protection associations, founded in 1990, and arguably the one that is most influential in the city. Evidence of its influence is evidenced by it being one of the few associations to have its own television programme aimed at educating consumers. In fact, the government anticipated that the television show, *Nay Leer* (translated from Wolof this means: 'It Has to be Transparent'), would rile the population and therefore did not permit it to air. After the association pursued the project for many years, *Nay Leer* eventually aired. The association's power is also evident in its increased ability to organize successful protests, such as the protest against the rising cost of living in Dakar in 2008, and the boycott against the RUTEL tax (*Redevance d'Utilisation de Télécommunications*), a 2 per cent tax on telecommunication products, in February 2009. These protests generated a lot of interest in Dakar because reports of them landed on YouTube. Many have access to the Internet in Dakar, thus YouTube has proved to be a successful means of politicizing consumer protection issues 'at home' while reaching out to an international community.

Like UNACOIS, ASCOSEN was a divided association before the arrival of Chinese trading. Differing visions of a consumer protection association prompted Massokhna Kane to leave ASCOSEN and found SOS Consommateurs, a group that is well known for its lawsuit against a sugar manufacturer in Senegal for raising its prices without justification. Differing views on Chinese traders in Dakar, in other words, deepened conflicts between consumer groups, and contributed to clarifying distinctions between two groups. For example, the associations' differences became clear in a live debate on national radio. Kane argued that Chinese traders take away jobs from Senegalese and dupe consumers by selling them poor-quality goods. In addition, Chinese traders live in 'ethnic enclaves', which does not lead to them patronizing Senegalese shops and integrating within the broader society. In effect, SOS's position on Chinese trading aligned the association with UNACOIS, an association that does not normally take the views of consumers into consideration.

Mohammed Ndao, the leader of ASCOSEN, vigorously argued in support of Chinese trading. He suggested that Chinese trading liberates the cost of goods in the market and provides consumers with choices. Those who criticize the legality of Chinese trading practices overlook the reality that Senegalese traders also benefit from the tolerance of extralegal practices. Ndao also asserted that associations against Chinese trading are xenophobic. He argued that it is contradictory to expect Senegalese in diaspora to be accommodated in guest countries while efforts are being made to exclude Chinese immigrants in Senegal. To advance this point, in 2005 ASCOSEN organized a march against racism towards Chinese traders in Dakar.

Unlike the UNACOIS associations in the past and present, the consumer protection associations tend to be extremely small-scale operations. They tend to project, however, an international image, owing to their organizing strategies. ASCOSEN, for example, seems like a well-funded and well-connected organization because news reports of ASCOSEN appear on CNN. Ndao frequently participates in consumer activist conferences in Europe, and in other parts of Africa. Many members of the association are Senegalese in diaspora in France, other parts of Europe, Canada and the USA. And many non-Senegalese intellectuals and activists support ASCOSEN. They are kept apprised of goings-on in the association through frequent email announcements.

Despite this image of an association that is linked to a variety of international communities, ASCOSEN is nearly a one-man show. The association has limited funding. Essentially, friends donate funds as needs arise. Members rarely attend meetings; thus, planning and strategizing are often accomplished through informal meetings. This is not to discredit ASCOSEN and to suggest that it is a shell association that serves Ndao's personal interests. Marc Edelman (2008) documents the rise of such associations in Costa Rica, where setting up and directing an association is an entrepreneurial strategy for individuals to generate a source of income in an economy with high unemployment. Rather, it is to highlight how ASCOSEN's image and power in Dakar's informal economy are fuelled by engagement with an international audience. Virtual power has become a significant element in the organizing strategies of small associations in Dakar's informal economy.

Chinese business associations Chinese have been living and working in Dakar for at least two decades; however, the community has increased in size since 2000. According to my conversations with Chinese leaders, there are approximately eight hundred to a thousand Chinese now living in Dakar.

The Chinese in Dakar are culturally and socially diverse. They are from various regions of China, including traditional trading centres such as Wenzhou, Shanghai and Hong Kong, and underdeveloped areas such as Henan and Hubei. These patterns resonate to an extent with findings reported in other studies of Chinese in Dakar and in Praia, the capital of Cape Verde, which is off the coast of Senegal (Bredeloup and Bertoncello 2006; Haugen and Carling 2005).

In addition to being culturally diverse, the community is socially diverse. Traders are recent college graduates (men and women), young couples with infants, married and unmarried middle-aged adults, elders who left farm work to help their children in Dakar, and elders who have worked in Dakar for over fifteen years and who have plans to retire in the homes of their children in Australia, France, the USA and other parts of the Chinese diaspora. The structure of their work in Dakar varies too. Individuals work as independent entrepreneurs who lease their own shops, import and sell their own merchandise. A number are employees of other small-scale Chinese importers. They sell merchandise, watch the shop during the boss's business trips to China, supervise Senegalese employees who are hired to communicate with customers, and some assemble merchandise. Yet others are employees of large Chinese transnational textile and footwear companies. Often in these cases vendors have worked in other African cities such as Banjul and Casablanca. Most of the individuals who work for larger transnational companies are men. Indeed, I found many women who sold their own merchandise in Dakar. Many women, however, migrated to Dakar to help their husbands.

The social and cultural diversity of Chinese traders in Dakar has been a factor in preventing traders from organizing. According to traders, there have been numerous attempts to develop business associations, but most efforts failed because groups were formed for certain classes of people, or dominated by particular cultural groups. Moreover, many traders see other Chinese traders rather than Senegalese traders as their primary source of competition. Therefore, they have no interest in participating in a group consisting of rivals.

In 2009, Chinese traders' attitudes towards organizing in Dakar changed, however, after the third murder of a Chinese national since 2003. Again it did not appear that the authorities would do much to find the perpetrators. Talk of creating a business association for small-scale Chinese vendors had already been under way, but this event became the tipping point that compelled many to join a new association, the 'Chinese Business Association of Senegal'. Among its first activities, the association arranged for the shut-down of businesses in Centenaire for three days in protest at the murder. A number of Senegalese traders in Centenaire also closed their shops in solidarity.

An additional factor that made it possible for traders to organize relates to the identity of the association's leader, George Qian. George was born in China, and migrated to the USA as a teenager. He eventually became an American citizen and attended a prestigious private school in the United States. George recently relocated to Dakar in order to open a small manufacturing business. His interest in opening a business in Senegal was fostered by Senegalese friends who live and work in the United States. Transnational links, in other words, made it possible for an activist to emerge in the Chinese community in Dakar.

George's dual identity as both a 'local' and a 'global' member of the immigrant community inspires participation in the Chinese business association among a broad range of people. For many traders, he is viewed as a local because of his birthplace, language and immigrant experiences. By others, he is viewed as a 'global' individual because of his American education, ability to speak English and relationships with Senegalese who have insider knowledge of Senegalese commercial laws and bureaucracy. George's rich and complex identity enabled many to identify with him and to see the value of organizing the community. In this light, knowing how to manipulate a mixed global/local identity is a useful strategy for organizing, and can be adapted in many ways in the context of an informal economy where actors are culturally and socially diverse, and resources are scarce.

Reflections on organizing in the informal economy

Several points about informal economies and collective organizing may be made from the case above. First, Dakar's informal economy reflects patterns commonly associated with globalization processes. For example, market liberalization has accelerated the informalization of Dakar and engendered the social and cultural diversification of actors in the informal economy. Today's informal economy is comprised of Chinese traders, a broader range of rural entrants, youth, and men and women who cross gender boundaries in the informal economy in order to make ends meet. In addition, new groups of activists – consumer advocates – are emerging on to the scene. Diverse actors and their new roles in the informal economy, therefore, reflect the outcomes of a host of contemporary globalization phenomena, including neoliberalism and its open-border policies, the intensification of informalization, and the formidable impact of international politics on 'local' urban space, among other processes.

Contemporary market liberalization creates new opportunities and conflicts in the informal economy. The arrival of Chinese traders has provided economically marginalized youth with a new source of employment, and economically marginalized consumers with an opportunity to participate in the economy. It has also created a moment for rival trader associations to reconcile and join forces. At the same time, Chinese trading has created a new competition for local merchants. This has resulted in the emergence of a discourse of belonging and intense 'Otherizing'. It has stirred new conflicts between Senegalese producers and consumers, and created divides among different consumer protection associations presumably working for the same cause.

Second, just as the forces of globalization are beginning to have an impact on Dakar's informal economy, local actors are engaging global connections to increase their power. As a result, local actors make the informal economy an arena of globalized social interactions. For example, the trader associations in Dakar discuss the insecurities in the informal economy with international organizations and seek funding from these organizations for projects to address these issues. Transnational members support the organizations financially as well as keeping members of the diaspora informed of the associations' work. Consumer protection associations organize protests against racism and broadcast their campaigns on international television. The Internet is a primary tool of communication and community-building within consumer protection organizations, and it is used specifically to reach out to interested parties, many of whom live outside of Africa and who are not Senegalese.

The developments point to the extent to which Dakar's informal economy is deeply embedded within global networks. The international trajectories of commodities have been a primary means for appreciating the global reach of informal economies. However, in the case of Dakar, and in the context of controversy created by Chinese trading, collective organizing is yet another domain through which the informal economy's global links are mediated. Given the history of Dakar's engagement with global networks, it comes as no surprise that the groups representing actors in the informal economy employ global resources to reach their goals. Local actors call on the forces of globalization for empowerment just as the forces of globalization create and exacerbate the inequalities and insecurities that call activists to collective action. The 'China Challenge' in Dakar, therefore, illuminates several ways of appreciating the global dimensions of an informal economy. It provides a poignant example of the ironic consequences of globalization, and allows us to rethink the assumptions about the nature of the informal economy, its actors and their organizing strategies.

Acknowledgement

I wish to thank Lydia Siu for assisting me with fieldwork in Dakar in 2009.

9 | Passport, please: the Cross-Border Traders Association in Zambia

Wilma S. Nchito and Karen Tranberg Hansen

Introduction

As new waves of informalization entangle urban economies in far-flung commodity circuits that expose them to global market forces, many regional distinctions in the level and intensity of market associational and organizational activity are disappearing. The Cross-Border Traders Association (CBTA) in Zambia invites attention for global and regional reasons. In global terms, the CBTA is inspired by, and sets into motion, new organizational forms and influences that span the bounds of the state, regional and international bodies, and NGOs (Nash 2005). In regional terms, the CBTA presents a special case because Zambia, unlike many countries in West Africa, Asia and Latin America, does not have a long history of market associational activity. While most recent associational activity in Zambia is trade specific or regional,[1] the CBTA comprises traders in many different commodities from across the wider region. The CBTA is a particularly interesting example of an informal sector organization because it interacts with large, formal, regional bodies such as the Common Market of Eastern and Southern Africa (COMESA) and the Southern African Development Community (SADC). Above all, the CBTA compels attention because it operates successfully in a highly contested urban economic space within a regulatory environment that – much as elsewhere in Africa (Lourenço-Lindell 2004) – is generally hostile towards urban informal activity.

Neoliberal policies of the 1990s adversely affected employment opportunities in Zambia, pushing more and more people into an already crowded informal economy. An important part of that economy comprises commerce and trade, including activities conducted across national borders by enterprising individuals who source goods abroad for the purpose of reselling them at home. Because Zambia is a landlocked country, surrounded by eight different countries that all have something to offer, cross-border traders bring in goods ranging from handkerchiefs produced in China to vehicles manufactured in Japan. Today many traders travel by air, bringing in goods in bulk. The number of cross-border traders has increased in recent years. Their shared experiences were instrumental in the formation the Cross-Border Traders Association, with branches in other countries throughout southern Africa.

What accounts for the success of the CBTA? In the pages that follow, we sketch the political and economic dynamics that fuelled the recent rapid growth of cross-border trade in Zambia and resulted in the formation of the CBTA in 1997. The association has opened up new space for economic activity through the development of a strategic organizational model. We identify its goals, organizational structure, membership and operational model, and describe its hub, the COMESA Flea Market in Lusaka. Analysing its national and regional linkages, we discuss the CBTA's future prospects as a regional association.

Background

Trade across borders is a phenomenon of long standing, dating back to the pre-colonial period's long-distance trade and continuing into the twenty-first century's liberalized trade regimes. The ease of cross-border trade depends on national and regional regulatory regimes, including foreign exchange availability, transportation and, above all, on the state of the national economy. The regional focus of the trade shifts not only in response to shortages but also to the needs and desires of specific consumers. During much of the colonial period in Zambia, import restrictions and limited purchasing power curtailed local people's engagement with foreign goods, and 'empire preference' privileged the import of commodities originating in the British Empire. But even colonial borders were penetrable and smuggling took place (Hansen 2000: 64–70). In the restricted economic climate of the socialist command economy of the 1980s, for example, enterprising individuals went on shopping trips to neighbouring countries to buy the commodities, including food staples, that were in short supply or of poor quality in Zambia. The reach of this type of 'suitcase' trade expanded when the border with Zimbabwe reopened at independence in 1980 after years of economic sanctions, and it also included Botswana, Swaziland, Malawi, Tanzania and Zaire. Following the transition to majority rule in South Africa in 1994, that country has become an integral part of the cross-border trade circuit. Frequent flight connections from South Africa to the world of global trade beyond the African continent enable cross-border traders to undertake long-haul trips to Asia, Europe and the United States.

Cross-border traders use many forms of transport: bus, boat, truck, train, plane, Scotch cart, wheelbarrow and even head-loading. They are constantly on the lookout for goods that may sell quickly once they are brought in or taken out of the country, always searching for new trade routes. After decades of civil war, peace in Angola recently saw the return of thousands of refugees who had spent many years in Zambia. These refugees were accustomed to Zambian products that were not available in their home country. Their need created a ready market for Zambian goods which cross-border traders were quick to notice. Traders were able to communicate because the former refugees spoke local Zambian languages. The advent of affordable air transport has enabled cross-border traders to develop new routes, among them the Lubumbashi route to the Democratic Republic of Congo (DRC).

The recent rapid growth in the scope and nature of the cross-border trade from Zambia is fuelled by two processes. One is the dismantling of the interventionist state in the wake of the neoliberal government voted into power in 1991. The second is the aggressive displacement by urban governments of informal vendors from streets and public places, which curtails the entrepreneurial freedom of traders. For many years, cross-border traders did not have a specific site or location for their local retail practices. Among these traders were many non-Zambians who intermittently experienced hostility in the competition for urban space. When crossing borders, many traders were harassed by immigration and customs officials. Because tariffs were high, some traders sought to evade them, thus operating illegally. The CBTA was formed to represent traders in negotiation with government, lobby for change in tariff rules, inform members of foreign-travel-related rules and regulations, and to provide social assistance and raise awareness about the long-distance travel risks of HIV/AIDS.

The Cross-Border Traders Association Informal cross-border trade is generally conducted, according to Mwaniki, by 'small-scale quasi professional traders including women, who use various means to move small quantities of goods across national frontiers' (Mwaniki 2007: 3). They range from small-scale suitcase travellers to importers of containerized goods. Cross-border traders encounter many obstacles to the successful pursuit of their work, stemming from poor infrastructure (road and rail networks), poor quality of goods, lack of access to capital, visa restrictions, customs control, and harassment, especially of women traders. Because the majority of traders conducting cross-border trade do not submit annual financial returns, their contribution to national economies is not recognized.

The Zambia Cross-Border Traders Association (CBTA) was formed in 1997 and formally registered in 1998. In addition to the general members, the association has twelve office-bearers, elected every three years (Taruvinga, interview, 2007). Cross-border traders experienced fairly similar problems throughout the southern African region. Officials at borders were hostile and customs regulations not conducive to cross-border trade. The traders faced both tariff and non-tariff barriers. Tariffs on textile products, for example, are very high, with many products attracting over 60 per cent customs duty (Hartzenberg 2003: 180). The non-tariff barriers are import prohibitions on certain goods by certain countries, language problems, poor security, and lack of trading venues, because cross-border traders do not have specific space in foreign markets. High transport costs and the lack of accommodation constituted other barriers. Many traders were forced to sleep at bus stations or in expensive hotels. Some traders had money and goods stolen. There were also instances of traders falling ill or dying while abroad.

The major problem at the time of the formation of the CBTA was the lack of specific government policies to facilitate intra-regional small-scale trade across southern African. The struggles the traders experienced pulled them together as an organization to put pressure on governments for a better trade regime. If the status quo remained, they would continue experiencing hardship because of their lack of recognition by governments within the region. No one was interested in their welfare. With little hope of entering the formal sector, the traders realized that the onus was on them to improve their lot. And owing to political and economic changes across the region, the ranks of traders grew to include people who had previously held formal sector jobs.

Zambia had just introduced multiparty politics in 1991 and the government of the day embraced a structural adjustment programme (SAP) with policies of economic liberalization. Privatization of many parastatal companies caused redundancies and massive job losses, accelerating unemployment, especially in urban areas. Of Zambia's total population estimated at 12.9 million, only 4.7 per cent (498,943) currently hold formal employment (GRZ 2006). With few new formal jobs created, the informal economy takes up the slack. It is not surprising that cross-border trade became an option that many pursued.

Not all cross-border traders are members of the CBTA. Some traders are so well established that they do not need an association to assist them. Such traders do not need a separate space to conduct their business because they have well-established suppliers and customers. And traders who travel beyond Africa, sourcing their goods from afar, do not benefit from tariff cuts across regional borders. A large group of traders travel frequently to the Far East on shopping trips. Some of these well-established traders remain members of CBTA because they started their business sourcing goods within the region, although they have now moved on to destinations farther away. Such traders often employ a relative or paid worker to oversee their regional trade while they themselves travel to the Far East.

Membership The association defines a cross-border trader as 'a person engaged in Cross Border Trade by importing or exporting goods from one COMESA or SADC country to another in small or medium quantities by using any means of transport across the border' (CBTA 2006: Article 1). The yearly membership fee in Zambia is US$10. To become a member, a person must rely on trade and carry it out frequently. Traders who join the CBTA must have valid travel documents and abide by the laws of each country they enter. The trader should not have a criminal record as this may cause problems when in a foreign country. Cross-border traders differ from the everyday market trader because of their skills: abilities to negotiate and pay for a passport or travel document, pass through customs, fill in necessary transit, entry and exit forms and documents, and conduct business in countries with unfamiliar currencies. Transacting profitably in a foreign currency entails literacy and business acumen. Not surprisingly, CBTA members have fairly advanced levels of education, some of them university degrees, acquired formally and strengthened through far-flung experiences on the ground (Shimukonka, interview, 2006).

Within Zambia there are an estimated 15,000 members of CBTA, and regionally the association has approximately 75,000 members in its forty branches, scattered throughout eastern and southern Africa (War on Want et al. 2006: 51). In Zambia, women form nearly 75 per cent and men 25 per cent of the membership (ibid.). This gender imbalance is striking. One frequently suggested explanation for this imbalance holds that informal trading is widespread among women without advanced education and that it can easily be combined with childcare (Mitullah 2004: 5). For the same reason, market trading has been considered to be a woman's domain. Widespread gender stereotypes are at work in such popular explanations (Clark 1994). Thus, according to Shimukonka, the general chairperson of the CBTA, women are better at sharing information and more ready than men to pass on useful information to persons intending to enter the trading sphere. Women, he argued, are also better managers and have a higher resilience when it comes to trading.

As we noted at the outset, women were among the early cross-border traders. 'Older women have traditionally been at the forefront of the informal cross-border trade. Now younger women have also joined business' (Guardian Weekly 2007). The term *bana makwebo*, meaning 'mothers of goods' in the Bemba language (*bana* meaning mothers and *makwebo* meaning buying and selling), was coined in the 1980s. A study from the closing years of the second republic details the journey by road, rail and air of mostly middle-class, well-educated women travelling abroad in groups of two or three, bringing in clothes, shoes and fabrics as well as vehicle and machinery spare parts, electrical goods and groceries (Siyolwe 1994: 100–110, 121–2). In some cases, wealthy and well-connected men financed women's long-distance trade.

Another factor propelling women into informal trade is the many job redundancies in the wake of SAP, particularly affecting men. In their effort to ensure household survival, more women launched informal economic activities (Hansen 1997). In addition to these economic reasons are the facts of demography, with men dying earlier than their spouses, leaving a high number of widows to fend for their families. The HIV/AIDS pandemic, sadly, accentuates this process.

In recent years, a new type of savvy cross-border trader has emerged who uses the Internet to search for and order goods, and transfer money for payments through banks. They use mobile phones to communicate and buy plane tickets to fly to and from the countries where they source their goods. These traders spend longer periods away from home and some ship container-loads of goods back to

Zambia. This trader is a stark contrast to the more ordinary trader who undertakes day trips across the nearest border and buys a few goods for resale in a small stall or by the roadside when returning. These new traders are well informed about what is happening within the region and beyond, and because they know their human rights, they will not allow customs officers to harass them.

The Zambian CBTA was the first to form, and others were established in neighbouring countries. Branches in other countries provide trading space for association members, and as a result, many countries in the region have a COMESA flea market. Association leadership in these markets settles any disputes that may arise between foreign and local traders. Because these markets are not governed by local government rules and regulations, the market fees collected there are used to improve the markets.

The COMESA Flea Market in Lusaka The COMESA markets so far established in Zambia offer a range of goods, depending on their geographical location and economic hinterland. At the Kasumbalesa market on the border with the DRC, for example, cross-border traders sell mainly foodstuffs. And whereas cross-border traders in Lusaka's Soweto market, on the fringe of the light industrial area, specialize in the sale of manufactured products, especially spare parts, the COMESA Flea Market, much closer to the Central Business District (CBD), has the reputation of specializing in clothing and apparel.

The COMESA Flea Market is located in an area of Lusaka's town centre that is easily accessible by foot traffic and car. First renting the space (measuring 5,435 square metres), the CBTA succeeded in purchasing it from the owner in 1998 for 600 million kwacha (K) (approximately US$150,000).[2] In the intervening years, traders who are members of the CBTA have constructed stalls and the space is maximally utilized. In fact, the market is severely crowded, giving rise to health issues, with highly visible drainage ditches that keep the area from flooding during the rainy season. Some traders own their stalls while others rent them from members of the association (Taruvinga, interview, 2007). In 2007, 1,094 registered members operated in the COMESA Flea Market.

The COMESA Flea Market is very popular with price- and style-conscious consumers who not only want value for money but also 'the latest'. The market offers goods and commodities for sale at better prices than Lusaka's new shopping malls, and in a setting where interpersonal bargaining is possible. Prospects for buying on credit are much better than in the shopping malls. The commodities on sale in August 2007 ranged from bedding to dry goods. A large section specialized in the sale of alcohol, both beer and hard liquor. Most of the market space was taken up with ready-made clothing and apparel, especially shoes. The market offers goods both for retail and wholesale purchase, providing an attractive outlet for many price-conscious out-of-town informal traders, who source their supplies from it.

Our brief market survey revealed a wide range of activities (see Appendix). We interviewed thirty-two traders, selected in order to illustrate the most common types of commodities, and their sources, that are sold in Lusaka's COMESA Flea Market. Twenty-five per cent of the stallholders had changed the commodity they initially traded, and 69 per cent sold more than one single commodity. They travelled to seven countries within the region to source their goods (Tanzania, Zimbabwe, South Africa, Kenya, Burundi, Namibia and DRC), as well as farther away, to Dubai and Hong Kong. Making an average of five trips a year, the majority of these traders travel with companions (69 per cent). Cross-border traders like to travel with companions for reasons of company, security and assistance, and they also like to have someone around in case of illness.

All cross-border markets are host to traders from several countries within the region. Our survey consisted of fifteen Zambians and seventeen non-Zambians. The non-Zambian traders were from Zimbabwe, Tanzania, DRC, Burundi and Kenya. Tanzania had the highest representation with eight traders, followed by four from DRC, three from Burundi and one each from Zimbabwe and Kenya. A little more than half of the traders we interviewed were men (53.1 per cent). Most were married and most were heads of household (19 were married, 3 widowed, 4 divorced and only 5 were single). They were adults, not youths, with ages ranging between 26 and 45 (94 per cent); only one trader was older than 46 and one younger than 25. Their education levels were high, with 72 per cent completing secondary education and 12 per cent attaining tertiary education.

More than half of these traders (63 per cent) gave unemployment as the reason for starting, while 6 per cent ventured into cross-border trade in order to expand existing business. Some referred to divorce, the death of a spouse or civil strife in the country of origin as reasons for conducting cross-border trade. Their sources of start-up capital varied, with 19 per cent borrowing money from friends and close family members. Some (25 per cent) obtained support from more distant relatives or pursued short-term work to raise funds (13 per cent). In some cases women used money they had obtained from divorce settlements or the estates of deceased spouses (13 per cent). Only one woman trader received money outright from her husband. The start-up capital of some derived from the sale of property of deceased parents (9 per cent), while a few used money they had received as a dowry for a daughter. Only 22 per cent obtained loans from banks, and most traders complained that the process of applying for bank loans was too long and the interest rate too high. In fact, most of the traders who started their business by borrowing money had obtained it through a variety of informal lending arrangements. Here, as elsewhere in the informal economy, social and family networks are at play in raising capital (Pratt 2006: 44).

Above everything else, our survey demonstrates the importance of the informal economy to economic survival in Lusaka. Most of the traders we interviewed came from households in which at least one other person earned an income within the informal economy. Twelve households in which other members held formal economy jobs also had earners in the informal economy. Only one trader came from a household with all members in formal employment. The average number of persons per household was nearly seven. The non-Zambian traders tended to live (88 per cent) on the western side of Lusaka in unplanned settlements, near the markets, in Zambian households, largely as tenants, whereas the Zambian traders lived farther away, although also in unplanned settlements (60 per cent).

All these traders had operated in the COMESA Flea Market for more than one year. The market, when we visited it, did indeed appear to be saturated and unable to accommodate any more traders. Although there has been a recent influx into Zambia of Zimbabwean traders owing to the upheavals in that country, according to the secretary-general there was no room to accommodate them. Because they had been chased away from the streets, the Zimbabwean traders were forced to hawk their goods in residential areas. The longest period a trader had been active in the flea market was nine years, while 50 per cent had traded in the market for less than four years and the remaining 50 per cent between five and nine years. Two traders started cross-border activities in 1994 and 34 per cent prior to the year 2000. The rest, 66 per cent, started in 2000 or later. Some of the cross-border traders in the flea market were also employers, with more than 59 per cent employing at least two people, and 25 per cent employing between three and six people to attend to the trade and assist customers.

Cross-border traders have developed new strategies for selling goods on credit. With improved access to telephone communication, customers and traders are able to communicate about the availability and pricing of goods. Traders are also able to arrange delivery to customers. In fact, some cross-border traders were more effective than formal sector operators in their innovative use of mobile phone technology.

Modus operandi of the CBTA The general role of the CBTA is threefold. In the first instance the association promotes greater cohesion by organizing a group of people who previously acted as single individuals. This cohesion gives the association a greater voice and a strategic approach to problem-solving. Second, the association lobbies for its members. Finally it seeks to educate members by disseminating information relevant to them concerning both their financial and their physical well-being.

Apart from bringing traders together, the association acts as a conduit of communication. The CBTA provides the platform on which regional bodies, government agencies and formal private sector entities can directly interact with traders in the informal sector. It also promotes its role as an informal economy organization within the Alliance for Zambia Informal Economy Associations (AZIEA), an umbrella organization formed in 2001 that we briefly describe later. Communicating effectively with larger regional bodies such as COMESA and SADC, the CBTA is able easily to dispense critical information to informal economy traders.

Lobbying When cross-border traders operated as individuals their views and grievances went unnoticed, and they were treated with hostility and considered to be a nuisance. The CBTA gives traders representation and a voice. A recent example is the Livingstone branch of the association, which appealed to headquarters in Lusaka over increased customs duties affecting those crossing the border into Zimbabwe. CBTA leaders made a presentation to the Ministry of Commerce, Trade and Industry, which in turn approached the corresponding ministry in Zimbabwe in an attempt to resolve the issue. CBTA members trust the ability of their leaders to lobby the relevant government departments to get a hearing.

The CBTA uses its voice to lobby for change. The association lobbies the Ministry of Home Affairs on immigration matters and the Ministry of Finance on customs issues (War on Want et al. 2006: 51). Tariff barriers may not be a priority issue for governments. But because the CBTA engages directly with the Ministry of Commerce, Trade and Industry though the permanent secretary, the ministry adds tariff concerns to the agenda for meetings of regional groups such as SADC and COMESA. Occasionally, the CBTA is invited to participate in general trade conferences in order to contribute to policy discussions. The CBTA lobbied vigorously for the effective formation of a free trade area that was launched in 2000 (Post 2006a). The establishment of the free trade area is to the advantage of the CBTA, as it will ensure the free movement of goods and services and the removal of tariff and non-tariff barriers within the COMESA region (E-COMESA 2006).

The CBTA lobbies for other issues, such as 'one-stop trading centres' in urban and rural areas of the COMESA and SADC countries. These are envisioned as trade centres CBTA members can reach easily and where they can find a variety of goods in one place. The current organization of the trade forces traders to move from store to store in the various cities they go to. Such movements not only make them vulnerable to theft but also add to the cost of conducting this type of trade. The CBTA also lobbies for access to credit in any member state without discrimination on the basis of nationality, gender, tribe or race (CBTA 2006: Article 6). The association recently called on the Zambian government to set up a revolving fund to help business people in the informal sector (Post 2006b). It is lobbying for a Simplified Trade Regime (STR) with a Simplified Trade Document (STD). The current process of certification for goods that qualify for duty exemptions is expensive and rigorous because in most cases the required documents are available only in the capital cities. The STR would apply to goods that do not exceed US$500, and the STD will be much easier to complete than the forms that are in use at the moment. Such a regime will help traders who are unable to obtain the documentation they need for tax exemption under the current duty- and quota-free provisions of the COMESA region (Times of Zambia 2007).

Information dissemination The third role of the CBTA is to educate its members about non-trade issues affecting their trade, the major one of which in the southern African region is HIV/AIDS. Providing more knowledge to its members, the CBTA holds workshops and seminars about finance management, travel requirements, immigration, customs rules and regulations, availability of goods, and HIV/AIDS prevention. Through seminars about COMESA, members of CBTA have learned what COMESA and other regional bodies are about and the advantages that such regional bodies offer to business. The CBTA has links with the Anti-Corruption Commission and the Drug Enforcement Commission, which educate members about the dangers of corruption and drug trafficking. Members also share information on transport routes and accommodation services in member countries.

National linkages Apart from the connections with regional bodies that we discuss below, the CBTA has links with the financial sector within Zambia. The economic and finance chairperson of the CBTA is in charge of identifying partners within the finance sector. The association has been successful, for instance, with Finance Bank, a local Zambian bank that has offered to promote small-scale trade by giving soft loans. The bank provides credit to CBTA members at the rate of 33 per cent per year (Shimukonka, interview, 2006). This rate is high and prohibitive. Association members also get loans from Pride Zambia, a micro-finance institution offering loans at a 30 per cent rate that is negotiable depending on the length of the repayment period. Recently, mainstream banks such as Barclays Bank plc and Stanbic Bank have begun to reduce their stringent loan requirements in ways from which cross-border traders may benefit.

Cross-border traders have long-standing linkages with traders in both the retail and wholesale sectors. In fact, cross-border traders supply beverages, cosmetics/lotions and jewellery/hair accessories to large retail outlets like Shoprite and Spar, both of them South African franchises with several Zambian outlets. Cross-border traders also supply beverages, printed cloth, blankets, curtains and household goods to many Asian shops and other small retail shops throughout the country (ibid.),[3] at times at the request of retailers.

Using different modes of transport, most cross-border traders travel without insurance. Road transporters tend to charge exorbitant rates to carry goods. Although a transport owner may have fixed rates per kilo of weight, truck or bus drivers are known to inflate such charges in order to make some money themselves. In 2006, Zambian Airways, a newly established local airline, started wooing the cross-border traders. The airline introduced an affordable fare and a lower charge for excess baggage in an attempt to encourage cross-border traders to fly on its Johannesburg and Dar es Salaam routes.[4] Travelling by air, traders spend less time while paying just as much or less than the cost of road transport (Post 2006b). Realizing that cross-border traders were potential clients, the airline tailored a product to suit them. This initiative has resulted in a marked increase in the number of cross-border traders who travel by plane.

Informal economy linkages Like the CBTA, informal economy organizations in many parts of the world have in recent years established networks and federations and made cross-national and international alliances in order to improve their situation. The CBTA is one of thirteen informal economy associations in Zambia and is part of an umbrella organization, the AZIEA, formed in 2001. AZIEA seeks to bargain with the government with the aim of making informal economy workers part of the recognized, protected and represented workforce that enjoys labour standards set by the ILO. For this purpose, AZIEA and the Workers Education Association of Zambia have approached the Zambia Congress of Trade Unions with a view to establishing an alliance and identifying initiatives to organize informal economy workers.

The secretary-general of CBTA in 2007 was the vice-president of AZIEA, working, he told us, on establishing a common voice across the informal sector in Zambia (Tavuringa, interview, 2007). AIEA in turn is an affiliate of StreetNet International, a South Africa-based organization that grew out of the Self-Employed Women's Association (SEWA), first established in India and then other countries, to organize workers in the informal economy. SEWA's work inspired the formation of StreetNet in 1995 and its formal establishment in Durban, South Africa, in 2002, to support the development of organizations of street vendors, informal market vendors and hawkers throughout the world. Indeed, StreetNet has branches in Africa, Asia and Latin America (War on Want et al. 2006: 27–8). The chief goal of StreetNet, inspired by a class-based organizational model, is to create alliances with labour and social movements rather than to focus on the micro-enterprise sector and the NGO development sector.

The organizational model of CBTA and its AZIEA supports contrasts sharply with network- and federation-based approaches pursued, for example, by informal sector organizations focused on informal housing, among them the Shack Dwellers Association International. Even if such community-based partners craft networks of 'globalization from below' (Appadurai 2001), they still depend on external NGO inputs, and because of that, they ultimately have less control over their own agenda (for similar observations, see Mitullah's chapter, this volume).

Regional linkages When the CBTA was established in 1997, the regional body, the Common Market for Eastern and Southern Africa (COMESA), had been in existence since 1993. Affiliating with COMESA, the CBTA discovered that some of the countries from which goods were sourced were not members of the regional body and were therefore not bound by its resolutions. These countries, South Africa, Botswana, Mozambique, Lesotho and Namibia, were members of a different regional body, the Southern African Customs Union (SACU). There was yet another regional body, the Southern African Development Community (SADC). All SACU member states are members of SADC but not necessarily of COMESA. Still other countries are members of both COMESA and SADC. These overlapping memberships lead to potential conflicts of interest for cross-border traders. For instance, while 'the SADC Treaty is concerned mainly with the issue of development in its multi-dimensional sense, the COMESA Treaty is much more focused at market-oriented economic growth' (Mwenda 1999: 145). COMESA and SADC have a variety of trade programmes aimed at trade liberalization and monetary union.

The CBTA represents the traders at important trade conferences to contribute to the formulation of policies and regulations that govern inter-regional trade. The association is present at all COMESA trade meetings. Because SADC is not primarily oriented towards trade promotion, the CBTA does not have a particularly strong relationship with SADC. Even so, SADC has worked with the CBTA in efforts to fight HIV/AIDS.

COMESA According to treaty Article 45, COMESA requires member states to establish a customs union over a transitional ten-year period from the time of entry.[5] The first customs union is set to start in 2008, and member nations of COMESA are likely to benefit from its formation (Grainger 2006). Other member nations are expected to form customs unions after this landmark year. But the CBTA has to await the Zambian government's decision about whether or not to remain in COMESA. Proponents of non-entry into any customs union and withdrawal from COMESA argue that a customs union will disadvantage Zambian manufacturers, who already face stiff competition from cheap imported products, among other places from China. Yet the CBTA argues that leaving COMESA is 'tantamount to committing economic suicide' (Shimukonka, interview, 2006). For COMESA has a potentially much wider market, including North African countries such as Sudan, Egypt and Libya, with which Zambia has yet to establish trade links.

The CBTA has such close ties with COMESA that Lusaka-based COMESA Assistant Secretary-General for Programmes Sindiso Ngwenya has been the patron (honorary head) of the CBTA. According to the CBTA constitution, starting from 2007 the secretary-general who is head of COMESA will be the patron (CBTA 2006: 3). The reason for this close relationship is probably that the headquarters of COMESA are located in Lusaka, within easy reach of the CBTA. CBTA members receive membership cards giving them preferential treatment within COMESA member countries. One result of preferential treatment is extra time allowances on visas from COMESA member countries.

SADC Initially referred to as the Southern African Development Coordination Conference (SADCC), the Southern African Development Community (SADC) was formed in 1980 as a loose alliance of nine majority-ruled countries in the region. The main aim at that time was to coordinate development projects in an effort to reduce regional dependence on apartheid South Africa. The founding members were Angola, Botswana, Malawi, Mozambique, Lesotho, Swaziland, Tanzania, Zimbabwe and Zambia. SADCC was transformed into SADC on 17 August 1992. The members of SADC today are the Democratic Republic of Congo, Lesotho, Madagascar, Malawi, Mauritius, Mozambique, Namibia, South Africa, Swaziland, Tanzania, Zambia and Zimbabwe. The headquarters are in Gaborone, Botswana (SADC 2007). SADC's objectives revolve around improving the general well-being of populations living within the region. It promotes political and economic integration, aiming to consolidate historical ties and achieve sustainable resource utilization.

Perhaps for reasons having to do with the organizational structure of SADC, the CBTA does not have particularly strong ties with it. In SADC, each member country hosts a different department. Zambia, for example, hosts the labour department, Tanzania the trade department and Zimbabwe the defence department. This fragmentation of responsibilities makes it difficult for the CBTA to lobby because its chief concerns are with the trade portfolio, based in Tanzania. Even so, the CBTA does lobby SADC to enable free movement of its members in SADC countries. It wants the regional body to support and facilitate cross-border trade. SADC lobbying takes place in press statements and written submissions to the regional body.

Conclusion

Cross-border traders in Zambia share much with workers who make a living in the informal economy elsewhere, ranging from home-based traders and street vendors to market stallholders (Brown 2006a: 5–7). Yet unlike many other informal workers, Zambia's cross-border traders have achieved marked successes, the most important of which is recognition. Much of this is due to the establishment in 1997 of the association of cross-border traders, which recognizes the importance of this trade and, by its registration as an association, has helped to lessen its shroud of informality. What is more, the CBTA was able to obtain land in Lusaka's CBD, where its members can legally conduct their retail trade. Because Zambia's cross-border traders operate in a hotly contested urban environment, the establishment of the COMESA Flea Market in Lusaka exclusively for members of the CBTA was a remarkable success.

How did this success come about? The CBTA does not have obvious local political linkages. In fact, several of its office-holders are not Zambian citizens. Starting from a point of disadvantage, the cross-border traders organized themselves into a pressure group, the CBTA. With the growth in movements of goods across national borders fuelled by shifts in politico-economic shifts across the region, the CBTA established branches abroad. Within Zambia, the CBTA developed close ties within the Ministry of Trade, Commerce and Industry and sought patronage at a regional level from the COMESA secretariat, headquartered in Lusaka, the capital. The CBTA involved itself in the national agenda by lobbying regional groupings such as COMESA and SADC with the aim of introducing flexibility in import regimes.

Rather than being considered a public nuisance, the CBTA is now held to be a partner in development. Will this last? The CBTA's development participation and entrepreneurship are central practices of current urban governance, yet the regulatory environment by and large remains hostile to the operation of the COMESA Flea Market. The Lusaka City Council's (LCC) recent ultimatum to the liquor traders in the market is just one example of the struggle over authority. At issue is the prohibition, according to LCC by-laws, on the sale of alcohol in the open. Invoking a new urban ordinance, the LCC also requested cross-border traders to move their business 2 metres away from the road. Although many other informal market participants in places other than the COMESA Flea Market site are not observing this ordinance, the LCC places special pressure on the cross-border traders. These and other examples of the intermittent yet continuous pressure under which cross-border traders work in the COMESA Flea Market dramatically illustrate their vulnerable position in relation to local authorities. In effect, while the CBTA solved the contentious issue of access to trading space some years ago, the traders remain vulnerable because of the vagaries of the urban regulatory environment. Of late, the CBTA has pursued a new strategy to lessen such interventions. Because Zambia's recently revised Market Act places all markets under the authority of the Ministry of Local Government and Housing, the CBTA recently changed its status to that of a trade centre in order to avoid hostile regulatory interventions having to do with the locus of control and authority (Taruvinga, interview, 2007). Yet although it has achieved so much already, the CBTA continues the struggle to be accepted as an autonomous player in the conflict-ridden urban regulatory environment in Zambia.

Acknowledgements

Wilma Nchito conducted most of the research on which this chapter is based; her assistant, Gilbert Zulu, carried out the survey in the COMESA market. Karen Tranberg Hansen drew on her previous research in Lusaka markets and added a comparative angle to the discussion. Both authors thank Mr Tadeo Taruvinga,

CBTA secretary-general and regional executive, for informative discussions and help in facilitating the COMESA market survey, as well as other members of the CBTA for providing important information.

Appendix: typology of goods sold at the COMESA Flea Market, Lusaka, and their sources

Apparel	*Source country*
Adult clothes	Tanzania, Zimbabwe, South Africa, Dubai
Baby/children's clothes	Tanzania, Hong Kong, Dubai
Chitenge (printed cloth)	Tanzania, Zimbabwe, DRC, Burundi
Shoes	Tanzania, Dubai
Ethnic sandals	Kenya

Beverages	
Alcoholic	Zimbabwe
Non-alcoholic	Zimbabwe

Household	
Blankets/duvets/sheets	Tanzania, Zimbabwe, Namibia
Curtains	Zimbabwe, South Africa

Accessories	
Handbags	Tanzania, Zimbabwe, South Africa
Cosmetics/lotions	Tanzania, Dubai
Jewellery/hair accessories	Tanzania, South Africa, Hong Kong

Interviews

Shimukonka, Greenwell, Chairman General, CBTA, 21 December 2006
Taruvinga, Tadeo, Secretary-General, CBTA, 20 March 2007, 28 August 2007, 9 October 2007

10 | Informal workers in Kenya and transnational organizing: networking and leveraging resources

Winnie V. Mitullah

Introduction

Informal economies in most African countries date back to the colonial period, when capitalism began penetrating the indigenous economy. The use of the concept 'informal sector', and later 'informal economy',[1] dates back to the Keith Hart study of 1971 in Ghana (Hart 1973), followed by the ILO study in Kenya on *Employment, Incomes and Inequality* of 1972. The ILO study highlighted the importance of the sector and urged governments to support it (ILO 1972). However, it was not until the 78th Session of the International Labour Conference in 1991 that the dilemma of the sector was discussed. This resulted in the ILO adopting an enterprise-based definition of the sector, which included only employees of informal enterprises, leaving out all other categories (ILO 1993). In 2002 the ILO, in collaboration with transnational organizations, undertook a critical examination of decent work and the informal economy (ILO 2002a). This resulted in the establishment of a platform ensuring that decent work, in particular for informal workers, remains an agenda for governments and international agencies, including transnational movements.

The 2002 ILO report observed that the sector was growing rapidly in almost every corner of the globe, and could no longer be considered a temporary or residual phenomenon. The report further noted that the bulk of new employment in recent years, particularly in the developing and transitional countries, had been in the informal economy, with most people relying on it. Informal employment as a percentage of non-agricultural employment is estimated to be over 70 per cent in sub-Saharan Africa, 65 per cent in Asia and over 50 per cent in Latin America, with wide variations among different countries. On average, the informal economy in Africa is estimated to represent 42 per cent of GDP and in Latin America 41 per cent of the GDP (Habitat Debate 2007). In Asia, the range is from Thailand at 52.6 per cent to Singapore with 13.1 per cent and Japan with 11.3 per cent (World Bank 2003, cited in Dey 2007).

While it is acknowledged that the sector provides a high percentage of employment, work in the sector is often seriously deficient in terms of workers' access to appropriate working conditions, legal and social protection, representation and voice, which are not comparable to the regulated work conditions in the formal economy (ILO 2002a). The *World Employment Report 2004/2005* (ILO 2004b) notes that, while it is clearly the case that employment is central to poverty reduction, it is decent and productive employment which matters and not employment alone. In this respect, labour rights should be founded on decent work, by reducing decent work deficits.

'International organizations' in this chapter refers to organizations such as the ILO and the United Nations, while 'transnational organizations' refers to networks and movements such as StreetNet International, Women in Informal Employment: Organizing and Globalizing (WIEGO) and the Unitarian Universalists Service Committee (UUSC), which are discussed later in the chapter. The concepts transnational organizations and transnational movements are used interchangeably.

Apart from secondary literature, the information used in this chapter is drawn from many sources. The author conducted a major study on street and informal traders in Kenya between 1998 and 2000, and also coordinated research focusing on street and informal trade in five African countries. Since then, the author has been facilitating the organization of street and informal traders in Kenya, as well as working closely with StreetNet International and WIEGO, which are transnational movements supporting the local organizing and networking of informal workers across the globe. While the author's direct engagement in both local and international organizing may colour her perceptions, it has facilitated close monitoring of the inner workings of both local and transnational organizations, as discussed in this chapter.

The desire to change the situation of informal economy workers has prompted the creation of grassroots movements using new strategies of organizing, which include working with networks of local, regional, national and international development organizations. Using the case of KENASVIT (the Kenya National Alliance of Street Vendors and Informal Traders), this chapter argues that the efforts of transnational organizations supporting informal workers have begun influencing the local working environment of informal workers. Through networks of transnational organizations, local organizations of workers are organizing, mobilizing resources and engaging public authorities in negotiating for recognition and inclusion in the public policy-making process, and the planning and management of resources.

The political economy of informal work

The contemporary predicament of many informal workers needs to be understood in the context of the global political economy of informal work. Knorringa and Pegler's (2006) analysis of globalization, firm upgrading and their impact on labour, using value chain analysis, reveals the negative impact of economic globalization. They argue that it results in increased insecurity, precariousness and longer working hours, as well as downward pressure on real wages. Thus, they call for the decent work approach to the informal economy, noting that 'any campaign to increase the probability of labour rights improvements must be based on a broader and more inclusive human development agenda, for example by integrating the decent work approach' (ibid.).

Stiglitz (2002a) argues that the international community, in particular financial institutions, has remained silent on labour issues as they foreground the Washington Consensus and macroeconomic policies. These policies have resulted in high unemployment, with *pro-cyclical* monetary fiscal policies, which include labour market flexibility. Second, they have resulted in workers bearing the brunt of their adverse consequences. Stiglitz further observes that macroeconomic indicators get enormous attention, while other issues, such as the level of employment, the level of wages, and disparities in pay, are virtually ignored. In his analysis, the international community has opposed or at least not supported demands for rights to collective action. He concludes that they should not only concentrate on promoting economic prosperity, but should push for decent work, for full employment and better working conditions.

The challenges of informal work require informal workers to organize, but most of these workers belong to business and welfare associations which are weak and not well positioned to engage in advocacy for the workers' rights to working space and protection from harassment by public authorities. The benefits of effective Micro and Small Enterprise (MSE) associations include influence on policies and issues affecting members' businesses, service provision to members and accumulation of social capital (McCormick et al. 2003). The weak associations of workers have exposed them to harassment by urban authorities, who view them not as workers but as intruders messing up the urban fabric. This has further contributed to their limited ability to independently influence their working environment, and subsequently their partnership with transnational movements and organizations (Mitullah 2007b). The lack of an 'enabling environment' and harassment from central and local authorities in Africa have partly prepared the way for organizing, *including joining transnational networks and organizations* (Macharia 1973).

The unprotected working environment has exposed workers to insecurity in the labour market, employment, skill reproduction, income and representation. They work without contracts, and are exposed to poor working conditions which include long hours of work without benefits, low pay and lack of social protection. This insecurity has been a major hindrance to organizing and improving their working conditions. At the same time, most governments' support has tended to 'push' the sector towards the formal economy by insisting on registration without facilitating the provision of the accompanying infrastructure, services and protection of labour rights through policy and legal provision (Mitullah 2006b).

For decades, many African governments believed that the informal economy could be formalized by deploying punitive control measures. However, as governments intensified their control, and continued with neoliberal reforms, the informal economy kept expanding and absorbing the labour force retrenched from the formal economy, including the public sector. Additionally, the punitive measures and abuse of human rights within the informal economy gave rise to various social movements[2] advocating for informal workers' rights. Some of these ended up institutionalizing themselves as organizations advocating for informal workers. These organizations began embracing informal workers' organizations, after the popularization of the decent work campaign by the ILO and transnational organizations, and the opening up of political space in Africa (Olukoshi and Wohlgemuth 1995).

Implementing the decent work approach, however, presupposes workers who are aware of their rights, and have access to basic needs and employment opportunities. These elements are not available to the majority of informal workers in Africa, and many of them have formed social movements aimed at addressing the challenges facing them. There are many theories applied in an attempt to understand these movements, namely political process (Tilly 1978; McAdam 1982), collective action (Olson 1965), moral economy (Thompson 1971), resource mobilization (McCarthy and Zald 1973) and culture, among others. The social movements have many faces, which include: independent local movements; local branches of international movements; associations and networks of existing organizations; and informal, unregistered movements without formal structures (Ballard et al. 2006).

Ballard et al. acknowledge that social movements are informed by three central aspects: the contextual prevailing structure of opportunities and constraints; network structures and other resources that actors employ to mobilize supporters; and the ways in which movement participants define or frame their movement. These forces work together to bridge approaches to 'old' and 'new' social movements. Ballard et al. observe further that local initiatives often overcome the constraints of their geographic focus by affiliating with movements elsewhere in the country or in the world (ibid.), as discussed later in this chapter. Other scholars, such as Keek and Sikkink (1998) and Della Porta and Tarrow (2004), also support this position by advocating for definition of opportunities, networks and identities which transcend national boundaries and which connect the 'local and the global'.

In the face of weak local organizing, transnational organizations have become important organizing forces at the local level. Transnational and social movements aim to effect larger social transformations that are linked to their members' beliefs. They enable people to generate new ideologies, redefine their own identities (Castells 1997) and counter elite economic perspectives and ideologies. While there are many theories of social movements, this chapter adopts the political process theory, which integrates three vital components of social movement formation: namely, insurgent consciousness, organizational strength and political opportunities. Insurgent consciousness is the collective sense of injustice that members of social movements feel and serves as the motivation for movement organization. The organizational strength aspect relates to the condition that in order for a social movement to organize, it must have strong leadership and sufficient resources, while the political opportunity aspect refers to the receptivity or vulnerability of existing political systems to change.

In applying the political process theory, it is acknowledged that social movements do not have consistency and coherent logic but rather several and contradictory social logics (Mamdani and Wamba-dia-Wamba 1995). It is therefore important to undertake a critical analysis of social movements and their projects, since each movement has its own characteristics and dynamics. Before delving into an analysis of social movements using KENASVIT as a case study, it is relevant to have a clear understanding of the informal economy on which the movement thrives.

The informal economy and organizing in Kenya

Kenya's informal economy has a long history, dating back to 1972 when the ILO conducted a major study on the informal sector (ILO 1972). The MSEs which are the pillars of informal economic activities create over 90 per cent of employment and contribute about 18 per cent of GDP. In 2002, the sector employed 5,086,400, up from 4,624,400 in 2001. This was an increase of 462,000 persons and constituted 74 per cent of total private sector employment in the economy (RoK 2003a). Despite the importance of the sector, it was not until 1992 that the government put in place a policy aimed at improving the operations of the sector. This was followed by another policy in 2005, but these policies were not translated into action, and those working in the sector continued to work in poor, unprotected conditions. The government policy acknowledges that the MSEs cut across all sectors of the Kenyan economy and are the most prolific sources of employment creation, income generation and poverty reduction. The policy further acknowledges that, despite the significant role played by the sector, it has continued to experience many constraints that have inhibited the realization of its full potential (RoK 2005).

A baseline survey on MSEs revealed a number of challenges facing the sector. Apart from lack of capital, credit and poor marketing, the MSEs lack security, they are harassed by local authority officials and lack work sites (CBS/ACEG/ K-REP 1999). A census of traders operating within the Central Business District (CBD) of the capital city of Nairobi revealed that out of the 3,488 traders covered in the survey, only 6 per cent trade on designated sites. The rest trade on undesignated street pavements (75.4 per cent) or in bus stations (11 per cent), while others are mobile (7.3 per cent) (NISCOF 2006). Lack of licences and traders working in unauthorized sites are often used to justify harassment and punitive measures against informal workers (Mitullah 2007a). However, the lack of effective associations that can advocate and lobby for workers' rights within the informal economy is viewed as a major factor contributing to harassment. Thus, site of operation is a major challenge to traders and a major source of conflict with urban authorities, since regulations require that any trader given a licence must have an authorized site of operation (Alila and Mitullah 2000).

Characteristics of local associations

Informal workers in Kenya are largely organized around welfare issues, with many operating Rotating Savings and Credit Schemes (ROSCAs). Their social orientation has a great deal to do with Kenya's past risky economic environment and lack of social safety nets. The associations differ in formation, size and focus, with most of them drawing their membership from small producers and traders (McCormick et al. 2003). A task force commissioned by the government of Kenya in 2003 to study and make recommendations on the challenges facing the MSE associations observed that the associations are weak and do not undertake activities that ensure the efficient operation of enterprises. The task force further noted that ensuring a dynamic MSE sector requires well-functioning associations that support entrepreneurs and lobby and hold dialogues with authorities for an improved working environment with provision of infrastructure and services (RoK 2003b).

KENASVIT and local organizing

KENASVIT is a budding national civil society organization with a vision of transforming street vending and informal businesses into corporate establishments. KENASVIT was established in 2005 with the support of the Institute for Development Studies (IDS) of the University of Nairobi and transnational organizations. The IDS, in collaboration with street vendors and informal traders, developed a proposal, while StreetNet International leveraged resources for rolling out activities leading to the establishment of the organization (Mitullah 2007a).

The organization is managed by a National Executive Committee (NEC) composed of a Management Committee (MC), Urban Alliance Committees (UACs) and Local Association Committees (LACs) drawn from seven urban local authorities in Kenya. The organization has three trustees, two drawn from institutions. This management structure is facilitated by a secretariat based in one of the urban authorities, Nakuru. The secretariat is backed up by the IDS, which provided the secretariat prior to the establishment of the KENASVIT secretariat. The secretariat is responsible for coordination of KENASVIT activities and also serves as a contact point for members and the link with other development partners.

The establishment of the alliance owes its origin to research conducted between 1998 and 2000 by the IDS on women and street vendors in Kenya. The research covered four urban areas located in three different regions of the country. One of the main findings of the study was that street vendors lacked the capacity to organize themselves in order to have a strong voice on matters affecting their trade at both local and national level (Alila and Mitullah 2000).

The research findings were disseminated to policy-makers and street and informal traders in the four urban authorities. This was followed in 2003 by a National Street Vendors Forum, which brought together policy-makers, representatives of street and informal traders and other stakeholders. During the conference, the street and informal traders' delegates decided to form an Interim Steering Committee to spearhead the formation of a National Alliance, which was eventually registered by the government in February 2006. The research findings and the subsequent workshops, conferences and policy dialogues stimulated the IDS to move beyond research, to support the vendors and informal traders by developing a proposal on the 'Facilitation of street vendors and informal traders' organizations in Kenya' (Mitullah 2005b). The project contributed to the birth of KENASVIT, and the organization was officially launched as a national organization on 18 March 2006 (Mitullah 2007b).

The author's experience in facilitating organizing reveals that a third neutral party is required during initial alliance-building. In the case of KENASVIT, the IDS, in collaboration with transnational organizations, in particular StreetNet, UUSC and WIEGO, played this role. The IDS continued to provide support in developing a strategic plan which provided a framework for the IDS withdrawal in August 2007, when KENASVIT managed to hire a full-time coordinator based at its secretariat in Nakuru.

The alliance has over three thousand members drawn from 140 local associations that form the seven (Nairobi, Mombasa, Kisumu, Nakuru, Eldoret, Migori and Machakos) urban alliances, largely organized around welfare. These members are for the most part traders and service providers. Their economic activities include hawking and selling fruit and vegetables, tree seedlings, second-hand clothes, electrical gadgets and domestic goods such as kitchen appliances, bedding, mats and carpets. These traders face a number of challenges, which range from lack of trading sites, credit facilities, infrastructure and services to harassment by local authorities.

KENASVIT has the task of moving the traders beyond welfare to business, lobbying and policy influence. Membership of the organization is open to street vendors and informal traders through Urban Alliances, which are constituted by local-level, street and informal traders' associations. Honorary and associate membership are open to non-political organizations and individuals who support the mission and objectives of the alliance. The organization has eight key leadership positions, including those of chair, secretary and treasurer, which are assumed through elections, held every four years. In addition, every Urban Alliance is entitled to elect one representative to sit on the NEC. The MC works closely with the secretariat and meets once a month, while the NEC and the Annual General Assembly meet quarterly and annually respectively (KENASVIT Constitution 2006).

The mission of the alliance is to organize and empower street vendors and informal traders, in order to improve their business through training, access to credit, dialogue with local authorities and other relevant organizations on appropriate by-laws and policies that give recognition to and bring to an end harassment and discrimination (ibid.). Article 2(f) and 2(g) of the KENASVIT constitution state that the organization shall 'engage and lobby the central government and stakeholders to develop appropriate policies, regulations, infrastructure and provide services for street vendors and informal traders'; and 'establish networks and close collaboration between street vendors' and informal traders' organizations and with other organizations nationally, regionally and internationally'. The latter provision is already being realized by the creation of networks and partnerships at local and international levels, as discussed later in this chapter.

KENASVIT's activities

The act leading to KENASVIT's launch was the development of a constitution, which was largely undertaken by an Interim Steering Committee. During the constitution-making process three meetings were held; these enabled the National Steering Committee to draft the constitution and share the draft with members of respective Urban Alliances. The second meeting integrated the feedback from this process and provided a second opportunity for the membership to offer further input. The third meeting, held on 18 March 2005, was attended by delegates drawn from the seven Urban Alliances. The meeting finalized and adopted the constitution and elected the national office-bearers; this marked the birth of KENASVIT. These processes were enabled by a grant of US$10,500 in seed funds leveraged by StreetNet International for facilitating and monitoring street vendors and informal traders' associations. Apart from the constitution-making process, funds were also used for policy dialogue with local authorities, national Interim Steering Committee meetings, and launching the alliance. These were very important steps towards the institutionalization of the alliance, and would not have been possible without the collaboration and support of both local and transnational partners.

Since the initiation of KENASVIT, the national alliance and its seven affiliate members, with the support of local civil society and transnational organizations, have managed to organize themselves and to undertake a number of activities, including lobbying and policy dialogue. In addition, the alliance and its affiliates have benefited from capacity-building, including training in organizing by local and international agencies (KENASVIT/IDS Report 2006). Informal workers in Africa are weak in lobbying and policy dialogue (Mitullah 2005c). This is because their access to resources is limited, and they wield minimum power, although in terms of numbers they constitute a critical mass. Street vendors and informal traders are also often poorly informed about the laws and regulations that govern their operations, and suffer from the failure of urban authorities to respect agreements they have made with the traders and to enforce the regulations that they have set (Mitullah 2005b).

Local authority by-laws require traders to operate in specific areas, and to avoid causing obstructions; however, vending and trading areas are not allocated. Cases have been cited where one regime of urban government allocates trading space to these workers, while a subsequent government evicts them from the spaces allocated. For example, in the city of Kisumu the vendors held a dialogue with the municipality and trading sites were allocated beside a park and in selected streets. However, upon election of a new council, the new team threatened to evict vendors from the allocated sites, and the vendors took the council to court (ibid.). Prior to the organization of street vendors and informal traders in Kenya, the vendors were not able to engage the urban authorities in any dialogue, they were harassed on a daily basis, and no attempt was made to allocate any spaces for their economic activities. At the same time, they had no say in determining licensing fees and operated officially without services and infrastructure (Alila and Mitullah 2000).

With the establishment of KENASVIT, there has been an improvement in the working environment of street vendors and informal traders through their intervention in a number of government initiatives. These include development of a national land policy, development of a Micro and Small Enterprises (MSE) Bill, development of Nairobi City Council by-laws, and the commissioning and development of a hawkers' market located within the periphery of the CBD of Nairobi by the president of Kenya in 2006. As indicated earlier, the alliance, through one of its affiliates, NISCOF, conducted a census of street vendors and informal traders operating within the CBD; this census attracted international interest. StreetNet International has popularized the census by publishing it on its website and in its newsletter and has further leveraged resources for an exchange visit between NISCOF and Nepal Street Traders (NEST). Sharing the census methodology and exchanging ideas on organizing and policy dialogue with authorities were the main objectives of the exchange visit.

KENASVIT participated in the formulation of a national land policy through the facilitation of the Kenya Land Alliance (KLA) – an umbrella local network of civil society organizations which facilitates networking and information sharing on land issues at local, regional and international level (KLA 2002). The organization collaborated with KENASVIT and its affiliates and played a key role in enabling KENASVIT to represent the interests of street vendors and informal traders in the national land policy-making process.

KENASVIT, with the facilitation of UUSC, has been engaged in the development of the MSE Bill. The draft bill defined an MSE as a business that is carried on with fewer than fifty employees. This definition was found by KENASVIT to be inappropriate and to overlook 'own-account workers', who have no employees. During the stakeholders' workshop, therefore, the alliance recommended that the title of the bill be changed to the Micro, Small Enterprises and Hawkers Bill of 2006. In defining MSEs to include businesses with fewer than fifty employees, the bill's ability to protect certain categories of MSEs is limited. KENASVIT leaders argued that 'the self-employed' and 'own-account workers' of micro-enterprises employing nobody and enterprises employing between one and five people cannot be grouped with formal workers.

The 'own-account workers' operate in different environments with different capacities. The formal workers have more capacities in terms of resources and organization as compared to street vendors, who are largely own-account workers. Apart from the definition, KENASVIT, with the support of its lawyer, provided input in the areas of administrative provision, establishment, composition and functions of a proposed Council for MSEs, registration of MSEs with the Council, and the powers of the minister with respect to the allocation of trading spaces (Mitullah 2007b). The development of the bill is still ongoing, and a second transnational organization, War on Want, has become involved in the process and has provided resources to enable KENASVIT to continue with its engagement.

The MSE policy is quite important for street vendors and informal workers since the traders face a number of challenges relating to policy and regulations; the bill is expected to specifically deal with those challenges. Sihanya (2006) has noted that the operation of street vendors and informal traders outside the law has encouraged rent-seeking by public officials and the illegalizing of their economic activities. Further, lack of legal provisions has resulted in no legal obligation being placed upon government, local authorities and other public bodies and officials to facilitate and support MSEs.

The alliance has also been involved in the review of the City of Nairobi (Hawkers) Amendment By-Laws, 2006. The draft by-laws made it an offence for any person to engage in hawking without a permit; and also an offence for 'any person who solicits, bargains, induces or negotiates with any hawker with a view to buy[ing] or sell[ing] any hawking goods in non designated areas'. KENASVIT and its affiliate NISCOF have raised concerns over the draft by-laws and through a forum organized by civil society networks have provided relevant input, which they expect to inform the revised by-law. If passed, this by-law is likely to affect a high percentage of informal workers who rely on street vending and informal trade as a source of employment and income. The city authority licenses fewer than 10,000 street vendors and informal traders, and yet there are over 100,000 traders operating within the city without any licences (Alila and Mitullah 2000). In order to change this situation the street traders have to engage the city authorities in dialogue and negotiation for trading space.

The seven affiliates of KENASVIT are also engaging urban authorities on issues relating to their operations and working environments. The membership of KENASVIT have increased their visibility, confidence and ability to influence urban policies in their own interests. For instance, the Migori Town Urban Alliance has been recognized and its members are represented on a number of local and central government community development committees. The recognition and good relations with the urban authority have effected tremendous changes in the relations of vendors and traders with the council. Harassment, which the traders used to experience, has diminished, and there is an improvement in service delivery by the local authority (KENASVIT/IDS Report 2006).

In Mombasa, the second-largest city in Kenya, the Urban Alliance facilitates resolution of disputes between the city council and the traders, and also negotiates with the city authorities and other stakeholders for trading spaces. The disputes include evictions, payment of daily fees and allocation of trading spaces. The affiliate has linked the traders with financial institutions which offer loans at modest interest rates and has also negotiated with the council on the weekly payment of fees. The affiliate negotiated with the council to ensure that at least 5 per cent of the weekly fees are given back to the affiliate for its operations. Further negotiations with Kenya Ferry Services for trading space resulted in the development of market stalls for traders in Likoni (ibid.).

In Nairobi, the census conducted by the Urban Alliance in collaboration with city authorities and the provincial administration has attracted international interest and has assisted the Urban Alliance in lobbying the city government. Considering that documentation of informal economic activities is generally poor in most African countries, the exercise undertaken by the Urban Alliance is remarkable. Most local authorities have no idea of the number of informal enterprises they are dealing with, and therefore the initiative, which no other local authority in Kenya and hardly any local authorities in other African countries has undertaken, is commendable (Mitullah 2007b).

Overall, the recognition of KENASVIT as an organization of street vendors and informal traders has earned the organization inclusion as a key stakeholder in important national processes. The organization continues to participate in national activities relating to the MSE sector. During the commissioning of a market for street and informal traders in Nairobi by the president of Kenya, both the chairman of KENASVIT and the Nairobi Urban Alliance affiliate NISCOF were invited. The market currently provides trading facilities for a significant percentage of street vendors and informal traders, who previously operated on sites considered illegal by the city authority.

KENASVIT was also helped by resources leveraged from the UUSC to participate in the launch of a concept paper on the National Integrated Employment

Creation Programme for MSEs. This enabled the chairman to identify the fact that street and informal traders were not adequately provided for in the concept paper. In a follow-up press conference, the chairman called for wider consultation on the concept paper. This led to the permanent secretary in the relevant ministry giving the chairman an appointment to explain his protest, which partly influenced an extension of the stakeholder consultation period on the concept paper, to KENASVIT's credit (KENASVIT/IDS Report 2006).

KENASVIT and transnational organizing

Since its creation, KENASVIT has linked up and partnered a number of local, regional and international networks and movements. Most of the activities that the organization has engaged in have been supported by resources leveraged by these organizations. The argument in this chapter concerning the benefits of global organizing to local associations is illustrated by the case of KENASVIT and the transnational organizations with which it collaborates. Since its inception, the alliance has partnered two global social movements, namely StreetNet International and WIEGO, and a non-sectarian organization, the UUSC, and has lately added to its network an international civil society organization, War on Want. The partnerships and working relations with these organizations have facilitated local organizing among KENASVIT members, and strengthened the internal organizational capacity, which has in turn enhanced the organizations' lobbying, advocacy and policy influence capacity.

StreetNet International is a global organization that was conceived by a network of individual street vendors, activists, researchers and organizations, who came together to focus on how to increase the visibility, voice and bargaining power of street vendors throughout the world (StreetNet 2000). The work of StreetNet International is supported through research promoted by another transnational network, WIEGO. StreetNet has twenty-four affiliates in twenty countries across the globe, representing over 300,000 street vendors, informal market vendors and hawkers. The objectives of StreetNet include expanding and strengthening street vendor networks at the international, regional and national levels; building an information base on street vendors in different parts of the world; documenting and disseminating information on effective organizing strategies; and working towards building a solid institutional base for carrying forward its mandate (StreetNet 2006).

WIEGO, a sister organization of StreetNet, is a global research policy network that seeks to improve the status of the working poor, especially women, in the informal economy by highlighting the size, composition, characteristics and contribution of the informal economy through improved statistics and research; by helping to strengthen member-based organizations of informal workers; and by promoting policy dialogues and processes that include representatives of informal worker organizations. The network comprises 150 active members and several hundred associates from over one hundred countries around the world (www.wiego.org). The network has remained in the forefront, collaborating with StreetNet and other international organizations, including the ILO, in advocating and seeking to improve the status of women in the informal economy.

UUSC dates back sixty-five years and is a non-sectarian organization, with more than 47,000 members and supporters, which advances human rights and social justice in the USA and around the world. The programmes of the organization are based on Unitarian Universalist principles that affirm the worth, dignity and human rights of every person – but one need not be a Unitarian Universalist to join UUSC. Through a potent combination of advocacy, education and partnerships with grassroots organizations, UUSC supports programmes and policies that promote workers' rights, defend civil liberties and preserve the rights of those affected by humanitarian crisis (uusc.org/info/about.html).

KENASVIT's initial contact with transnational organizations was through the international coordinator of StreetNet International during the IDS National Dissemination Workshop on the research findings of the women street vendors study in March 2000. The coordinator and other colleagues in WIEGO were part of the team that contributed to the development of the proposal on research on street vendors in Africa. The coordinator of StreetNet International, in collaboration with the IDS, leveraged resources to support the organizing of street vendors and informal traders in Kenya, through their various associations, identified during research.

Information on the activities of the budding alliance was shared in the Street-Net newsletters and also in various forums attended by members of the IDS, StreetNet and WIEGO, where the author was the director of the Urban Policies Programme. Meanwhile, organizing among KENASVIT members, and new activities such as gathering, documenting and packaging relevant information and initiating policy dialogues, was taking place. This required substantial funding, and at the right time a senior officer of the UUSC, who had heard about the budding organization, contacted the IDS, requesting funding through the UUSC Economic and Justice Programme.

The IDS developed a second proposal on behalf of KENASVIT and managed to leverage funds from UUSC for one year to establish a secretariat for KENASVIT, supporting urban alliances, the official launch of KENASVIT and three issues of *The Trader*, a KENASVIT quarterly newsletter. This was followed up by a second, one-year tranche of funding covering: project monitoring; undertaking a rapid assessment of the KENASVIT NEC and of the Urban Alliances; induction seminars for the KENASVIT NEC and for the Urban Alliances; a national conference to discuss the Hawkers Bill; and personnel costs. The third one-year (2007/08) tranche of funding from UUSC supported the consolidation of KENASVIT and its affiliates, and has enabled the employment of a full-time coordinator based in the KENASVIT office in Nakuru. In addition, the funding supported office operations, dialogue with urban authorities, project coordination and monitoring. At the time of writing, UUSC had supported KENASVIT in responding to the 2007 post-election violence through peace-building among traders and a revolving loan fund.

The collaboration between KENASVIT and its transnational development partners goes beyond funding. Both StreetNet and UUSC have enhanced the capacity of KENASVIT by providing training in leadership, team-building, conflict resolution and negotiation. Dealing with these issues has been a major challenge for KENASVIT. Indeed, in 2006 two senior officials of UUSC made a visit to Kenya, during the launch of KENASVIT, and conducted training for KENASVIT NEC members. The training emphasized the need for leaders to be visionary and creative, and to continuously look for opportunities for collaboration, including local, regional and international exchange visits. Apart from the training, UUSC officials also visited three urban alliances and were able to share their global experiences with the street vendors and informal traders.

In 2007, UUSC made a second visit and visited three other Urban Alliances. In each of the Urban Alliances UUSC accompanied the KENASVIT affiliates to meet government authorities, and lobby for the traders' interests. They also met Urban Alliance leaders and representatives of the primary membership and motivated them by sharing their experiences in transnational organizing across the globe (KENASVIT/IDS Report 2006, 2007).

UUSC applies the 'eye to eye' partnership approach, which ensures that power is shared with the people that are supported (KENASVIT/IDS Report 2006). This has been demonstrated in their partnership with KENASVIT, where personal visits are made, and information and ideas are shared both electronically and through face-to-face interaction. The first visit of UUSC officials to KENASVIT and its affiliates was appreciated by the traders, who noted that the UUSC had put Kenyan informal workers on the global map, and had facilitated interaction among street vendors and informal traders in Kenya. To quote one of the chairpersons of an affiliate alliance, 'KENASVIT is taking traders to places they never knew or would reach on their own.'

Transnational organizations such as StreetNet, WIEGO and UUSC are able to influence international development organizations that shape policies and global events. StreetNet and WIEGO have remained in the forefront in the campaign for decent work for informal workers. WIEGO's Urban Policies Programme conducted studies on street and informal trade in Africa and has used the data to influence the policies of key international organizations such as the World Bank and the ILO. Thus, KENASVIT's affiliation to these organizations has exposed the organization to the international dynamics of organizing. In 2006, StreetNet organized a pre-World Social Forum (WSF) meeting in Nairobi, which provided a training ground for KENASVIT members. They benefited from attending the sessions, bonding in solidarity with StreetNet International and its global affiliates. KENASVIT exploited the opportunity fully and organized a press conference which exposed its struggles and the efforts it was making using transnational networks. The international participants encouraged the members of KENASVIT to forge ahead if they wished to change their situation as informal workers. A Korean representative, who had been organizing Korean street vendors and informal traders for over twenty years, encouraged the Kenyan informal workers to sustain the struggle for their rights. He noted that the Koreans had also gone through the rough phase of harassment, but every time they were harassed, they came together, protested and negotiated for their rights.

Through the facilitation of StreetNet and two local civil society organizations, Kenya Land Alliance and Pamoja Trust, Kenyan street vendors and informal traders were able to attend the WSF, whose theme was 'Another world is possible'. The forum provided a further opportunity for Kenyan street vendors and informal traders to interact globally and to make their agenda visible. KENASVIT was able to interact with other StreetNet International affiliates from Nepal, India, Korea, Nicaragua, Mexico, Senegal, Benin, Ghana, Zambia, Malawi, Zimbabwe, Uganda and Tanzania. This cluster of countries, with unique experiences, provided a good seedbed for knowledge- and experience-sharing among workers, who have a common identity as informal workers whose rights are often abused by both local and central governments.

The climax of the WSF was a street vendors' rally whose theme was 'No to poverty and inequality'. The venue of the rally was Uhuru Park, the opening and closing venue of the WSF. The rally was organized by KENASVIT and attended by all the international StreetNet delegates. In spite of the rally being listed among the WSF activities, a hitch was experienced when the city authority insisted that the rally could not take place. This delayed the start of the rally, by two hours, as KENASVIT, supported by the IDS, struggled to ensure that it took place. This hitch made StreetNet International observe in its report on the WSF that street vendors might continue to experience harassment by municipal authorities even if the slogan of the WSF, 'Another world is possible', was realized.

During the WSF, the members of KENASVIT, in particular the seven Urban Alliances, and their banners were visible everywhere, including in the march from the biggest slum in Kenya to the opening and closing venues of the forum. In its report on the forum, StreetNet acknowledges the participation of KENASVIT by noting that 'StreetNet is particularly proud of the way in which KENASVIT members from different Urban Alliances made their presence felt, drew attention to the issues facing street vendors in Kenya and participated with their local allies to add their voices to a range of other socio-economic struggles as well' (KENASVIT 2007). The participation of StreetNet and its affiliates, including KENASVIT, put the issues of street vendors and informal traders on the civil society agenda.

A key contribution of these transnational organizations is putting issues on the global table, where they are picked up by governments, other international development organizations and both international and national civil society organizations. The transnational organizations are able to leverage resources and support local grassroots movements such as KENASVIT. The support provides capacity, boosts the image of local organizations and enables them to negotiate with local governors. It is the international and national civil society organizations which often leverage funds from and push international development organizations and governments to respond to issues relating to the working conditions of informal workers.

Local achievements and challenges

KENASVIT has achieved much through the collaboration and support of transnational organizations, as discussed in this chapter. The support has resulted in the KENASVIT membership regularly meeting and exchanging ideas, establishing a secretariat, engaging in dialogue with authorities, lobbying and influencing policies on informal work, and interacting with informal workers globally. KENASVIT's engagement in land and MSE policy development are two major achievements. Through the support of transnational organizations and a local civil society network, KENASVIT has made tangible contributions to the policy-making process, and authorities are aware of their demands and take their written inputs seriously. However, these two processes are still to be concluded, and it is not possible to judge whether KENASVIT contributions will be well integrated into the final policy outputs. This implies that lobbying and policy influence should not stop until the policy output is realized.

The transnational connections and facilitation have contributed to the KENASVIT NEC beginning to network with its transnational partners and their collaborators though tele-conferences and regular e-mail communication. These communication channels have provided the KENASVIT leadership with an opportunity for networking beyond Kenya. They are able to receive information from other social movements across the globe and to contribute to the ongoing debates on informal economy and decent work.

The achievements are not without challenges. The key challenges facing KENASVIT relate to organizing the affiliates whose capacities are inadequate and who expect support, including skills and finances, from KENASVIT. The urban alliances also require capacity-building. Only two urban alliances out of seven have established secretariats, manned by local officials on a voluntary basis. Two other affiliates established secretariats but these subsequently closed since they could not sustain the offices; one urban alliance uses the KENASVIT secretariat in Nakuru for meetings, while two others have never attempted to establish offices. The latter two, and those that have closed their offices, use the business premises of their officials as contact points and for keeping alliance records. Funds, leveraged by KENASVIT with the support of the IDS in collaboration with transnational organizations, have provided basic support to the Urban Alliances' secretariats. This has included the provision of resources such as stationery and finances for organizing forums, which bring the membership and other stakeholders together to hold dialogues on issues relating to the informal economy and to decent work, including engaging urban authorities.

The capacity of the KENASVIT leadership and that of the affiliate alliances and their membership has been a concern. KENASVIT notes in its Draft Strategic Plan that capacity development seminars will be held on an annual basis for the NEC, the Urban Alliances and the primary association's management committees to improve governance, which is critical to the growth and stability of KENASVIT and its affiliates. The Strategic Plan further notes that KENASVIT will continue to seek collaboration and partnership with relevant government ministries, departments and other development partners in order to realize its objectives (KENASVIT 2007).

Ineffective communication between traders and their leaders, and other key stakeholders such as urban authorities, is another challenge, the reason for which is partly that the traders are yet to develop a sense of common interest as members of the same organization. In addition, communication forums for the members of KENASVIT are limited. Meetings are not held regularly in the Urban Alliances, and in cases where members are located far from each other, and have no unifying activities, the exchange of ideas is rare. Ineffective communication contributes to suspicion and has the potential to destroy the synergy so far generated through transnational organizing.

The reliance on resources leveraged by transnational movements is another challenge. Since its inception, KENASVIT has largely relied on the financial support of its international partners, mobilized with the support of the IDS, and with the IDS overseeing the management of the funds. This framework was initially used because KENASVIT was not registered. Since January 2006, when the organization was registered, the organization has opened a bank account and most Urban Alliances have begun contributing to the organization, although the contributions are minimal and irregular. The estimated cost of US$80,000 per year for the efficient running of the organization is way above the financial capacity of KENASVIT, and the organization has to put more effort into generating funds to sustain the organization, rather than relying on transnational organizations.

Concluding remarks

This chapter has demonstrated that in the face of weak local organizing, transnational networks are an important driving force at the local level. With the support of transnational organizations, local associations are able to organize, lobby and influence policy to their advantage. However, such initiatives are difficult to sustain if local associations do not expand their local resource base. For sustainability, local associations such as KENASVIT have to enlarge their local networks, improve their businesses, generate more income and contribute to the running of the organization. In order for this to occur, capacity-building in the areas of organizing, resource mobilization, leadership and conflict resolution is required, especially among the Urban Alliance leadership and their primary affiliates. Such efforts will not only provide knowledge but will also enhance interaction and information-sharing among the membership and provide the necessary exposure.

Transnational networks and support tend to focus on national bodies, while the local-level associations which are the bedrock of national organizing remain largely untouched. A focus on lower levels has the potential to build strong foundations for the national alliance and create a well-resourced, knowledgeable and well-networked constituency from which the national alliance can draw support, including resources for expanding networks and sustainability.

Organizations of informal workers face challenges in mobilizing relevant resources for organizing their activities, influencing policy and developing capacity for undertaking planned activities. An examination of the roles played by transnational organizations in providing back-up to organizations such as KENASVIT shows enormous support in organizing and capacity-building for leadership and policy dialogue. Most transnational organizations have to compete for funds, and the only difference between them and local associations is their ability to write proposals, fund-raise and network across countries, and indeed continents. Some of them are members of international organizations, while others have an observer status at the United Nations and international organizations. These links provide transnational organizations with the opportunity to gather information in their areas of focus and to build relevant networks in order to push their agenda and support local organizations across nations and continents.

This chapter has discussed how local organizations have partnered transnational organizations in organizing and leveraging resources for lobbying and negotiating with public authorities for enabling policies, among them inclusion in the planning and management of urban resources. This process requires efficient mobilization of local resources, including networks, adequate capacity-building and efficient management of conflict and resources. Thus, we can conclude that, as local associations of workers come together and engage in joint action with support from transnational organizations, they become visible and are recognized by governments and other development partners. This recognition earns them inclusion in local and national processes which influence their working environment and livelihoods.

Notes

Introduction

1 This anthology results from a conference with the theme 'Informalizing economies and new organizing strategies in Africa', held in Uppsala, Sweden, 20–22 April 2007. A second collection resulting from the same conference is being published as a Special Issue in *African Studies Quarterly* (see Lindell 2010c), available at www.africa.ufl.edu/asq/index.htm. I wish to thank the Nordic Africa Institute for sponsoring the conference, and all the participants and discussants for contributing to stimulating discussions during the conference. I am grateful to Amin Kamete, Gunilla Andrae, Amanda Hammar and Andrew Byerley for their comments on this chapter as well as to the two external peer reviewers. Thank you to Birgitta Hellmark-Lindgren and Sonja Johansson for their assistance and to Magnus Calais and Peter Colenbrander for stylistic and language improvements respectively.

2 Among the important exceptions, see Fernández-Kelly (2006), Cross and Morales (2007a) and Roy and Alsayyad (2004).

3 See Fernández-Kelly (2006: 1) for a critique of this view. See also Pieterse (2008: chs 5, 6). Lindell (2010c) discusses the continuum of forms of agency among informal workers, from the individual to the collective.

4 For a discussion of informalization and casualization as a facet of global late capitalism, see Castells and Portes (1989), Cross and Morales (2007a) and Gallin (2001). On the impacts of structural adjustment policies on informal economies, see Hansen and Vaa (2004), Lourenço-Lindell (2002) and Bryceson (2006). On the impacts of interventions by local authorities see Amis (2004) and Brown (2006a). See Lourenço-Lindell

(2002) for a thorough discussion of the multiple and contradictory forces involved in the production of informality – including the state, foreign and domestic capital and popular groups.

5 See Amis (2004), Brown (2006a), Hansen (2004), Lindell and Kamete (forthcoming), Roy (2004a) and Setšabi (2006).

6 'Divide' in this context is not to be interpreted in terms of economic separation between an informal and a formal 'sector'. Rather, it refers to the *organizational* divide that has kept apart workers at both ends of the formal–informal continuum.

7 See, for a discussion, Fernandéz-Kelly (2006: 4) and Potts (2008).

8 See, for example, Centeno and Portes (2006: 29) and Potts (2008: 163). See also Cross and Peña (2006) for a discussion.

9 Rural informality has been left out of this book, although this omission is not intended to deny its importance.

10 See Lindell (2010a) for a discussion of conceptions of class in relation to informality.

11 Personal communication with Pat Horn, Coordinator of Streetnet International, 2006.

12 This understanding of informality is visible in academic work across the political spectrum. See, for example, Bayat's (2004) 'quiet encroachment of the ordinary'; the earlier 'disengagement' perspective (MacGaffey 1988); Centeno and Portes (2006); and the influential works of Castells and Portes (1989) and de Soto (1989).

13 Agamben (1998). See Sad and Poole (2004) for a discussion of this notion in relation to 'the margins' and Roy (2005) for its application to the realm of informality.

14 See Sad and Poole (2004) for a discussion of the illegible practices of the state.

15 This is exemplified by Roy (2003), Cross (1998a) and Lindell (2008a) for Calcutta, Mexico City and Maputo respectively.

16 As Cross (1998a) illustrates for vendors' associations in Mexico, Gay (2006) for neighbourhood associations in Brazil and Dill (2009) on water management associations in Dar es Salaam.

17 For example, a marketers' association in Maputo sometimes appeals to key politicians at central level as a way of seeking protection from the hostilities of the local authorities (Lindell 2008a).

18 See Hansen (2004) and Potts (2008). Personal communication with Amanda Hammar. See also Cross (1998a) and Gay (2006) for examples beyond Africa.

19 As clarified earlier, 'divide' here refers to the *organizational* divide that has kept apart workers at both ends of the formal–informal continuum.

20 Gallin (2001), Horn (2005), Lindell (2008b), ILO (1999) and chapters by Andrae and Beckman, Jimu, Jordhus-Lier and Boampong in this collection.

21 See Gallin (2001: 531–49), Horn (2005: 25–6). See also the chapter by Andrae and Beckman for a discussion.

22 This bridging of urban and rural popular concerns suggests an interesting development that has been noted elsewhere, in the Latin American context (Harvard Trade Union Program 2001).

23 Such institutions include not only international financial institutions, but also regional and international organizations regulating international economic exchanges.

2 The politics of vulnerability

1 The Igbo were a stateless society in pre-colonial times, and tend to identify more strongly with their local sub-communities, based on genealogical and political groupings that share a common dialect of Igbo.

2 Interview with president and secretary of Aba Garment Manufacturers' Cooperative, Aba, 5 November 1999 and 7 April 2000.

3 Interview with chairman, Umuehilegbu Industrial Shoe Makers Union, Umuehilegbu Shoe Production Zone (aka Bakassi), 22 November 1999.

4 Interview with chairman, United Shoe Manufacturers Association of Nigeria, Imo Avenue Shoe Production Zone, Aba, 26 August 2000; interview with chairman, Umuehilegbu Industrial Shoe Makers Union, Umuehilegbu Shoe Production Zone (aka Bakassi), 22 November 1999, 14 August 2000.

5 President, Aba Garment Manufacturers' Cooperative, Aba, 24 August 2000.

6 Meeting between president of Aba Garment and official of NUTGTWN, 10 May 2001.

3 Women leaders

1 Perham (1970); Paulme (1963); Lebeuf (1963); Marshall (1964); Van Allen (1976); Okonjo (1976); Clark (1994); Cordonnier (1987); Eames (1988); Humarau (1996, 1997); Amadiume (1987, 1995, 1997); Coquery-Vidrovitch (1994: 115, 2001); Heilbrunn (1997a, b); Rosander (1997); Sarr (1998).

2 Membership figures are seldom reliable, because actors tend to boost them to signal their influence. Moreover, her contacts at the market in Parakou seemed to be scarce, and her influence is probably strongest in the south.

3 The state institution which centralizes all tax and other state income.

4 Syfia International,15 March 2002; Grâce Victoire Oussa, www.enmarche.be/ Cooperation/Femmes_actrices.htm.

5 At the end of January 2007, Lucienne Carrena Azonhoumoun was dismissed on suspicion of having set up an illegal network selling falsified tickets at Dantokpa. A new woman, Denise A. H. Houngninou, was appointed to the position. She was later accused of multiple cases of embezzlement and irregularities (*Le Matin*, 25 August 2007) and sacked in November 2007, when Joseph Tamègnon, former

RB politician, was appointed. Chodaton's union SYNAVAMAB was involved in the firing of both the second and the third woman in 2007.

5 Self-organized workers in Malawi

1 'Now the street beggars have been cleared from the streets', *The Times* (Malawi), 5 January 1967.

2 Chimyeke Tembo, 'Vendors to sue mayor', *The Nation*, 30 November 1995.

3 'Over 80 street peddlers fined', *Daily Times*, 9 July 1990.

4 'No end to street vending problem', *Daily Times*, Wednesday, 26 January 1994.

5 The first ever multiparty general elections that took place in May 1994 ousted the autocratic rule of late Dr Banda. See 'Cheated – Vendors cry out for freedom', *Daily Times*, 15 July 1994.

6 'Street vendors present a petition to city', *Daily Times*, 25 January 1994.

7 Based on an interview with Councillor Anna Kachikho, the former deputy mayor who is now a member of parliament and minister, on 31 October 2002, and the chairman of the Limbe Street Vendors on 25 October 2002.

8 'BT City Council demolishes structures', *Daily Times*, Wednesday, 24 January 1996.

9 Emmanuel Muwamba reported that NABW training aims at fighting poverty and uplifting the economic status of women. 'NABW trains 25 women', *The Nation*, 30 October 2006.

6 Moments of resistance

1 This chapter is based on a paper presented at this conference.

2 At the time of writing, senior management in the city of Cape Town claimed that the widespread use of labour broker staff was being phased out owing to operational requirements.

7 Collective organization in Ghana

1 Lawson (1992) disaggregates employment relations to include nature of contract, regularity of job, wages and income, benefits enjoyed by workers, training and skill acquisition, career progression and health and safety issues.

2 The NRC/SMC government led by General Acheampong ousted the Progress Party in 1972 in a military coup.

3 Before the retrenchment these casual workers had been converted to permanent staff, according to Manuh.

4 The composition of casual workers at the port today is not made up of individuals from northern Ghana only. The workers come from diverse geographical and ethnic backgrounds, including from neighbouring countries (Boampong 2005).

5 The casual workers interviewed persistently referred to themselves as 'permanent casual workers' because of their long tenure of employment with the port authority. This notion of permanent employment status assumed by the casual workers was reinforced by the readiness of GPHA to pay compensation to the workers when it decided to lay them off, even though there was no formal employment agreement between them (Ghanaian Chronicle 2002).

6 The exact number of these local unions in Tema, as well as those which are members of MDU, could not be ascertained in the field.

7 Subsection 75(1) stipulates that 'a temporary worker who is employed by the same employer for a continuous period of six months and more shall be treated under this Part as a permanent worker'. The act defines a temporary worker as a worker who is employed for a continuous period of not less than one month and is not a permanent worker, or employed for work that is seasonal in character. On the other hand it defines a casual worker as a worker engaged in work which is seasonal or intermittent and not for a continuous period of more than six months and whose remuneration is calculated on a daily basis. Since a distinction is made between casual workers and temporary workers, it is not clear if the subsection which specifically mentions temporary workers also covers casual workers.

8 This is an old practice, which has

been maintained and elaborated through the efforts of the local union and implemented in tandem with the agency.

9 The minimum wage as at 2004 was 11,000 cedis or approximately US$1.2. The basic wages for the same period for GDLC regular gang members and headmen were 21,894 cedis or US$2.4 and 26,370 cedis or US$2.8 respectively. The casual workers were paid a transport allowance of 9,150 cedis (Boampong 2005: 59–61).

9 Passport, please

1 Among them are: Zambia Fisheries and Marketeers Union, Tinsmith Association of Zambia (Lusaka), Chibolya Carpentry, Shoe and Fence Wire Making and Blacksmith Association (Kitwe), Mansa Carpenters Association (Mansa), and Tuntemba Association of Zambia (Kalulushi, Kitwe).

2 The exchange rate at the time was approximately K4,000 to US$1.

3 As a legacy of colonial history, persons from the Indian subcontinent still have a large presence in commerce and trade in Zambia.

4 Zambian Airways charges US50 cents per kilogram of excess baggage.

5 COMESA defines a customs union as the 'merger of two or more customs territories into a single customs territory, in which customs duties and other measures that restrict trade are eliminated for substantially all trade between the merged territories' (COMESA 2004).

10 Informal workers in Kenya

1 Informal economy includes all types of 'non-standard' wage employment including 'sweatshop production', homework, temporary and part-time work, and unregulated workers, all of which have direct and indirect links with the formal economy (Carr and Chen 2002).

2 Social movements consist of diffuse agglomerations of individuals within civil society who are linked together by ideology, belief or collective identities. Organizations created by social movements bridge the social and political spheres, translating the beliefs of the social movement participants into political action. Organizations may catalyse the creation of such agglomerations or may be generated by them. Thus the relationship between organizations and social movements is co-causal (Rubin 2001).

Bibliography

Ackerman, J. (2004) 'Co-governance for accountability: beyond "exit" and "voice"', *World Development*, 32(3).

Adu-Amankwah, K. (1999) 'Ghana', *Labour Education*, 3(116).

Agamben, G. (1998) *Homo Sacer: Sovereign Power and Bare Life*, Palo Alto, CA: Stanford University Press.

Agarwala, R. (2007) 'Resistance and compliance in the age of globalization: Indian women and labor organizations', *ANNALS of the American Academy of Political and Social Science*, 610(1).

Aguilar, E. E., A. Pacek and D. S. Thornton (1998) 'Political participation among informal sector workers in Mexico and Costa Rica', Paper presented at a meeting of the Latin American Studies Association, Chicago, IL, 24–26 September.

Aina, T. (1997) 'The state and civil society: politics, government and social organization in African cities', in C. Rakodi (ed.), *The Urban Challenge in Africa*, Tokyo/New York/Paris: United Nations University Press.

Alila P. A. and W. V. Mitullah (2000) 'Enhancing the lobbying capacity of women street vendors: the challenges in the Kenyan policy environment', IDS Occasional Paper, University of Nairobi, Nairobi.

Allen, J. (2004) 'The whereabouts of power: politics, government and space', *Geografiska Annaler, Series B*, 86(1).

Alsayyad, N. (2004) 'Urban informality as a "new" way of life', in A. Roy and N. Alsayyad (eds), *Urban Informality: Transnational Perspectives from the Middle East, Latin America, and South Asia*, Lanham, MD/Boulder, CO/New York/ Toronto/Oxford: Lexington Books.

Altman, M. (2005) 'The state of unemployment', in J. Daniel, R. Southall and J. Lutchman (eds), *State of the Nation: South Africa 2004–2005*, Cape Town: HSRC Press.

Alves, P. and P. Draper (2006) 'Introduction: China's growing role in Africa', in G. le Pere (ed.), *China in Africa: Mercantilist Predator or Partner in Development?*, Midrand/Johannesburg: Institute for Global Dialogue/South African Institute of International Affairs.

Amadiume, I. (1987) *Male Daughters, Female Husbands: Gender and Sex in an African Society*, London: Zed Books.

— (1995) 'Gender, political systems and social movements: a West African experience', in M. Mamdani and E. Wamba-dia-Wamba (eds), *African Social Movements and Democracy*, Dakar: CODESRIA.

— (1997) *Reinventing Africa – Matriarchy, Religion and Culture*, London: Zed Books.

Amarteifio, G. W. et al. (1966) *Tema Manhean, a Study of Resettlement*, Accra: Ghana Universities Press.

Amis, P. (2004) 'Regulating the informal sector: voice and bad governance', in N. Devas (ed.), *Urban Governance, Voice and Poverty in the Developing World*, London: Earthscan.

Anderson, B. (2003) 'Porto Alegre: a worm's-eye view', *Global Networks*, 3(2).

Andrae, G. (2006) 'Urban labour, livelihood and land in South Africa and Nigeria: workers' reproduction relations and their politics of production', Paper presented to the World Congress of the International Sociological Association (RC44), Durban, 23–29 July.

Andrae, G. and B. Beckman (1998) *Union Power in the Nigerian Textile Industry. Labour Regime and Adjustment*, Uppsala: Nordic Africa Institute.

Anyemedu, A. (2000) 'Trade unions responses to globalization: case study on Ghana', Labour and Society Programme Discussion Papers no. 121.

Appadurai, A. (2001) 'Deep democracy: urban governmentality and the horizon of politics', *Environment and Urbanization*, 13(2).

Baah-Boateng, W. (2004) 'Employment policies for sustainable development: the experience of Ghana', GOG/UNDP/ILO, Golden Tulip, Ghana.

Baker, J., J. Obama, N. Sola and H. Wallevik (2002) *The Local Government Reform Process in Tanzania: Towards a Greater Interdependency between Local Government and Civil Society at the Local Level?*, Report from the collaboration between Mzumbe University, Tanzania, and Agder University College, Norway, Kristiansand: Agder Research Foundation.

Balbo, M. and G. Marconi (2005) 'Governing international migration in the city of the South', *Global Migration Perspectives*, 38.

Ballard, R. (2005) 'Social movements in post-apartheid South Africa: an introduction', in P. Jones and K. Stokke (eds), *Democratising Development: The Politics of Socio-economic Rights in South Africa*, Leiden/Boston, MA: Martinus Nijhoff Publishers.

Ballard, R., A. Habib and I. Valodia (2006) 'From anti-apartheid to post-apartheid social movements', in R. Ballard, A. Habib and I. Valodia (eds), *Voices of Protest: Social Movements in Post-Apartheid South Africa*, Scottsville: University of KwaZulu-Natal Press.

Banda, J. (1997) 'Address by Joyce Banda on the occasion of receiving the 1997 Africa Prize for Leadership', available online at africaprize.org/97/jb097.htm, accessed 19 April 2007.

Banégas, R. (1998) 'Marchandisation du vote, citoyenneté et consolidation démocratique au Bénin', *Politique Africaine*, 69.

— (2003) 'La démocratie à pas de caméléon – transition et imaginaires politiques au Bénin', Paris: Editions Karthala.

Barnes, J. S. (1986) *Patrons and Power: Creating a Political Community in Metropolitan Lagos*, Manchester: Manchester University Press.

Bayart, J.-F. et al. (eds) (1999) *The Criminalization of the State in Africa*, Oxford/Bloomington: James Currey/Indiana University Press.

Bayat, A. (1997a) 'Uncivil society: the politics of the "informal people"', *Third World Quarterly*, 18(1).

— (1997b) *Street Politics: Poor People's Movements in Iran*, New York: Columbia University Press.

— (2004) 'Globalization and the politics of the informals in the global South', in A. Roy and N. Alsayyad (eds), *Urban Informality: Transnational Perspectives from the Middle East, Latin America, and South Asia*, Lanham, MD/Boulder, CO/New York/Toronto/Oxford: Lexington Books.

BBC (2009) 'Timeline: Nepal', available online at new.bbc.co.uk/1/hi/world/south_asia/1166516.stm, accessed June 2008.

Beckman, B. (2005a) 'The politics of reform: responses of African trade unions with a South African case', Paper presented to the African Studies Seminar, St Antony's College, Oxford, 27 April.

— (2005b) 'Unions versus free trade: trade unions and globalization in South Africa's clothing and textiles industry', Paper presented to the conference on Globalization: Overcoming Exclusion, Strengthening Inclusion, organized by the Globalization Studies Network and CODESRIA, Dakar, 29–31 August.

Beckman, B. and S. Lukman (2006) 'The failure of Nigeria's Labour Party', Paper presented to the workshop on Trade Unions and Party Politics: Africa in a Comparative Perspective, Johannesburg, 21/22 July, and the World Congress of the International Sociological Association (RC44), Durban, 23–29 July.

Bennet, J. R. (1998) 'Business associations and their potential contribution to the competitiveness of SMEs', *Entrepreneurship and Regional Development*, 10(3).

Bieler, A., I. Lindberg and D. Pillay (2008) 'The future of the global working class: an introduction', in A. Bieler, I. Lindberg and D. Pillay (eds), *Labour and the Challenges of Globalization: What Prospects for Transnational Solidarity*, London: Pluto Press.

Bigsten, A. and A. Danielson (2001) *Tanzania: Is the Ugly Duckling Finally Growing Up?*, Research Report 120, OECD Project on Emerging Africa, Uppsala: Nordic Africa Institute.

Blunch, N.-H., S. Canagarajah and D. Raju (2001) 'The informal sector revisited: a synthesis across space and time', Social Protection Discussion Paper no. 0119, World Bank.

Boampong, O. (2005) 'Formalising the informal, recruiting through intermediaries: a way out or a way to the bottom', Unpublished master's thesis, Department of Sociology and Human Geography, University of Oslo.

Bond, P. (2000) *Elite Transition: From Apartheid to Neoliberalism in South Africa*, London: Pluto Press.

Boumedouha, S. (1990) 'Adjustment to West African realities: the Lebanese in Senegal', *Journal of the International African Institute*, 60(4).

Bourdieu, P. (1984/2002) *Questions de Sociologie*, Paris: Les Editions de Minuit.

Brecher, J. and T. Costello (1990) *Building Bridges: The Emerging Grassroots Coalition of Labor and Community*, New York: Monthly Review Press.

Bredeloup, S. and B. Bertoncello (2006) 'La migration chinoise en Afrique: accélérateur du développement ou "sanglot de l'homme noir"?', *Afrique Contemporaine*, 2(218).

Breman, J. (2004) *The Making and Unmaking of an Industrial Working Class: Sliding Down the Labour Hierarchy in Ahmedabad, India*, Amsterdam: Amsterdam University Press.

Bromley, R. D. F. (1998) 'Informal commerce: expansion and exclusion in the historical center of the Latin American City', *International Journal of Urban and Regional Research*, 22(2).

Bronfenbrenner, K., S. Friedman, R. W. Hurd, R. A. Oswald and R. L. Seeber (eds) (1998) *Organizing to Win: New Research on Union Strategies*, Ithaca, NY: Cornell University Press.

Brown, A. (ed.) (2006a) *Contested Space: Street Trading, Public Space, and Livelihoods in Developing Cities*, Rugby: ITDG Publishing.

— (2006b) 'Social, economic and political influences on the informal sector in Ghana, Lesotho, Nepal and Tanzania', in A. Brown (ed.), *Contested Space: Street Trading, Public Space, and Livelihoods in Developing Cities*, Rugby: ITDG Publishing.

Brown, A. and T. Nnkya (2006) 'Rights to the city: contested space and urban livelihoods', Paper presented at the World Planning Schools Conference, Planning for Diversity and Multiplicity, 12–16 July, Mexico.

Bryceson, D. (2006) 'African urban economies: searching for sources of sustainability', in D. Bryceson and D. Potts (eds), *African Urban Economies: Viability, Vitality or Vitiation?*, New York: Palgrave Macmillan.

Buckley, G. (1997) 'Microfinance in Africa: is it either the problem or the solution?', *World Development*, 25(7).

Buggenhagen, B. (2003) 'At home in the black Atlantic. Circulation, domesticity and value in the Senegalese Murid trade diaspora', Unpublished PhD thesis, University of Chicago.

Buhlungu, S. (2003) 'The state of trade unionism in post-apartheid South Africa', in J. Daniel, A. Habib and R. Southall (eds), *State of the Nation: South Africa 2003–2004*, Cape Town: HSRC Press.

Bureau des Echanges Extérieurs (1996) *Annuaire des Statistiques du Commerce Extérieur*, Tome 4/8, Dakar: Produit-Pay.

— (2005) *Annuaire des Statistiques du Commerce Extérieur*, Tome 4/8, Dakar: Produit-Pay.

Callaghy, T. (1994) 'Civil society, democracy, and economic change in Africa: a dissenting opinion about resurgent societies', in J. W. Harbeson, D. Rothchild and N. Chazan (eds), *Civil Society and the State in Africa*, Boulder, CO: Lynne Rienner.

Carr, M. and M. A. Chen (2002) *Globalization and the Informal Economy: How Global Trade and Investment Impact on the Working Poor*, Geneva: International Labour Office.

— (2004) 'Globalization, social exclusion and work: with special reference to informal employment and gender', Working Paper no. 20, Geneva: International Labour Organization.

Carter, D. (1997) *States of Grace: Senegalese in Italy and the New European Immigration*, Minnesota: University of Minnesota Press.

Castells, M. (1997) *The Rise of the Network Society*, Oxford: Blackwell.

Castells, M. and A. Portes (1989) 'World underneath: the origins, dynamics and effects of the informal economy', in A. Portes, M. Castells and L. Benton (eds), *The Informal Economy: Studies in Advanced and Less Developed Countries*, London: Johns Hopkins Press.

CBS/ACEG/K-REP (1999) *Micro and Small Enterprises: Baseline Survey*, Central Bureau of Statistics, African Centre for Economic Growth and K-REP, Nairobi.

CBTA (2006) *The Cross Border Traders Association Constitution*, Lusaka: CBTA.

Centeno, M. and A. Portes (2006) 'The informal economy in the shadow of the state', in P. Fernández-Kelly and J. Shefner (eds), *Out of the Shadows: Political Action and the Informal Economy in Latin America*, Pennsylvania: Pennsylvania State University Press.

Cheadle, H. and M. Clarke (2000) 'Country study: South Africa', *ILO Report: National Studies on Worker Protection*, 1(52).

Chen, M., R. Jhablava and F. Lund (2002) 'Supporting workers in the informal economy: a policy framework', Working Paper on the Informal Economy, Geneva: International Labour Organization, www.wiego.org, accessed 15 November 2007.

Chimombo, D. (2006) 'Malawi street traders seek dialogue: letter from Davis Chimombo', Malawi Union for the Informal Sector (MUFIS), 9 March 2006, available online at www.streetnet.org.za/English/newsarchive06.htm, accessed 19 April 2007.

Chun, J. (2005) 'Public dramas and the politics of justice: comparison of janitors' struggles in South Korea and the United States', *Work and Occupations*, 32(4).

CIPE (1998) 'Strengthening the voice of businesses', *Economic Reform Today*, 4, Centre for International Private Enterprise, available online at www.cipe.org/publications/ert/e30/E30_5.pdf, accessed 19 April 2007.

Clark, G. (ed.) (1988) *Traders versus the State: Anthropological Approaches to Unofficial Economies*, Boulder, CO: Westview Press.

— (1994) *Onions are My Husband: Survival and Accumulation by West African Women*, Chicago, IL: Chicago University Press.

— (2010) 'Loyalties and scapegoats: relations between market traders and governments from the past to the present, Kumasi, Ghana', in I. Lindell (ed.), *Between Exit and Voice: Informality and the Spaces of Popular Agency*, Special Issue of *African Studies Quarterly*, 11(2/3), available online at www.africa.ufl.edu/asq/index.htm.

Cohen, B. (2003) 'Urban growth in developing countries: a review of current trends and a caution regarding existing forecasts', *World Development*, 32(1).

Cohen, M., M. Bhatt and P. Horn (2000) 'Women street vendors: the road to recognition', *Seeds*, 20, New York: Population Council.

Coleman, J. (1988) 'Social capital in the creation of human capital', *American Journal of Sociology*, 94.

COMESA (2004) www.comesa.int/trade/Folder.2004-04-19.2132, accessed 27 February 2007.

Coquery-Vidrovitch, C. (1994) *Les Afric-aines – Histoire des femmes d'Afrique noire du XIXe au XXe siècle*, Paris: Editions Desjonquères.

— (2001) 'Des femmes colonisées aux femmes de l'indépendence, ou du misérabilisme au développement par les femmes: approche historique', Paper presented at the Colloque Internationale Genre, Population et Développement en Afrique, available online at www.ined.fr/coll_abidjan/publis/pdf/session2/coquery.pdf, accessed 30 August 2009.

Cordonnier, R. (1987) *Femmes africaines et commerce – les revendeuses de tissu de la ville de Lomé (Togo)*, Paris: Editions l'Harmattan.

COSATU (1997) *September Commission Report*, Congress of South African Trade Unions.

Cross, J. (1998a) *Informal Politics: Street Vendors and the State in Mexico City*, Stanford, CA: Stanford University Press.

— (1998b) 'Co-optation, competition, and resistance: state and street vendors in Mexico City', *Latin American Perspectives*, 25(2).

— (2000) 'Organizing the informal sector: notes from the field', Paper written for a panel presentation as part of an ILO conference on the potential for trade union organization of the informal sector.

— (2007) 'Pirates on the high streets: the street as a site of local resistance to globalization', in J. Cross and A. Morales (eds), *Street Entrepreneurs: People, Place and Politics in Local and Global Perspective*, London/New York: Routledge.

Cross, J. and A. Morales (2007a) 'Introduction: locating street markets in the modern/postmodern world', in J. Cross and A. Morales (eds), *Street Entrepreneurs: People, Place and Politics in Local and Global Perspective*, London/New York: Routledge.

— (2007b) *Street Entrepreneurs: People, Place and Politics in Local and Global Perspective*, London/New York: Routledge.

Cross, J. and S. Peña (2006) 'Risk and regu-lation in informal and illegal markets', in P. Fernández-Kelly and J. Shefner (eds), *Out of the Shadows: Political Action and the Informal Economy in Latin America*, Pennsylvania, Pennsylvania State University Press.

Cruise O'Brien, R. (1975) 'Lebanese entre-preneurs in Senegal: economic integra-tion and the politics of protection', *Cahiers d'Études Africaines*, 15(15).

Cumbers, A., P. Routledge and C. Nativel (2008) 'The entangled geographies of global justice networks', *Progress in Human Geography*, 32(2).

DCC (Dar es Salaam City Council) (1999) *Strategic Urban Development Planning Framework: Draft for the City of Dar es Salaam*, Dar Es Salaam: Dar Es Salaam City Council.

De Neve, G. (2004) *The Everyday Politics of Labour: Working Lives in India's Informal Economy*, Delhi: Social Science Press.

De Soto, H. (1989) *The Other Path*, New York: Harper and Row.

Debroux, M. (2002) 'Informal solidarity, yes! Informal exploitation, NO!', *Unpro-tected Labour: What Role for Unions in the Informal Economy? Labour Educa-tion*, 2(27).

Della Porta, D. and S. Tarrow (2004) 'Transnational processes and social activism: an introduction' in D. Della Porta and S. Tarrow (eds), *Trans-national and Global Activism*, Oxford: Rowman & Littlefield.

Desai, A. (2003) 'Neoliberalism and resist-ance in South Africa', *Monthly Review*, 54(8).

Devas, N. (ed.) (2004) *Urban Governance, Voice and Poverty in the Developing World*, London: Earthscan.

— (2005) 'Metropolitan governance and urban poverty', *Public Administration and Development*, 25(4).

Devenish, A. and C. Skinner (2006) 'Col-lective action in the informal economy: the case of the Self-Employed Women's Union, 1994–2004', in R. Ballard, A. Habib and I. Valodia (eds), *Voices of Protest*, Scottsville: University of KwaZulu-Natal Press.

Dey, D. (ed.) (2007) *The Informal Sector in a Globalized Era*, Hyderabad: Icfai University Press.

Dill, B. (2009) 'Reap what you sow: governmentality and the agency of community-based organizations', Paper presented at the 3rd European Conference on African Studies, Leipzig, 4–7 June.

Diouf, M. (1999) 'The French colonial policy of assimilation and the civility of the Originaire of the Four Communes (Senegal): a nineteenth century globalization project', in B. Meer and P. Geschiere (eds), *Globalization and Identity: Dialectics of Flow and Closure*, Oxford: Blackwell.

— (2000) 'The Senegalese Mourid trade diaspora and the making of a vernacular cosmopolitanism', *CODESRIA Bulletin*, 1.

Dudrah, R. K. (2003) 'Constructing city spaces through Black popular cultures and the Black public sphere', *City*, 6(3).

Eames, E. A. (1988) 'Why the women went to war: women and wealth in Ondo Town, southwestern Nigeria', in G. Clark (ed.), *Traders versus the State: Anthropological Approaches to Unofficial Economies*, Boulder, CO: Westview Press.

Ebin, V. (1995) 'International networks of a trading diaspora: the Mourids of Senegal abroad', in P. Antoine and A. B. Diop (eds), *La Ville à Guichets Fermés? Itinéraires, Réseaux et Insertion Urbaine*, Dakar: ORSTOM.

E-COMESA (2006) No. 48, 7 July.

Edelman, M. (2008) 'Transnational organizing in agrarian Central America: histories, challenges, prospects', in S. M. Borras, M. Edelman and C. Kay (eds), *Transnational Agrarian Movements Confronting Globalization*, New York: Wiley-Blackwell.

Englund, H. (2000) 'The dead hand of human rights: contrasting Christianities in post-transition Malawi', *Journal of Modern African Studies*, 38(4).

— (2002) 'The village in the city, the city in the village: migrants in Lilongwe', *Journal of Southern African Studies*, 28(1).

Evans, A. and E. Ngalewa (2003) 'Tanzania', in D. Booth (ed.), *Fighting Poverty in Africa: Are PRSPs Making a Difference?*, London: Overseas Development Institute.

Faloya, T. (1990) 'Lebanese traders in southwestern Nigeria, 1900–1960', *African Affairs*, 89(357).

Fernández-Kelly, P. (2006) 'Introduction', in P. Fernández-Kelly and J. Shefner (eds), *Out of the Shadows: Political Action and the Informal Economy in Latin America*, Pennsylvania: Pennsylvania State University Press.

Fernández-Kelly, P. and J. Shefner (eds) (2006) *Out of the Shadows: Political Action and the Informal Economy in Latin America*, Pennsylvania: Pennsylvania State University Press.

Fidler, P. and L. Webster (1996) 'The informal sector of West Africa', in L. Webster and P. Fidler (eds), *The Informal Sector and Microfinance Institutions in West Africa*, Washington, DC: International Bank for Reconstruction and Development/World Bank.

Fisher-French, M., N. Tolsi, R. Tabane and T. Makgetla (2007) 'Towards a social democracy?', *Mail and Guardian*, 16 February.

Forrest, T. (1994) *The Advance of African Capital: The Growth of Nigerian Private Enterprise*, Edinburgh: Edinburgh University Press for the International African Institute.

Foster, D. and P. Scott (1998) 'Conceptualising union responses to contracting out municipal services, 1979–97', *Industrial Relations Journal*, 29(2).

Freund, W. (1988) *The African Worker*, Cambridge: Cambridge University Press.

Friedman, S. (2006) 'Participatory governance and citizen action in post-apartheid South Africa', Discussion paper DP164/2006, Geneva: International Institute for Labour Studies/International Labour Organization.

Gallin, D. (2001) 'Propositions on trade

unions and informal employment in times of globalization', *Antipode*, 33(3).

— (2002) 'Organizing in the informal economy', *Unprotected Labour: What Role for Unions in the Informal Economy? Labour Education*, 2(29).

— (2004) 'Organizing in the global informal economy', Paper presented at the Social Policy Forum: The Changing Role of Unions in the Contemporary World of Labour, Istanbul, 26/27 November, available online at www.global-labour.org, accessed 17 October 2007.

Gallin, D. and P. Horn (2005) 'Organizing informal women workers', StreetNet International.

Gay, R. (2006) 'The even more difficult transition from clientelism to citizenship: lessons from Brazil', in P. Fernández-Kelly and J. Shefner (eds), *Out of the Shadows: Political Action and the Informal Economy in Latin America*, Pennsylvania: Pennsylvania State University Press.

Gelb, S. (2005) 'An overview of the South African economy', in J. Daniel, R. Southall and J. Lutchman (eds), *State of the Nation: South Africa 2004–2005*, Cape Town: HSRC Press.

Gellar, S. (1982) *Senegal: An African Nation between Islam and the West*, Boulder, CO: Westview Press.

Ghanaian Chronicle (2002) 'Calm returns to Tema port', 30 May.

Goldie, C. (2002) 'Living in public space: a human rights wasteland', *Alternative Law Journal*, 27(4).

Government of Malawi (1995) 'Policy framework for Poverty Alleviation Programme', PAP Coordinating Unit, Ministry of Economic Planning and Development, Lilongwe.

— (2000a) 'The state of Malawi's poor: their economic characteristics', Poverty Monitoring Systems (PMS) briefing no. 6.

— (2000b) 'The state of Malawi's poor: the incidence, depth and severity of poverty', Poverty Monitoring Systems (PMS) briefing no. 6.

— (2000c) *GEMINI Micro and Small Enterprise (MSE) Baseline Survey*, Zomba: National Statistical Office.

Grainger, S. (2006) 'Growing together', *Focus on Africa*, British Broadcasting Corporation, January–March, pp. 52–3.

Green, C. and S. Baden (1994) *Women and Development in Malawi*, Report prepared for the Commission of European Communities Directorate-General for Development, Institute of Development Studies, University of Sussex, Brighton.

GRZ (Government of the Republic of Zambia) (2006) *2006 Formal Sector Employment and Earnings Inquiry Report*, Lusaka: Central Statistical Office.

Guardian Weekly (2007) 'Risky business of informal cross border trade', 24 February–2 March.

Gutkind, P. W. C. (1973) 'From the energy of despair to the anger of despair: the transition from social circulation to political consciousness among the urban poor in Africa', *Canadian Journal of African Studies*, 7(2).

Habib, A. and H. Kotzé (2002) *Civil Society, Governance and Development in an Era of Globalization*, Durban: University of Natal.

Habitat Debate (2007) 13(12).

Hall, D., J. Lethbridge and E. Lobina (2005) 'Public–public partnerships in health and essential services', Occasional Paper Series, No. 9, Municipal Services Project, Queen's University.

Hansen, K. T. (1997) *Keeping House in Lusaka*, New York: Columbia University Press.

— (2000) *Salaula: The World of Secondhand Clothing and Zambia*, Chicago, IL: University of Chicago Press.

— (2004) 'Who rules the streets? The politics of vending space in Lusaka', in K. Hansen and M. Vaa (eds), *Reconsidering Informality: Perspectives from Urban Africa*, Uppsala: Nordic Africa Institute.

Hansen, K. T. and M. Vaa (eds) (2004) *Reconsidering Informality: Perspectives from Urban Africa*, Uppsala: Nordic Africa Institute.

Harrison, P. (2006) 'Integrated development plans and Third Way politics', in U. Pillay, R. Tomlinson and J. du Toit (eds), *Democracy and Delivery: Urban Policy in South Africa*, Cape Town: HSRC Press.

Hart, K. (1973) 'Informal income opportunities and urban employment in Ghana', *Journal of Modern African Studies*, 11(6).

— (2005) 'Formal bureaucracy and the emergent forms of the informal economy', United Nations University, Wider, Research Paper no. 2005/11, available at www.wider.unu.edu/publications/working-papers/research-papers/2005/en_GB/research_papers_2005/?startAt=31&sortField=2&sortDir=asc, accessed 11 September 2009.

Hartzenberg, T. (2003) 'The new SADC agreement', in D. Hansohm, W. Breytenbach and T. Hartzenberg (eds), *Monitoring Regional Integration in Southern Africa: Yearbook, Volume 3*, Windhoek: Gamsberg Macmillan Publishers.

Harvard Trade Union Program (2001) 'Report on the Conference on Organizing Informal Workers in the Global Economy: Unions, Co-operatives, Advocacy Networks, and Emerging Labor Organizations', Harvard University, October 2001, available online at www.wiego.org, accessed 12 November 2007.

Hashim, Y. (1994) *The State and Trade Unions in Africa: A Study of Macro-Corporatism*, The Hague: Institute of Social Studies.

Haugen, H. Ø. and J. Carling (2005) 'On the edge of the Chinese Diaspora: the surge of Baihuo business in an African city', *Ethnic and Racial Studies*, 28(4).

Heath, D. (1990) 'Fashion, anti-fashion and heteroglossia in urban Senegal', *American Ethnologist*, 19.

Heilbrunn, J. R. (1997a) 'Market, profits and power: the politics of business in Benin and Togo', *Travaux et Documents*, 53, Centre d'Etude d'Afrique Noire (CEAN), Institut d'Etudes Politiques de Bordeaux.

— (1997b) 'Commerce, politics and business associations in Benin and Togo', *Comparative Politics*, 29(4).

Hermochova, S. (1997) 'Reflections on living through the changes in Eastern Europe', *Annals of the American Academy of Political Science*, 552.

Herod, A. (1998) 'The spatiality of labor unionism: a review essay', in A. Herod (ed.), *Organizing the Landscape*, Minneapolis: University of Minnesota Press.

Hickey, S. and G. Mohan (2005) *Participation: From Tyranny to Transformation?*, London/New York: Zed Books.

Hill, E. (2001) 'Women in the Indian informal economy: collective strategies for work life improvement and development', *Work, Employment, Society*, 15(3).

HMG CBS (2002) *Population Census, 2001, National Report*, Kathmandu: His Majesty's Government of Nepal, National Planning Commission Secretariat, Central Bureau of Statistics (HMG CBS) and the United Nations Population Fund.

Hope, K. R., Sr (2001) 'Indigenous small enterprises development in Africa: growth and impact of the subterranean economy', *European Journal of Development Research*, 13(1).

Horn, P. (2002) 'The realities, the organizing strategies, and the policy priorities of street vendors and their organization', Paper presented at the conference 'Rethinking labor market informalization', Cornell University, 18/19 October.

— (2003) 'Voice regulation in the informal economy and new forms of work', available online at www.global-labour.org.

— (2005) 'Unions targeting the unorganised', *South African Labour Bulletin*, 29(3).

Humarau, B. (1996) 'Les marches d'Ibadan – pivots de la construction d'une identité feminine et de son rapport au politique', *Travaux et Documents*, 49, Centre d'Etude d'Afrique Noire (CEAN), Institut d'Etudes Politiques de Bordeaux.

— (1997) 'Grand commerce féminin, hiérachies et solidarité en Afrique de l'Ouest', *Politique Africaine*, 67, Institut d'Etudes Politiques de Bordeaux.

Hutchful, E. (2002) *Ghana's Adjustment Experience: The Paradox of Reform*, Oxford/Accra: UNRISD in association with James Currey/Woeli.

ILD (2005a) *Volume I: Executive Summary, the Diagnosis*, available online at www.tanzania.go.tz/mkurabita/mkurabita_report_index.html, accessed 10 September 2009.

— (2005b) *Volume II: The Extra-legal Economy: Its Archetypes and Sizes*, available online at www.tanzania.go.tz/mkurabita/mkurabita_report_index.html, accessed 10 September 2009.

ILO (1972) *Employment, Incomes and Inequality*, Geneva: International Labour Organization.

— (1991) 'The dilemma of the informal sector', Report of the Director-General (Part 1) to the International Labour Conference, 78th Session, Geneva: International Labour Organization.

— (1993) '15th International Conference of Labour Statisticians', Geneva: International Labour Organization.

— (1999) 'Trade unions in the informal sector: finding their bearings', *Labour Education*, 3(116), Geneva: International Labour Organization.

— (2002a) 'Decent work and the informal economy', International Labour Conference, 90th session, Geneva: International Labour Organization.

— (2002b) 'Resolution concerning decent work and the informal economy', Geneva: International Labour Organization.

— (2002c) *Women and Men in the Informal Economy: A Statistical Picture*, Geneva: International Labour Organization/ILO Employment Sector.

— (2002d) *Reducing the Decent Work Deficit. A Global Challenge*, Geneva: International Labour Organization.

— (2004a) 'Gender in East Africa (Kenya, Uganda and Tanzania) employment dimensions of poverty: policy issues, challenges and responses', Geneva: International Labour Organization.

— (2004b) *World Employment Report 2004/2005*, available online at www.ilo.org/public/english/employment/strat/wer2004.htm, accessed 16 March 2006.

— (2007) 'For debate and guidance, the informal economy', Geneva: International Labour Organization.

ILO, UNIDO, UNDP (2002) *Roadmap Study of the Informal Sector in Mainland Tanzania*, Dar es Salaam.

IMF (2006) 'United Republic of Tanzania: Poverty Reduction Strategy Paper – Joint Staff Advisory Note', IMF Country Report no. 06/144.

Isaac, T. and W. Franke (2000) *Local Democracy and Development: People's Campaign for Decentralized Planning in Kerala*, New Delhi: Left Word Books.

Isichei, E. A. (1976) *A History of the Igbo People*, London: Macmillan.

Jason, A. and J. Wells (2007) 'Organization among informal construction workers: findings from recent studies and reflections on strategies and objectives', Paper presented at the NAI conference on 'Informalizing economies and new organizing strategies in Africa', Uppsala.

Jessop, B. (2002) *The Future of the Capitalist State*, Cambridge: Polity Press.

Jimu, I. M. (2003) 'Appropriation and mediation of urban spaces: dynamics and politics of street trading in Blantyre, Malawi', MA dissertation, University of Botswana, Gaborone.

— (2005) 'Negotiated economic opportunity and power: perspectives and perceptions of street vending in urban Malawi', *Africa Development*, 30(4).

Kaduna State Tailors Union, Doka Zone (n.d., c. 2006) 'Constitution and rules', Kaduna.

Karki, T. (2004) *An Assessment of Regional and Urban Development Policies and Programmes in Nepal*, FIG (International Federation of Surveyors) Working Week, Athens, Greece, 22–27 May, available online at www.fig.net/pub/athens/papers/ts24/TS24_5_karki.pdf, accessed August 2008.

Kasinitz, P., J. Mollenkopf and M. C.

Waters (eds) (2004) *Becoming a New Yorker: Ethnographies of the New Second Generation*, New York: Russell Sage.

Keek, M. and K. Sikkink (1998) *Activities beyond Borders: Transnational Activist Networks in International Politics*, Ithaca, NY: Cornell University Press.

Keith, M. (1995) 'Shouts of the street: identity and the spaces of authenticity', *Social Identities*, 1(2).

KENASVIT (2007) 'The trade', *Newsletter*, 2.

KENASVIT Constitution (2006) Kenya National Alliance of Street Vendors and Informal Traders office/University of Nairobi/IDS, Nakuru.

KENASVIT/IDS Report (2006) Kenya National Alliance of Street Vendors and Informal Traders office/University of Nairobi/IDS, Nakuru.

— (2007) Kenya National Alliance of Street Vendors and Informal Traders office/University of Nairobi/IDS, Nakuru.

King, R. (2006) 'Fulcrum of the urban economy: governance and street livelihoods in Kumasi, Ghana', in A. Brown (ed.), *Contested Space: Street Trading, Public Space and Livelihoods in Developing Cities*, Rugby: ITDG Publishing.

KLA (Kenya Land Alliance) (2002) 'Eradication of poverty through assured security of access to land and natural resources', Report of the National Civil Society Conference on Land Reform and the Land Question in Kenya, Kenya College of Communication Technology, Mbagathi.

Knorringa P. and L. Pegler (2006) 'Globalization, firm upgrading and impacts on labour', in *Tijdschrift voor Economische en Sociale Geografie*, 97(5).

Kumar, K. B. and J. G. Matsusaka (2005) *Village versus Market Social Capital: An Approach to Development*, Mimeo, Marshall School of Business, University of Southern California.

LACSO (2005) 'Resolutions', Lagos: Labour and Civil Society Coalition.

Laguerre, M. S. (1994) *The Informal City*, London: Macmillan.

Landau, L. B. (2005) 'Urbanization, nativism and the rule of law in South Africa's "Forbidden" Cities', *Third World Quarterly*, 26(7).

Lawson, A. V. (1992) 'Industrial subcontracting and employment forms in Latin America: a framework for contextual analysis', *Progress in Human Geography*, 16(1).

Lazar, S. (2004) 'Personalist politics, clientelism and citizenship: local elections in El Alto, Bolivia', *Bulletin of Latin American Research*, 23(2).

Lebeuf, A. M. D. (1963) 'The role of women in the political organization of African societies', in D. Paulme (ed.), *Women in Tropical Africa*, Berkeley/Los Angeles: University of California Press.

Lemarchand, R. (1988) 'The state, the parallel economy, and the changing structure of patronage systems', in D. Rothchild and N. Chazan (eds), *The Precarious Balance. State and Society in Africa*, Boulder, CO: Westview Press.

Lier, D. C. and K. Stokke (2006) 'Maximum working class unity? Challenges to local social movement unionism in Cape Town', *Antipode*, 38(4).

Lindberg, S. and S. Sverrisson (1997) 'Introduction', in S. Lindberg and S. Sverrisson (eds), *Social Movements in Development: The Challenge of Globalization and Democratization*, London/New York: Macmillan Press.

Lindell, I. (2008a) 'The multiple sites of urban governance: insights from an African city', *Urban Studies*, 45(10).

— (2008b) 'Building alliances between formal and informal workers: experiences from Africa', in A. Bieler, I. Lindberg and D. Pillay (eds), *Labour and the Challenge of Globalization: What Prospects for Transnational Solidarity?*, London: Pluto Press.

— (2009) '"Glocal" movements: place struggles and transnational organizing by informal workers', *Geografiska Annaler*, 91(2).

— (2010a) 'Informality and collective organizing: identities, alliances and transnational activism', *Third World Quarterly*, 31(2).

— (2010b) 'The transnational activism of

informal workers: networks, boundaries, mediation and a different politics of scale', *Global Networks*, forthcoming.

— (2010c) (ed.) *Between Exit and Voice: Informality and the Spaces of Popular Agency*, Special Issue of *African Studies Quarterly*, 11(2/3), available online at www.africa.ufl.edu/asq/index.htm.

Lindell, I. and A. Kamete (forthcoming) 'The politics of "non-planning" strategies in African cities: international and local dimensions', *Journal of Southern African Studies*.

Lipietz, A. (1987) *Mirages and Miracles: The Crisis of Global Fordism*, London: Verso.

Loayza, N. (1994) 'Labour regulation and the informal economy', Policy Research Working Paper Series, 1335, World Bank.

Lohani, K. (1997) *Urban Informal Sector*, Unpublished course manual, Institute of Engineering, Tribhuvan University, Lalitpur.

Lopez, S. H. (2004) *Reorganizing the Rust Belt: An Inside Study of the American Labor Movement*, Berkeley: University of California Press.

Lourenço-Lindell, I. (2002) *Walking the Tight Rope: Informal Livelihoods and Social Networks in a West African City*, Stockholm Studies in Human Geography no. 9, Stockholm: Acta Universitatis Stockholmiensis, available online at su.diva-portal.org/smash/record.jsf?pid=diva2:189997&rvn=1.

— (2004) 'Trade and the politics of informalization in Bissau', in K. T. Hansen and M. Vaa (eds), *Reconsidering Informality*, Uppsala: Nordic Africa Institute.

Lund, C. (2006) 'Twighlight institutions: an introduction', *Development and Change*, 37(4).

Lund, F. and C. Skinner (1999) 'Promoting the interests of women street traders: an analysis of street trader organizations in South Africa', Research Report no. 19, CSDS, Durban: University of Natal.

Lyons, M. (2005) 'Seen but not heard? On the extension of participatory governance to the informal sector', Invited presentation to the Seminar on the Globalizing City, Technische Hochschule, Berlin.

Lyons, M. and A. Brown (2007) 'Bearding the Asian Tiger in his den? African traders in Southeast China', Paper presented at the Institute of British Geographers, 28–31 August.

Lyons, M. and C. Msoka (2007) 'Microtrading in urban mainland Tanzania: the way forward', Report for HTSPE Development Consulting Services for the Development Partner Group, Tanzania.

Lyons, M. and S. Snoxell (2005a) 'Sustainable urban livelihoods and marketplace social capital: a comparative study of West African traders', *Urban Studies*, 42(8).

— (2005b) 'Creating urban social capital: some evidence from informal traders in Nairobi', *Urban Studies*, 42(7).

McAdam, D. (1982) *Political Process and the Development of Black Insurgency, 1930–1970*, Chicago, IL: Chicago University Press.

McCarthy, J. and M. N. Zald (1973) *The Trend of Social Movements in America: Professionalization and Resource Mobilization*, Morristown, NJ: General Learning Corporation.

McCormick, D. (1999) 'African enterprise clusters and industrialization: theory and reality', *World Development*, 27(9).

McCormick, D., W. V. Mitullah and M. Kinyanjui (2003) 'How to collaborate: associations and other community based organizations among Kenyan micro and small-scale entrepreneurs', IDS Occasional Paper no. 70.

MacGaffey, J. (1987) *Entrepreneurs and Parasites*, Cambridge: Cambridge University Press.

— (1988) 'Economic disengagement and class formation in Zaire', in D. Rothchild and N. Chazan (eds), *The Precarious Balance*, Boulder, CO/London: Westview Press.

— (1994) 'Civil society in Zaire: hidden resistance and the use of personal ties in class struggle', in J. W. Harbeson, D. Rothchild and N. Chazan (eds), *Civil*

Society and the State in Africa, Boulder, CO: Lynne Rienner.

MacGaffey, J. and R. Bazenguissa-Gango (2000) *Congo-Paris: Transnational Traders on the Margins of the Law*, Bloomington: Indiana University Press.

Macharia, K. (1973) 'The informal African city and development of Jua Kali associations: which way?', IDS Working Paper no. 494.

Mamdani, M. and E. Wamba-dia-Wamba (1995) *African Studies in Social Movements and Democracy*, Dakar: CODESRIA.

Manuh, T. (1994) 'Women in the public and informal economy under the Economic Recovery Programme', in P. Sparr (ed.), *Mortgaging Women's Lives: Feminist Critiques of Structural Adjustment*, London: Zed Books.

Marais, H. (2001) *Limits to Change: The Political Economy of Transition*, London: Zed Books.

Marshall, G. (1964) *Women, Trade and the Yoruba Family*, PhD thesis, Columbia University, New York.

Marwell, N. (2004) 'Ethnic and postethnic politics in New York City', in P. Kasinitz, J. Mollenkopf and M. C. Waters (eds), *Becoming a New Yorker: Ethnographies of the New Second Generation*, New York: Russell Sage.

Mayer, M. (2003) 'The onward sweep of social capital: causes and consequences for understanding cities', *International Journal of Urban and Regional Research*, 27(1).

Mboup, M. (2000) *Le Sénégalais d'Italie: Émigrés, Agents du Changement Social*, Paris: Editions l'Harmattan.

Meagher, K. (1995) 'Crisis, informalization and the urban informal sector in sub-Saharan Africa', *Development and Change*, 26(2).

— (2003) 'A back door to globalization? Structural adjustment, globalization and transborder trade in West Africa', *Review of African Political Economy*, 30(95).

— (2005) 'Social capital or analytical liability? Social networks and African informal economies', *Global Networks*, 5(3).

— (2006) 'Social capital, social liabilities and political capital: social networks and informal manufacturing in Nigeria', *African Affairs*, 105(421).

— (2007) 'Hijacking civil society: the inside story of the Bakassi Boys vigilante group of south-eastern Nigeria', *Journal of Modern African Studies*, 45(1).

— (2009) 'Culture, agency and power: theoretical reflections on informal economic networks and political process', Working Paper 2009:27, Copenhagen: Danish Institute for International Studies.

Minde I. J. and T. O. Nakhumwa (1998) *Unrecorded Cross-border Trade between Malawi and Neighbouring Countries*, USAID, available online at www.afr-sd.org/publications/90malawitrade.pdf, accessed 8 September 2009.

Mitlin, D. (2001) 'Civil society and urban poverty: examining complexity', *Environment and Urbanization*, 13(2).

— (2004) 'Civil society organizations: do they make a difference to urban poverty?', in N. Devas (ed.), *Urban Governance, Voice and Poverty in the Developing World*, London: Earthscan.

Mitullah, W. (2003) 'Street vending in African cities: a synthesis of empirical findings from Kenya, Ghana, Zimbabwe, Uganda and South Africa', available online at www.wiego.org, accessed 12 November 2007.

— (2004) 'A review of street trade in Africa', Working draft commissioned by Women in Informal Employment Globalizing and Organizing (WIEGO), Kennedy School of Government, Harvard University.

— (2005a) 'Tapping opportunities in decentralized governance and informal activities for urban development in East African countries', Background paper prepared for the World Bank initiative on 'Preparing Africa for an urban future', Washington, DC: World Bank.

— (2005b) 'Street trade in Kenya: the contribution of research in policy dialogue and response', in N. Hamdi (ed.), *Urban Futures: Economic Growth and Poverty Reduction*, Rugby: ITDG Publishing.

— (2005c) 'Street vending in African cities: a synthesis of empirical findings from Kenya, Côte d'Ivoire, Ghana, Zimbabwe, Uganda and South Africa', Background paper for the *World Development Report 2005*, Washington, DC: World Bank.

— (2006a) 'Challenges of protecting labour rights in an informalizing Kenyan economy', *Thematic Survey on Labour Rights for the High Level Commission on Legal Empowerment of the Poor*, Nairobi: UN-HABITAT.

— (2006b) 'From research to action: a case study of the Kenya National Alliance of Street Vendors and Informal Traders (KENASVIT)', *IDS Policy Brief*, 5(1).

— (2007a) 'Street vendors and informal trading: the struggle for the right to trade', in P. Burnett and F. Manji (eds), *From the Slave Trade to 'Free' Trade: How Trade Undermines Democracy and Justice in Africa*, Oxford: Fahamu.

— (2007b) 'Socio-economic engagement in contested city spaces: a case study of street vending and informal trade in Nairobi', Paper presented at the conference on 'Towards creating inclusive cities: experiences and challenges in contemporary African cities', University of Witwatersrand, Johannesburg, 5–8 March.

Moody, K. (1997) *Workers in a Lean World*, London: Verso.

— (2005) 'Toward an international social-movement unionism', in L. Amoore (ed.), *The Global Resistance Reader*, London/New York: Routledge.

Msoka, C. (2007) 'An assessment of the informal economy associations in Tanzania: the case study of VIBINDO Society in Dar es Salaam', Paper presented at the conference on Informalizing Economies and New Organizing Strategies in Africa, Nordic Africa Institute, 20–22 April.

Munck, R. (2004) 'Globalization, labor and the "Polanyi problem"', *Labor History*, 45(3).

Mwamadzingo, M. (2002) 'Unions and the informal economy in Africa', *Unprotected Labour: What Role for Unions in the Informal Economy? Labour Education*, 2(27): 33–42.

Mwaniki, J. (2007) *The Impact of Informal Cross Border Trade on Regional Integration in SADC and Implications for Wealth Creation*, available online at www.streetnet.org.za/english/CORN.pdf, accessed 27 February 2007.

Mwenda, K. K. (1999) *Legal Aspects of Corporate Capital and Finance*, Washington, DC: Penn Press.

Naidoo, R. (ed.) (2000) *Unions in Transition: COSATU into the New Millennium*, Johannesburg: NALEDI.

Nash, J. (2005) 'Introduction: social movements and global processes', in J. Nash (ed.), *Social Movements: An Anthropological Reader*, Oxford: Blackwell.

Navarro, Z. (2005) 'Decentralization, participation and social control of public resources: "Participatory Budgeting" in Porto Alegre (Brazil)', in I. Licha (ed.), *Citizens in Charge. Managing Local Budgets in East Asia and Latin America*, Washington, DC: Inter-American Development Bank.

Ninsin, K. A. (1991) *The Informal Economy in Ghana's Political Economy*, Accra: Freedom Publications.

NISCOF (2006) *Nairobi Central Ward Informal Traders Census Update*, Nairobi Informal Sector Confederation, Nairobi.

NLC (2007) 'NLC and TUC express concerns over the situation in the textile industry with particular reference to the closure of UNTL, Kaduna', Letter to the president of Nigeria, signed by the presidents of NLC and TUC, 15 October.

Nnkya, T. (2006) 'An enabling framework? Governance and street trading in Dar es Salaam, Tanzania', in A. Brown (ed.), *Contested Space: Street Trading, Public Space and Livelihoods in Developing Cities*, Rugby: ITDG Publishing.

Novy, A. and B. Leubolt (2005) 'Participatory budgeting in Porto Alegre: social innovation and the dialectical relationship of state and civil society', *Urban Studies*, 42(11).

NSAC (1998) *Nepal Human Development Report, 1998*, Kathmandu: Nepal South Asia Centre.

Nyamnjoh, F. (2006) *Insiders and Outsiders: Citizenship and Xenophobia in Contemporary Southern Africa*, London/New York/Dakar: Zed Books/CODESRIA.

Ocran, S. (1998) *Dignity and Sustenance: Social Watch Country Report on Ghana*, available online at www.socialwatch.org/en/informesNacionales/256.html, accessed 8 September 2009.

Okonjo, K. (1976) 'The dual-sex political system in operation. Igbo women and community politics in mid-western Nigeria', in N. J. Hafkin and E. G. Bay (eds), *Women in Africa: Studies in Social and Economic Change*, Stanford, CA: Stanford University Press.

Oldfield, S. and K. Stokke (2007) 'Political polemics and local practices of community-organizing in South Africa', in H. Leitner, J. Peck and E. Sheppard (eds), *Contested Neoliberalism: Urban Frontiers*, New York: Guilford.

Olson, M. (1965) *The Logic of Collective Action*, Cambridge, MA: Harvard University Press.

Olukoshi, A. (2005) 'Changing patterns of politics in Africa', in A. Boron and G. Lechini (eds), *Politics and Social Movements in a Hegemonic World: Lessons from Africa, Asia and Latin America*, Buenos Aires: CLACSO.

Olukoshi, A. O. and L. Laakso (eds) (1996) *Challenges to the Nation States in Africa*, Uppsala: Nordic Africa Institute.

Olukoshi, A. O. and L. Wohlgemuth (eds) (1995) *A Road to Development: Africa in the 21st Century*, Uppsala: Nordic Africa Institute.

Onibon-Doubougan, Y. (2001) *Femmes entrepreneurs au Bénin: stratégies d'organization, impact économique, social et politique*, Unpublished PhD thesis, Université de Paris Sud XI Faculté Jean Monnet – Sceaux.

Orr, A. and S. Orr (2002) 'Agricultural and micro enterprise in Malawi's rural south. ODI Agricultural Research and Extension Network', Network Paper no. 119.

Pape, J. (2001) 'Poised to succeed or set up to fail? A case study of South Africa's first public–public partnership in water delivery', Occasional Papers Series, No. 1, Municipal Services Project, Queen's University.

Paulais, T. and L. Wihelm (2000) *Marchés d'Afrique*, Paris: Editions Karthala.

Paulme, D. (1963) *Women in Tropical Africa*, Berkeley/Los Angeles: University of California Press.

Peck, J. (1996) *Work-place: The Social Regulation of Labour Markets*, New York: Guilford Press.

Peil, M. (1969) 'Unemployment in Tema: the plight of the skilled worker', *Canadian Journal of African Studies*, 3(2).

Perham, M. (1970) 'The Aba market women's riot in Nigeria, 1929', in W. Cartey and M. Kilson (eds), *The African Reader*, vol. 1, New York: Vintage Books.

Perry, D. (1997) 'Rural ideologies and urban imaginings: Wolof immigrants in New York City', *Africa Today*, 44(2).

Phillips, S. (2002) 'Social capital, local networks and community development', in C. Rakodi and T. Lloyd-Jones (eds), *Urban Livelihoods: A People-Centred Approach to Reducing Poverty*, London: Earthscan.

Pickvance, C. (2003) 'From urban social movements to urban movements: a review and introduction to a symposium on urban movements', *International Journal of Urban and Regional Research*, 27(1).

Pieterse, E. (2008) *City Futures: Confronting the Crisis of Urban Development*, London/New York/Cape Town: Zed Books/UCT Press.

Pillay, D. (2006) 'Globalization and the informalization of labour: the case of South Africa', Draft paper presented to the Workshop on Global Labour, Runö, Sweden, 12–15 January.

Popke, E. J. and R. Ballard (2004) 'Dislocating modernity: identity, space and representations of street-trade in Durban, South Africa', *Geoforum*, 35(1).

Portes, A. and R. Schauffler (1993) 'Competing perspectives on the Latin American informal sector', *Population and Development Review*, 19(1).

Portes, A. and J. Walton (1981) *Labour, Class and the International System*, New York: Academic Press.

Portes, A. et al. (1989) *The Informal Economy: Studies in Advanced and Less Developed Countries*, Baltimore, MD: Johns Hopkins University Press.

Post (2006a) 'COMESA summit to launch regional integration fund', 15 November.

— (2006b) 'Zambian Airways' daily flights to Tanzania cheer CBTA', 8 November.

Potts, D. (2008) 'The urban informal sector in sub-Saharan Africa: from bad to good (and back again?)', *Development Southern Africa*, 25(2).

Prag, E. (2004) *Women Making Politics – Women's Associations, Female Politicians and Development Brokers in Rural Senegal*, PhD thesis, International Development Studies, Roskilde University, Roskilde.

Pratt, N. (2006) 'Informal enterprise and street trading: a civil society and urban management perspective', in A. Brown (ed.), *Contested Space*, Rugby: Intermediate Technology Publishing.

Putnam, R. D. (1993) *Making Democracy Work: Civic Tradition in Modern Italy*, Princeton, NJ: Princetown University Press.

Putzel, J. (1997) 'Policy arena. Accounting for the "dark side" of social capital: reading Robert Putnam on democracy', *Journal of International Development*, 9(7).

Rakodi, C. (2003) 'Politics and performance: the implications of emerging governance arrangements for urban management', *Habitat International*, 27(4).

Rakodi, C. and T. Lloyd-Jones (eds) (2002) *Urban Livelihoods: A People-centred Approach to Reducing Poverty*, London: Earthscan.

Rakowski, C. (ed.) (1994) *Contrapunto: The Informal Economy Sector Debate in Latin America*, Albany, NY: SUNY Press.

Reis, E. P. and M. Moore (2005) *Elite Perceptions of Poverty and Inequality*, London/New York: Zed Books.

Reno, W. (1995) *Corruption and State Politics in Sierra Leone*, African Studies series no. 83, Cambridge: Cambridge University Press.

— (2000) 'Clandestine economies, violence and states in Africa', *Journal of International Affairs*, 53(2).

— (2002) 'The politics of insurgency in collapsing states', *Development and Change*, 33(5).

Republic of Ghana Labour Act (2003) *Act 651*, Accra: Assembly Press.

Robinson, W. I. (2001) 'Social theory and globalization: the rise of a transnational state', *Theory and Society*, 30(2).

Rogerson, C. M. and E. L. Nel (2005) *Local Economic Development in the Developing World: The Experience of Southern Africa*, New Brunswick, NJ: Transaction.

Roitman, J. (1990) 'The politics of informal markets in sub-Saharan Africa', *Journal of Modern African Studies*, 28(4).

— (2004) *Fiscal Disobedience: An Anthropology of Economic Regulation in Central Africa*, Princeton, NJ: Princeton University Press.

RoK (2003a) *Economic Survey*, Republic of Kenya, Nairobi: Government Printer.

— (2003b) *Report by the Task Force on Micro and Small Enterprises*, Republic of Kenya, Nairobi: Ministry of Labour and Human Resource Development.

— (2005) *Sessional Paper no. 2 of 2005 on Development of Micro and Small Enterprises for Wealth and Employment Creation for Poverty Reduction*, Nairobi: Government Printer.

Rosander, E. E. (ed.) (1997) *Transforming Female Identities*, Uppsala: Nordic Africa Institute.

Roy, A. (2003) *City Requiem, Calcutta:*

Gender and the Politics of Poverty, Minneapolis: University of Minnesota Press.

— (2004a) 'The gentlemen's city: urban informality in the Calcutta of new communism', in A. Roy and N. Alsayyad (eds), *Urban Informality: Transnational Perspectives from the Middle East, Latin America, and South Asia*, Lanham, MD/Boulder, CO/New York/Toronto/Oxford: Lexington Books.

— (2004b) 'Transnational trespassings: the geopolitics of urban informality', in A. Roy and N. Alsayyad (eds), *Urban Informality: Transnational Perspectives from the Middle East, Latin America, and South Asia*, Lanham, MD/Boulder, CO/ New York/Toronto/Oxford: Lexington Books.

— (2005) 'Urban informality: toward an epistemology of planning', *Journal of the American Planning Association*, 71(2).

Roy, A. and N. Alsayyad (eds) (2004) *Urban Informality: Transnational Perspectives from the Middle East, Latin America, and South Asia*, Lanham, MD/Boulder, CO/ New York/Toronto/Oxford: Lexington Books.

Rubin, E. (2001) 'Passing through the door: social movement literature and legal scholarship', *Pennsylvania Law Review*, 150 U Penn. L. Rev. 1.

Rutsch, H. (2001) 'From "planning the city" to a "city that plans": the experience of Dar es Salaam', *United Nations Chronicle*, 38(1), available online at www.un.org/Pubs/chronicle/2001/issue1/0101p62.html, accessed November 2007.

Sad, V. and D. Poole (eds) (2004) *Anthropology in the Margins of the State*, Santa Fe, NM/Oxford: School of American Research Press/James Currey.

SADC (2007) www.sadc.int/english/about/profile/index.php, accessed 28 February 2007.

Samson, M. (2004) 'Organizing in the informal economy: a case study of the municipal waste management industry in South Africa', ILO Report: SEED working paper no. 66.

Sarr, F. (1998) *L'Entrepreneuriat féminin au*

Sénégal. La transformation des rapport de pouvoir, Paris: Editions l'Harmattan.

Sassen, S. (1998) *Globalization and Its Discontents. Essays on the New Mobility of People and Money*, New York: New Press.

Savage, L. (1998) 'Geographies of organizing: Justice for Janitors in Los Angeles', in A. Herod (ed.), *Organizing the Landscape: Geographical Perspectives on Labor Unionism*, Minneapolis: University of Minnesota.

Schaffer, C. F. (1998) *Democracy in Translation. Understanding Politics in an Unfamiliar Culture*, Ithaca, NY/London: Cornell University Press.

Scheld, S. (2007) 'The "China challenge": activists' responses to new traders in Dakar, Senegal', Paper presented at the conference on Informalizing Economies and New Organizing Strategies in Africa, Nordic Africa Institute, 20–22 April.

Setšabi, S. (2006) 'Contest and conflict: governance and street livelihoods in Maseru, Lesotho', in A. Brown (ed.), *Contested Space: Street Trading, Public Space, and Livelihoods in Developing Cities*, Rugby: ITDG Publishing.

Shrestha, S. (2006) 'The new urban economy: governance and street livelihoods in the Kathmandu Valley, Nepal', in A. Brown (ed.), *Contested Space: Street Trading, Public Space and Livelihoods in Developing Cities*, Rugby: ITDG Publishing.

Sihanya, B. (2006) 'An outline of shortcomings in the Micro and Small Scale Enterprises Bill, 2006', Study commissioned by the Kenya National Alliance of Street Vendors and Informal Traders (KENASVIT), Innovative Lawyering, Nairobi.

Simone, A. (2004) *For the City Yet to Come*, Durham, NC/London: Duke University Press.

Siyolwe, Y. W. (1994) 'Makwebo women: a study of the socio-economic activities of a select group of women traders in Lusaka, Zambia, 1980–1990', Master of Letters thesis, University of Oxford.

Skinner, C. (2008) 'Street trade in Africa: a review', School of Development Studies Working Paper no. 51, University of KwaZulu Natal, Durban.

Smith, N. (1986) 'Gentrification, the frontier and the restructuring of urban space', in N. Smith and P. Williams (eds), *Gentrification of the City*, London/ New York: Allen and Unwin.

Soane, J., E. Taddei and C. Algranati (2005) 'The new configurations of popular movements in Latin America', in A. Boron and G. Lechini (eds), *Politics and Social Movements in an Hegemonic World*, Buenos Aires: CLACSO.

Sommerville, C. (1991) 'The impact of the reforms on the urban population: how the Dakarois view the crisis', in C. Delgado and S. Jammeh (eds), *The Political Economy of Senegal under Structural Adjustment*, New York: Praeger.

Soumaré, M. (2002) 'Local initiatives and poverty reduction in urban areas: the example of Yeumbeul, Senegal', *International Social Science Journal*, 54(172).

Souza, C. (2001) 'Participatory budgeting in Brazilian cities: limits and possibilities in building democratic institutions', *Environment and Urbanization*, 13(1).

Statesman (2007) 'Dockworkers fight IRS over income tax', 5 January.

Sthapit, D. (1998) 'Urban informal sector in Kathmandu City: a case study of commercial vendors', Master's thesis, Institute of Engineering, Tribhuvan University, Lalitpur.

Stiglitz, J. (2002a) *Globalization and Its Discontents*, London: Penguin Books.

— (2002b) 'Employment, social justice and societal well-being', *International Labour Review*, 141(1/2).

Streefkerk, H. (2002) 'Casualization of the workforce: thirty years of industrial labour in South Gujarat', in G. Shah et al. (eds), *Development and Deprivation in Gujarat, in Honour of Jan Breman*, New Delhi: Sage.

StreetNet (2000) *Newsletter*, 1, available online at www.streetnet.org.za/english/ newsa1.htm, accessed 8 September 2009.

— (2003) 'Nepal: street vendors' leader arrested in mass protest against Government repression', *StreetNet News*, 2, October, available online at www. streetnet.org.za/english/nepal2.htm, accessed 30 August 2009.

— (2006) *Newsletter*, 8, available online at www.streetnet.org.za/english/ Stnetnews8.htm, accessed 8 September 2009.

— (2009) StreetNet International, Home page, available online at www.streetnet. org.za/, accessed 30 August 2009.

Taylor, L. (2004) 'Client-ship and citizenship in Latin America', *Bulletin of Latin American Research*, 23(2), Oxford: Blackwell.

Taylor, L. and F. Wilson (2004) 'The messiness of everyday life: exploring key themes in Latin American citizenship studies. Introduction', *Bulletin of Latin American Research*, 23(2).

Thioub, I., M. C. Diop and C. Boone (1998) 'Economic liberalization in Senegal: shifting politics of indigenous business interests', *African Studies Review*, 41(2).

Thompson, E. P. (1971) 'The moral economy of the English crowd in the eighteenth century', *Past and Present*, 50.

Thulare, P. (2004) 'Trading democracy?: Johannesburg informal traders and citizenship', *Policy: Issues and Actors*, 17(1).

Tilly, C. (1978) *From Mobilization to Revolution*, Reading, MA: Addison-Wesley.

Times of Zambia (2007) 'Intra-COMESA trade growing', 14 September.

Tostensen, A., I. Tvedten and M. Vaa (eds) (2001) *Associational Life in African Cities: Popular Responses to the Urban Crisis*, Uppsala: Nordic Africa Institute.

Tripp, A. (1997) *Changing the Rules: The Politics of Liberalization and the Urban Informal Economy in Tanzania*, Berkeley/Los Angeles: University of California Press.

— (2000) *Women and Politics in Uganda*, Oxford: James Currey.

— (2001) 'Non-formal institutions, informal economies, and the politics of inclusion', Discussion Paper no. 2001/108, UNU/WIDER.

Tufts, S. (1998) 'Community unionism in Canada and labour's (re)organizing of space', *Antipode*, 30(3).

Ukiwo, U. (2002) 'Deus ex machina or Frankenstein monster? The changing roles of Bakassi Boys in eastern Nigeria', *Democracy and Development*, 3(1).

UN-Habitat (2007) 'The downside of informal trading – evictions', *Habitat Debate*, 13(2).

UNIFEM (2005) *Progress of the World's Women – Women, Work and Poverty*, New York: UNDP.

Union Network International (2006) 'Malawi union organizes informal economy workers', UNI-Africa News, 12 January, available online at www.union network.org/uniafrican.nsf/412fe820c3 a106a3c1256d7b003985e1/e1b430c8ca 8720fdc12570f90056e083?Open Document, accessed 28 January 2007.

United Nations (1996) *Informal Sector Development in Africa*, New York: United Nations.

Vailliancourt-Laflame, C. (2005) 'Trade unions and informal worker associations in the urban informal economy in Ecuador', Geneva: International Labour Organization.

Van Allen, J. (1976) '"Aba riots" or Igbo "women's war"? Ideology, stratification, and the invisibility of women', in N. J. Hafkin and E. G. Bay (eds), *Women in Africa: Studies in Social and Economic Change*, Stanford, CA: Stanford University Press.

Von Holdt, K. (1992) 'What is the future of labour?', *South African Labour Bulletin*, 16(8).

— (2003) *Transition from Below – Forging Trade Unionism and Workplace Change*, Scottsville: University of Natal Press.

Walsh, J. (2000) 'Organizing the scale of labour regulation in the United States: service sector activism in the city', *Environment and Planning A*, 32(9).

War on Want (n.d.) 'Helping street traders and market vendors in Malawi: Malawi Union for the Informal Sector (MUFIS)', available online at www.waron want. org/Helping+street+traders+and+ market +vendors+in+Malawi+10527. twl, accessed 29 January 2008.

War on Want, Alliance for Zambia Informal Economy Associations, and Workers Education Association of Zambia (2006) *Forces for Change: Informal Economy Organizations in Africa*, London: War on Want.

Waterman, P. (1999) 'The new social unionism: a new union model for a new world order', in R. Munck and P. Waterman (eds), *Labour Worldwide in the Era of Globalization*, London/New York: Palgrave.

— (2005) 'The forward march of labour (and unions?) recommenced: reflections on an emancipatory labour internationalism and international labour studies', *Antipode*, 37(2).

Webster, E. (1994) 'The rise of social-movement unionism: the two faces of the black trade union movement in South Africa', in E. Webster, L. Alfred, L. Bethlehem, A. Joffe and T. A. Selikow (eds), *Work and Industrialization in South Africa: An Introductory Reader*, Randburg: Ravan Press.

— (2006) 'Trade unions and the challenge of the informalization of work', in S. Buhlungu (ed.), *Trade Unions and Democracy: COSATU Workers' Political Attitudes in South Africa*, Cape Town: HSRC Press.

Webster, E. and K. von Holdt (2005) *Beyond the Apartheid Workplace*, Durban: University of KwaZulu Natal Press.

Webster, E., R. Lambert and A. Bezuidenhout (2008) *Grounding Globalization: Labour in the Age of Insecurity*, Antipode Book Series.

Widner, J. (1991) 'Interest group structure and organization in Kenya's informal sector: cultural despair or a politics of multiple allegiances?', *Comparative Political Studies*, 24(1).

WIEGO (n.d.) 'Rights, voice, protection and opportunities: a policy response to the informal economy', available online at www.wiego.org, accessed 12 November 2007.

— (2002) 'Women in informal employment: globalizing and organizing', Third General Meeting, Ahmedabad, 19–21 January.

Wild, L. and D. Mepham (eds) (2006) *The New Sinosphere: China in Africa*, London: Institute for Public Policy Research.

Wills, J. (2005) 'The geography of union organising in low-paid service industries in the UK: lessons from the T&G's campaign to unionise the Dorchester Hotel', *Antipode*, 37(1).

Woodford-Berger, P. (1997) 'Associating women – female linkage, collective identities and political ideology in Ghana', in E. E. Rosander (ed.), *Transforming Female Identities*, Uppsala: Nordic Africa Institute.

Woolcock, M. (1998) 'Social capital and economic development: toward a theoretical synthesis and policy framework', *Theory and Society*, 27(2).

World Bank (2005) *World Development Report 2005: A Better Investment Climate for Everyone*, Oxford: Oxford University Press.

Xaba, J., P. Horn and S. Motala (2002) *Employment Sector 2002/10, Working Paper on the Informal Economy, the Informal Sector in sub-Saharan Africa*, available online at www.wiego.org/papers/2005/unifem/29_ILO_WP_10_IS_Sub Saharan_Africa_Horn.pdf, accessed 9 September 2009.

About the contributors

Gunilla Andrae is a reader and researcher in the Department of Human Geography, Stockholm University. Her work includes studies of the formal–informal nexus in industry (*Industry in Ghana: Production Form and Spatial Structure*, 1981) and, with Björn Beckman, food policy and wheat dependence (*The Wheat Trap: Bread and Underdevelopment in Nigeria*, 1985), and trade unions in the textile industry (*Union Power in the Nigerian Textile Industry*, 1998). As coordinator of a programme on *People, Provisioning and Place* she has also been engaged in studies on governance in urban provisioning in different parts of Africa.

Björn Beckman is a professor and researcher in the Department of Political Science, Stockholm University. His works include *Organising the Farmers: Cocoa Politics and National Development in Ghana* (1976) and, with Gunilla Andrae, *The Wheat Trap: Bread and Underdevelopment in Nigeria* (1985) and *Union Power in the Nigerian Textile Industry* (1998). He taught at Ahmadu Bello University, Zaria, from 1978 to 1987. He has edited books on African trade unions with Lloyd Sachikonye and Sakhela Buhlungu and is currently working on a comparative study of Nigerian and South African trade unions.

Owusu Boampong is a PhD candidate at the International Development Department, University of Birmingham. His PhD research focuses on the role of institutional arrangements and market practices of small-scale Ghanaian exporters in mitigating local market imperfections and export market risks. His academic interests are in the areas of informal economy, market institutions, trade and industrial development.

Alison Brown is a reader at the School of City and Regional Planning, Cardiff University, and director for the MSc course International Planning and Development. She has research expertise in planning practice and the informal economy, with recent projects on street trading and public space and the impact of global value chains on informal trade in West Africa. She is a member of the steering committee for UN-Habitat's World Urban Campaign, a consultant to the UNESCO/UN-Habitat project on the *Right to the City*, and planning adviser to the global advocacy group WIEGO and to DfID's Technology, Infrastructure and Urban Planning resource centre.

Karen Tranberg Hansen is professor of anthropology at Northwestern University in the United States. She has conducted urban research in Zambia since the early 1970s on several issues related to the informal economy, including housing, gender and youth. Her most recent publications are *Salaula: The World of Secondhand Clothing and Zambia* (2000) and Hansen et al., *Youth and the City in the Global South* (2008).

Ignasio Malizani Jimu is a senior lecturer in human geography at Mzuzu University, Malawi. He is currently enrolled as a PhD candidate in social anthropology with the University of Basle, Switzerland. His research interests include the informal economy, provision of potable water to the urban poor and informal land transactions. He is also author of a book entitled *Urban Appropriation and Transformation*.

David Christoffer Jordhus-Lier is a human geographer and a senior researcher at the Norwegian Institute for Urban and Regional Research (NIBR), where he is based at the Department for International Studies. He recently completed his PhD at the University of Manchester. His research has focused on contested public sector reforms and the politics of labour in Cape Town, South Africa. His academic output is related to labour geography and the politics of work. He also works as a guest lecturer at the University of Oslo.

Michal Lyons is professor of urban development and policy at London South Bank University in the United Kingdom. For over a decade she has carried out comparative research on street trade in South Africa, Tanzania, Kenya, Togo, Mali and Senegal. Her research has covered a range of issues, including livelihoods and social capital, urban policy and voice, national reform agendas and power, and impacts of the China–Africa trade. Her work has been published in respected journals. She is also active in advocacy and advises NGOs and international agencies.

Kate Meagher is a lecturer in development studies at the Development Studies Institute (DESTIN), London School of Economics. She worked as a lecturer at Ahmadu Bello University in Nigeria from 1991 to 1997 before obtaining a DPhil in Sociology from Oxford. She has published widely on various aspects of African informal economies and social change. Publications include *The Bargain Sector: Structural Adjustment and the Non-Farm Sector in the Nigerian Savanna* (2001) and *Identity Economics* (forthcoming). Current research interests include informal institutions and economic governance, the comparative study of informal economic networks, the role of China in African economies, and vigilantism and organized crime in Africa.

Winnie V. Mitullah is a researcher and a lecturer at the Institute for Development Studies (IDS), University of Nairobi. She holds a PhD in political science and public administration from the University of York, United Kingdom. Her PhD thesis was on urban housing, with a major focus on policies relating to low-income housing. She has researched, written and consulted in the areas of development. Most of her recent publications focus on local governance with reference to the management of resources; the use of ICT as a governance tool; gender; informal economy, participatory governance and decentralized service delivery.

Wilma S. Nchito has been a lecturer in urban geography at the University of Zambia since 1993. She is currently a PhD candidate in geography at the University of Zambia, studying small-town functions and development in Zambia. Her other research interests are urban poverty, the urban informal sector, and urban sanitation and waste management.

Ebbe Prag is a part-time lecturer at the University of Roskilde, in the Department of Society and Globalization. He specializes in politics, women and trade in francophone Africa, with an emphasis on Senegal and Benin. His contribution to this book is part of his postdoctoral research carried out in Benin between 2006 and 2008.

Suzanne Scheld is assistant professor of anthropology at California State University, Northridge. She obtained her PhD in 2003 from the Graduate Center of the City University of New York. Her research interests are in urbanization, globalization, youth culture and consumerism in Africa. She is the author of several articles on youth culture and the politics of markets in Senegal.

Index

cut-offs of services, 120, 121, 125

Dakar (Senegal), 23, 26, 37, 45; informal
    economy in, 153–68; social structure
    of, 39–40
Dantopka market, Benin, 67–8
Dar es Salaam, 26, 37, 41–2, 44, 45
debt, 99
decent work, 6, 8, 20, 86, 97, 184, 186, 187
decentralization, urban poor within, 34
decollectivization of labour process, 132
decriminalization of informal activities, 9
Della Porta, D., 187
democracy, 34, 54, 63; among street
    vendors, 104; in informal associations,
    47
deregulation: of employment standards,
    116; of Nigerian petroleum market, 91;
    of wage labour, 86
differentiation in informal economy,
    10–15
Diop, Moustapha, 163
Diouf, Adbou, 160
divisions and hierarchy in informal
    economy, 12
Doka zone tailors' association (Kaduna,
    Nigeria), 96
donor funding, 111, 113; effect of, on
    trade unions, 112
Drug Enforcement Commission (Zambia),
    178
drugs, trafficking of, 16, 178
dual-sex associations, 12, 14
Durban, South Africa, street traders in, 37

education, 135–6
eight-hour day, 109
Ekwe female leaders, 72
electoral racketeering, 54
electricity: access to, 61; cut-offs of service,
    125 (resistance to, 120); restructuring
    of distribution of, 124
embezzlement of association funds, 74, 77
empowerment: of the poor, 35; through
    globalization, 168
ethnic relations, 12, 14, 18, 25
eviction, 15, 50; of small traders, 42;
    resistance to, 45, 120, 121
exclusion, 7, 14, 62
exit, 46–64
externalization of services see outsourcing

extortion rackets, in informal economy, 47

family labour, 99
Fangbédji, association leader in Benin,
    78, 79
Fédération Nationale des Organisations
    et Associations des Marchés du Bénin
    (FAOMAB), 68, 75, 81
federations, creation of, 8
Finance Bank (Zambia), 178
flexible labour market, 116, 134, 141, 148,
    186
formal channels, assessment of, 59–60
formal economy, 90; as minority sector,
    87; definition of, 85; downsizing of, 130
formal–informal divide, 4, 19–22, 27,
    85–98
free trade area, 177
fuel prices, contestation of, 91

Gallin, D., 133
gangs, 13; entry conditions for, 143; in
    port work in Ghana, 137–9, 140, 148
garment industry, 49; in Aba (Nigeria),
    51–2; in Nigeria, 85–98 (Hausa gowns,
    93)
gender boundaries, crossing of, 167
gender relations, 12, 14, 18, 25, 63, 64
General Agricultural Workers' Union
    (Ghana), 100, 137
Ghana, 10, 12, 19, 37, 66; Accelerated
    Development Plan for Education, 135;
    port workers' organization in, 130–49
Ghana Cocoa Marketing Company, 147
Ghana Dock Labour Company (GDLC),
    139–40, 141, 142, 143, 144, 145
GDLC Non-permanent Workers of MDU,
    144
Ghana Ports and Harbours Authority
    (GPHA), 138–9, 140
Ghana Private Road Transport Union, 11
Ghuthi trust (Nepal), 43
global networks of informal workers, 14,
    15
globalization, 22, 107, 115, 119, 156, 167,
    185; as means of empowerment, 168
governance, urban, 35–7
groundnut trade in Senegal, 158
Groupement Professionnel des
    Commerçants et Industriels Libanais
    du Sénégal, 159

Groupement Professionnel des Vendeurs et Vendeuses des Marchés du Bénin (GPVMB), 70

Guinea-Bissau, 11, 132, 142; casual work in, 139

Gujarat, women textile workers in, 65

Gyanendra, King, 43

Hansen, Karen Tranberg, 161–2

Harare (Zimbabwe), street vending in, 106

harassment of street vendors, 49, 52, 65, 104, 194

Hart, Keith, 184

headmen of work gangs, 135, 137, 139, 143, 145

health and safety, 99, 143

HIV/AIDS, 109, 110, 111, 173, 180; risks in cross-border trade, 171

Hlumani Wasteman (Pty) Ltd, 126

homeworking, 115

Hong Kong Confederation of Trade Unions, 100

Hong Kong Domestic Workers' Union, 100

Human Development Index (HDI), 39

Ibrahim, Kabiru, 93, 95–6

Igbo ethnic group, 48, 54

illiteracy of women traders, 73, 77; struggle against, 78

imagineers, 24

Independent Municipal and Allied Trade Union (IMATU) (South Africa), 118

Industrial and Commercial Workers Union (ICU) (Ghana), 147

informal economy: as divided and contentious space, 157, 162; as permanent aspect of economy, 99; as sphere of political competition, 3; diversity of, 21, 156; forms of struggle in, 134; global dimensions of, 156; growth of, 130, 184; in Africa, study of, 102; in Kenya, history of, 188–9; in relation to globalization, 155; in Senegal (colonial, 158; post-colonial, 160–1); internationalization of, 22; mass mobilization of workers in, 100; organizing in, 167–8 (in Malawi, 99–114); public attitudes to, 102; research into, 1; unionization of, 110; variety of actors in, 15–16; viewed as

inchoate mass, 46; viewed as marginal, 9; viewed as safety net, 155

informal employment: definition of, 131; recognition of, by state, 9; political economy of, 185–8; redefinition of, 6

informal workers: fluidity of, 133; in Kenya, 184–201; lack of visibility of, 134; organization of, in Ghana, 130–4

informality: as category of practice, 5; as set of processes, 120–1; changing politics of, 1–30; complexity of politics of, 30; historical development of, in Dakar, 154–7; in view of local actors, 5; of the poor, 6; use of term, 4

informalization, 46, 57, 89, 98, 128, 148, 167; and organization, 131–5; history of, 132; in Cape Town, 115–29; in Ghana, 135–43; in South Africa, 96, 115–29; organizing strategies against, 118; research into, 135

Institute for Development Studies (IDS) University of Nairobi, 189–90, 200; IDS National Dissemination Workshop, 196

insurgent citizenship, 2

Internal Revenue Service (IRS) (Ghana), 146–7

international dimensions of organizing, 28–9

International Labour Conference (1991), 184

International Labour Organization (ILO), 6, 8, 20, 34, 86, 97, 163, 187; *Decent Work and the Informal Economy* report, 64; definition of informal economy, 6; report on municipal waste services, 125; study on Keny, 184; *World Employment Report*, 185

International Monetary Fund (IMF), 99

international organizing *see* transnational organizing

international trajectory of commodities, 168

Internet: access to, 24; as tool of communication, 168, 173

Iran, street politics in, 100

Islam, 44 *see also* Muslims

Islamic brotherhoods, in Senegal, 44

Iyolade female leaders, 73

Johannesburg, traders' associations in, 37, 47

Mozambique, 10, 11
multi-class associations, 11–12
multiparty politics, locus of informal sector within, 18
municipal sector, job losses in, 136–7
Municipal Workers' Union (South Africa), 144
Muslim brotherhoods, 13
Muslims, in Dakar trading structures, 39–40

National Agency for Food and Drug Administration and Control (NAFDAC) (Nigeria), 49, 52–3, 60
National Association of Business Women (NABW) (Malawi), 101, 111
National Fish Stevedore Association (NFSA) (Ghana), 140–1, 145
National Integrated Employment Creation Programme (Kenya), 194
National Liberation Council (Ghana), 136
National Metalworkers' Union of South Africa (NUMSA), 124
National Redemption Council/Supreme Military Council (NRC/SMC) (Ghana), 136
National Street Vendors Forum (Kenya), 190
National Union of Harbour Employees (Ghana), 147
National Union of Textile, Garment and Tailoring Workers of Nigeria (NUTGTWN), 59, 88, 92–3
Nay Leer TV show (Senegal), 164
Ndao, Mohammed, 164–5
neoliberalism, 2, 87, 117, 121, 128; contestation of, 121–8; failure of, 161
Nepal, 37; traders' associations in, 42–3
Nepal Street Vendors' Union (NEST), 43, 44, 192
networking, 17–18, 34; importance of, 79; of informal workers, 179, 184–201; personal, 1–2
new organized actors, emergence of, 7–10
Ngwenya, Sindiso, 180
Nigeria, 27, 66, 68, 85–98; military coup in, 69
Nigeria Labour Congress (NLC), 59, 90–1, 97
night guards employed by market traders, 55, 78

NISCOF (Nairobi Informal Sector Confederation), 192, 193, 194
NLC-Civil Society Pro-Democracy Network (Nigeria), 92
non-govenmental organizations (NGOs), 36, 58, 179
Nordic Africa Institute, 117
Nwakwuo, Ify, 95

Obasanjo, Olusegun, 92
okada (motorcycle) drivers, 92
Omenka Shoe Manufacturers' Union (Nigeria), 50
'Opération villes mortes' (Senegal), 162
'organizing the unorganized', 107 see also transnational organizing
Oshiomhole, Adams, 91
outsourcing, 98, 121, 125, 126, 128, 130, 132

'Pagnes pour tous' association (Benin), 72
Pamoja Trust (Kenya), 198
Parti du renouveau démocratique (Benin), 69
participation: in Igbo culture, 54, 55; in market associations, 79–80; mobilization of, 56
participatory approach: to budgeting, in Porto Alegre, 36; to city planning, 41
Pillay, Devan, 87
police: corruption of, 61; harassment of informal traders, 60; relations with, 55
political process theory, 188
poor: not unified category, 11; organizational limitations of, 36 see also working poor
Porto Alegre, participatory budgeting in, 36
post-apartheid trade unionism, 119–21
post-Fordism, 117
Poverty Reduction Strategy Papers (Tanzania), 42
Powerline shoe producing area (Aba, Nigeria), 50
pre-paid meters, 121; campaign against, 124
precariousness of work, 3
price undercutting, 56, 57
Pride Zambia micro-finance institution, 178

234